TCHOUKAFALA

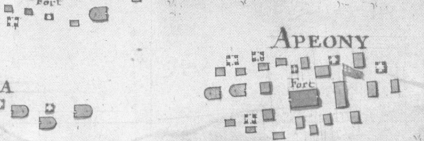

Fort

APEONY

Fort

AHEQUIA

Fort

Pêchez

Pêchez

CHICKASAW LIVES

VOLUME ONE: **EXPLORATIONS IN TRIBAL HISTORY**

By Richard Green

CHICKASAW PRESS

ISBN 978-0-9797858-1-8

Book and Cover Design by Skip McKinstry
Cover Illustration by Joshua D. Hinson

Chickasaw Press
P. O. Box 1548
Ada, Oklahoma 74820

For my children, Jed, Hart and Mary Green

CHICKASAW LIVES

VOLUME ONE: EXPLORATIONS IN TRIBAL HISTORY

Foreword

By Governor Bill Anoatubby

This volume literally has been more than ten years in the making. These articles written by tribal historian Richard Green appeared in tribal publications from 1994 into 2005. Aptly, this volume begins with an article on the tribe's versions of how it came to be. This was also the first article in Volume 1, Number 1 of the *Journal of Chickasaw History*, which Richard developed in late 1994.

This was two years after he came to work for the tribe. Initially, we asked him to research the tribe's twentieth century history. (Arrell Gibson's book, *The Chickasaws*, concluded with the turn of the twentieth century.) All of the articles that appear in the twentieth-century section of this anthology resulted from that work. All are based on original research covering subjects that are illuminated for the first time primarily from the Chickasaw point of view.

Richard has researched both our better-known historical events, such as the Battle of Ackia, and those that had faded with time. His articles are based on solid research and plausible speculation to bridge sometimes large gaps in our understanding. These gaps owe to sketchy or missing colonial documentation but even more so from the lack of a significant Chickasaw written record prior to the twentieth century.

When you think about it, it's quite a task to write balanced history when the record is so one-sided. But as you will see, Richard has given fresh perspective to old records. And he has worked diligently and successfully to turn up new sources of information.

As it was fitting to begin this book with stories of the tribe's origin, it is likewise fitting to conclude with articles on events that were and are pivotal to our future. The development of the tribe's constitution of 1983 was filled with conflict, as Richard's articles make painfully clear, especially to those of us who participated. The process was worth it, though, because that constitution has been the foundation of the tribe's unprecedented achievements.

The last article brings the book back full circle—to our ancient ancestors. But in this case the emphasis is not on describing their life and times. The article involves tribal government's enduring role in dealing with their unearthed remains.

Introduction

By Richard Green

In the summer of 1992, I contacted five Oklahoma-based tribes with a business idea. With years of experience writing relatively lengthy profiles of retired physicians for the state medical journal, I proposed writing similar profiles of tribal elders. I sent letters and writing samples to the first five tribes in alphabetical order. The Chickasaw Nation responded, and in due course made a counter-offer. This anthology is the fruit of that offer and what evolved from it. The initial work was to research and compile a twentieth century tribal history. Two years later in late 1994, Governor Bill Anoatubby named me tribal historian and approved my idea to be the founding editor of *The Journal of Chickasaw History*, a quarterly periodical for members of the newly constituted Chickasaw Historical Society.

Not surprisingly, the first issues of the *Journal* were top-heavy with articles on twentieth century Chickasaw history, while I tried to absorb as much of the earlier tribal history as possible. Simultaneously, the tribe's first director of cultural resources, Gary White Deer, was tutoring me on the process and issues involved in the repatriation of Chickasaw human remains and the possessions of these ancestral Chickasaws. I wrote an article on the subject in Volume 1 Number 1 of the *Journal*, and have written others as events warranted.

Aside from research articles on history and culture, I also produced oral histories and profiles of notable Chickasaws, which constituted some of the first expanded accounts of the lives of living Chickasaws. This work appeared in the *Journal* through 1999 and subsequently in the monthly tribal newspaper, the *Chickasaw Times.*

Most of the pre-twentieth century articles emerged out of the primary and secondary source material from archives in Oklahoma, across the Chickasaws' ancestral home in the Southeast, and through the microfilmed colonial records at the Library of Congress in Washington, D.C. This occurred as I hopped about the eighteenth and nineteenth centuries, as research bore fruit and promising leads materialized. Sometimes I skimmed the secondary sources—articles and books—for general information on a topic I would develop later. Sometimes I dug as deeply as I could, extracting and interpreting published sources and some combination of the primary material found in colonial records, archaeological and anthropological reports and articles, and later in time, the voluminous records of the United States.

After I began researching a book-length tribal social history—starting before colonial contact and traversing the eighteenth century—I wrote several associated articles for the *Times*. This work has become more of an odyssey than anything I have attempted. After I had written several chapters, a critical new source of information became available when three Tupelo, Mississippi-area artifact collectors with a storehouse of knowledge on Chickasaw history began sharing it with the tribe. Since that information is still being evaluated, only a small amount has been used in any of the articles presented here.

This important new source of information about eighteenth century Chickasaws is just the latest (albeit most dramatic) example of a lesson that I have been learning through hands-on experience since 1992. The history writing I do is my version of events based on my sources and my judgment. Some of these articles are more difficult to evaluate because I'm exploring pristine territory. But whether or not the subject has been examined before, no history article here is immutable. Some have needed alterations since they were published in the two tribal publications between 1995 and 2005.

Although the history articles are arranged chronologically, I have by no means attempted to compose a comprehensive Chickasaw history through them. As will be readily apparent to most readers, the chronology contains gaps, and with only a couple of exceptions, I did not attempt to bridge them with new articles. Most of the articles appear essentially as they were published. Some have been shortened to conform to a more uniform length throughout this book. Also, whenever I had good evidence that something needed to be updated or changed, I did that.

Some of the subjects were suggested by readers of the *Journal* and some came from tribal staff, but all of them were selected and developed by me. In general, the history articles in the research periodical, the *Journal*, were longer and usually were footnoted. Those in the tribal newspaper, by necessity, were shorter and contained a bibliography.

Usually curiosity was my main criterion for selection. Where did the Chickasaws originate? I wanted to know every detail of the contact between the Chickasaws and the army of Hernando de Soto during the winter of 1540-41. How were the Chickasaws able to defeat the French forces at Ackia in 1736? And for that matter how did the Chickasaws survive all of the calamitous events of the eighteenth century when so many other small tribes did not? What factors made the Chickasaw Trail of Tears unique? Why did the Chickasaws build an impressive new capitol building in 1898, the year after they had signed an agreement with the United States calling for an end to tribal government in 1906? How did the tribe survive the twentieth century with no tribal land or government?

My first few years as tribal historian were a very rich experience, much better I was sure than any conventional academic program. Of course, I wasn't a student, not officially, but most often I felt like a student with the luxury to pursue knowledge in several different ways and then report the results, via the *Journal* and *Times*, to the readers who were most interested, most critical, and most appreciative. Little did I know in 1999 when I stopped editing the *Journal* that the best, most fruitful and exciting times would span the several years ahead. Today, more people are studying Chickasaw tribal history and lives than ever before. There are good leads in many directions that will result in new and compelling insights and stories. I usually take on two or three simultaneously, for variety's sake, and there is no end in sight.

As originally planned, this anthology was also to contain a section of oral histories of tribal elders and one of profiles of notable Chickasaws. But the editors of Chickasaw Press believed that these two sections could and should be combined in a separate volume. So sometime soon a companion volume to this one will be published: *Chickasaw Lives, Volume 2: Profiles and Oral Histories*.

CHICKASAW LIVES

PRE-HISTORY TO EIGHTEENTH CENTURY

Origin: The Migration Stories

It is fitting that the first article of Volume 1, Number 1, of our new *Journal* should involve the origin of the Chickasaw tribe. Although different versions have emerged out of the people's ancient oral tradition, every account features a divinely inspired pole that leads the people to a place ordained for them by the Great Spirit.

The story of the Chickasaws' part of the "Trail of Tears" that resulted in the establishment of the tribe in Indian Territory is well documented. But before that tragedy took place, the tribe for several centuries inhabited various portions of the southeastern United States.

How the Chickasaws got there is revealed in stories of their origin and development. The stories reflect legend, conjecture, and even scientific discoveries. All accounts of the Chickasaws' origin involve a prolonged, divinely inspired migration and versions of how they and the Choctaws arose and were separated from their common ancestry. The sketches were passed down through many generations by a succession of tribal story tellers who were charged with honoring this obligation. Then, in the seventeenth and eighteenth centuries, some Europeans who heard the migration stories wrote them down and their versions were published. Probably the most widely read and quoted version was written by English trader James Adair. As generations went by, modifications and embellishments were added by others who either made them up or repeated what they had heard from tribal elders.

These versions involve two brothers, Chikasah and Chatah, leading the people in the quest of a new homeland. They navigated by means of a sacred pole that leaned in the proper direction; when the pole no longer leaned but stayed upright in the ground the people knew they had reached their destination. Some other southeastern tribes' origination legends also involved people following a leaning pole, and these variations have been a part of their oral traditions over the ages. In the Creek version, the legend started in the "land where the earth shook."

In the mid-1700s, the Chickasaws told James Adair that they were descended from a people called the Chickamacaws. Adair lived among the tribe and in time gained the trust of many of the members. He took meticulous notes on his observations and what he was told by elders about the tribe's history and culture. In a book published in 1775, Adair wrote that the tribe began their migration in the Mexican Empire along with another closely related tribe, the Choccomaws. Unfortunately, none of these legends included information that would help to identify where in the vast Mexican Empire the trek was begun, and so the physical evidence (artifacts and DNA testing of skeletal remains) or linguistic evidence needed to suggest the trek's origin was absent.

Adair said the migration took forty-three years, for the tribe traveled on foot and was loaded down with the bones of their ancestors. They fished and hunted on the way, but it was also necessary periodically to plant corn and wait for it to be harvested. It was probably not coincidental that forty-three years closely coincided with the number of years that the Hebrews followed Moses out of Egypt in their quest for freedom and a new home. Adair found other similarities between the Hebrews and the Muskogean tribes (Chickasaw, Choctaw and Creek) and in time developed the theory and later the belief that the tribes were the lineal descendents of the Hebrews. So preposterous was this theory to some scholars that they tended to denigrate all of Adair's work. But influential ethnologist John R. Swanton still considered Adair to be the premier authority on early Chickasaw development because Adair faithfully recorded only what he saw and heard.

H.B. Cushman, who grew up with and lived with the Choctaws, wrote in his 1899 book that some aged Choctaws recounted that their ancestors had been conquered many generations before by a more powerful tribe. After years of oppression, the chiefs and medicine men called out to Ubabeneli, the Great Spirit, for help. In the 1965 published account of tribal elder Jess Humes, the ancestral tribe had not been conquered but had grown weary of the continuous attacks and sought a solution from the tribal prophets.

At any rate, after many days of prayer and supplication, Ubabeneli revealed to the prophets and doctors the directions for the tribe's deliverance to the prophets and medicine men. A great council was called and Ubabeneli's instructions were related to the people.

They would immigrate to another land. Ubabeneli would lead them by means of a sacred pole. According to the story told by Alice Marriott, Ubabeneli inspired an old medicine man who selected the twin brothers and told them to make the pole from a sweet gum tree. Then, the old medicine man painted the pole with red and white stripes; the red symbolized war and white represented peace. He admonished them to never make war if they could make peace. Finally, he told them to go in the direction that the pole leaned.

In some versions the pole is identified in the Muskogean language as *fa-bus-sah*; in others, it is *kohta falaya* (long pole). Every evening, one from among the prophets, often Chikasah, would stick this long pole perpendicularly into the ground. A mystical force caused the pole to move slightly during the night. At sunrise, the pole would be leaning, indicating the direction for the day's travel.

After a lengthy migration from the west the leaders disagree over whether the divinely inspired pole is signifying that this is their new homeland. Chata's folded arms indicate his belief that the people have reached their destination. His twin brother Chikkasah points east. Their separation, according to tribal stories, marks the beginning of the Chickasaw and Choctaw nations. (Painting by Tom Phillips titled, *Chickasaw Migration Legends, The Parting of the Ways*. Courtesy the Chickasaw Nation)

The two brothers, Chahtah and Chikasah, had demonstrated bravery and honor in battle and wisdom in tribal affairs. From all accounts, this decision to leave and follow the pole had the total support of the people. Adair was told that some 10,000 people packed their belongings and set out together, following *fa-bus-sah*, always moving east-northeast in the direction of the rising sun.

Some accounts include mention of a large, white dog that led the people on their migration. Aside from serving as the tribe's guide and scout, this dog had mystical powers and may have been among the Indians' pantheon of deities. Nevertheless, the people endured great hardships as the weeks turned into months and then years. Unfortunately, none of the accounts deals anecdotally with the migration until its last stages; Humes speaks generally about much sickness and death on the journey (despite the powers of the medicine men and the white dog) and the fact that the people often had to fight their way through the lands of other Indians.

If, as many authorities believe, the people began their migration somewhere in what is now central Mexico, then they must have traversed parts of Texas, Louisiana and perhaps even Arkansas before many years later reaching an immense body of flowing water that stopped them cold, both physically and emotionally. Their astonishment and reverence was such

that they named it *misha sipokni*, beyond all age. Later, the name *misha sipokni* was corrupted by whites into "Mississippi." Physically, the vast river was so inspiring that many believed it was a sign they had reached their destination.

Nevertheless, at the next sunrise, the *fa-bus-sah* was again leaning toward the east. H.B. Cushman wrote that the people accepted the evidence "without a murmur" and immediately began constructing canoes and rafts for what would be a monumental crossing, taking weeks before everyone would be safely across. In other accounts, such as one by the late U.S. Congressman and Chickasaw citizen Charles Carter, the white dog was a casualty of the crossing.

At this point in particular, the versions of the migration legend diverge, regarding how the people got separated into the two groups that eventually became the Chickasaws and the Choctaws. Some sources of ethnologist Swanton told him that the brothers and their followers were separated during a snow storm while reconnoitering the land east of the Mississippi River. In another version, the brothers Chikasah and Chatah disagreed over where their new homeland was to be located and led their followers to different lands. Many more people had followed Chatah, who took his people to what is now central Mississippi. There they erected a huge mound and sacred place where they buried their ancestors' bones. They called this place *Nanih Waiya* (leaning mountain).

In another version, the split didn't take place until after the people had settled near *Nanih Waiya*. Jess Humes understood that the sacred pole wobbled crazily before stopping in an upright position. To Chatah, this was their destination; but the random wobbling had unnerved Chikasah and when he could not persuade his brother to join him, he took the pole and told the people that if they believed the promised land was still to the east, they should follow him.

Consequently, the followers of Chikasah kept moving east, as *fa-bus-sah* indicated, until they came to a location near what is now Huntsville in north-central Alabama. At sunrise, the pole remained embedded perpendicular to the ground. There, the people established their original Old Fields and became, in effect if not yet in fact, Chickasaws. How long they dwelled there is unknown.

Then, one morning the pole was discovered to be leaning to the west. Again, unhesitating, the Chickasaws abruptly abandoned their Old Field and set off again. As always, their fate depended on Ubabeneli, who would tell them all they needed to know through the leaning of *fa-bus-sah*. This time, their trek was relatively short. The pole retained its upright stature in the Tombigbee Highlands of northern Mississippi.

Dr. Gideon Lincecum's version (cited in James Malone's book, *The Chickasaw Nation*) provides a much more circuitous route back to northern Mississippi. Linceceum wrote that the tribe remained in northern Alabama only one winter and then followed the leaning pole to the northeast and then south to an area near present-day Savannah, Georgia. After many winters, a plague (probably yellow fever) wiped out many of the members; the survivors followed a *fa-bus-sah* over a course that retraced much of their earlier journey, ending back in northern Mississippi. They settled less than a hundred miles from the Choctaws.

The Chickasaws were living in this region in 1540 when Hernando de Soto arrived. He referred to the land of the Tombigbee Highlands as the Province of Chicaca and established both incentives (trading) and intimidation in dealing with the Chickasaws. A new and eventually calamitous epoch in the history of the tribe was just getting underway.

Moundville Linked to Chickasaw Past

History's first glimpse of the Chickasaws occurred when Hernando de Soto's Spanish expedition settled in December 1540 into a village the Indians had abandoned. Although the Spaniards stayed into March and had frequent contact with the Chickasaws, "glimpse," unfortunately, is the word that best characterizes the written accounts of the Spanish chroniclers.

Apparently these Spanish were too single-minded to be curious about or interested in the people they had encountered. Of course, as is evident from the chroniclers' accounts of the expedition's four-year trek across the Southeast, they recorded few details about the culture of any of the tribes they met.

Thus, a golden opportunity was lost to note their observations of Chickasaw culture at the earliest point in the tribe's recorded history. This is particularly unfortunate because it is likely that less than a century before—and maybe only a few years before—the Chickasaws who encountered de Soto had been living in very different circumstances. In fact, it is possible that within that relatively short time-span the people had come together from various settlements to form what would first be recognized at Chicaca as the Chickasaw tribe.

Trying to work back into tribal history prior to December 1540 in a step-wise fashion may be an impossible task. We don't know where precisely the Chickasaws were living then, let alone prior to that time. But archaeologists who have studied Southeastern prehistoric human remains and artifacts believe that the ancestors of the Chickasaws and most other Southeastern tribes were the highly centralized, mound-building Indians of the so-called Mississippian Period (roughly 900 to 1600 A.D.).

De Soto came along when this 700-year period was collapsing, and, as a result, many of the groups of Indians were moving permanently away from the period's characteristic centralized chiefdoms to more decentralized and democratic tribes. Descriptions in the de Soto chronicles suggest that the Chickasaws were going through this period of transition.

During the collapse, it is possible that migrating Indians from different locations in the Southeast had come together to form upland settlements overlooking rivers and streams. That this convergence may have happened is one reason why Governor Bill Anoatubby initiated Chickasaw Nation claims with the federal government involving Mississippian Period human remains and artifacts recently unearthed in construction projects in the Nashville area. The claims were initiated not to take possession of the material, but in keeping with tribal policy, to expedite the reburial of the remains and artifacts as near the original sites as possible. No one can say that none of the thousands of Indians who lived in the Nashville area during the Mississippian Period were or were not ancestral Chickasaws. But it is well-known that between 1400 and 1500 A.D., most of the Mississippian Indians abandoned the area. Why they left and where they went has been the subject of years of speculation and debate.

Similar upheavals were taking place at approximately the same time in other Southeastern locations. One of the best documented by archaeologists occurred at Moundville. Because it is only sixty to seventy miles southeast of where some experts on de Soto's expedition believe that the Spaniards wintered over near the Chickasaws, Moundville may have been a prime site for ancestral Chickasaws. This does not suggest that Moundvillians wound up settling in Chicaca. Artifacts do suggest, however, that the Moundvillians dispersed throughout the Black Warrior River Valley of western Alabama. But Moundville pottery that dates from 1100 to almost 1500 has been found west of the Tombigbee River in Mississippi. This means that not only Moundvillians but also descendants of prior generations of Moundvillians could be ancestral Chickasaws. More specifically, some of the Moundville artifacts have been unearthed just northeast of Starkville, Mississippi, at Lyon's Bluff, which archaeologist Marvin Smith, among others, thinks could have been the location of Chicaca.

The evidence linking Moundville to the Chickasaw is circumstantial, and archaeologists don't like to go out on limbs. But, Moundville is a window to the tribe's distant past, at the very least as a symbol of an epoch through which Southeastern Indians passed.

Archaeologists have been digging at the Moundville site on and off for nearly a century, and each excavation yields new information that increases understanding or is fodder for new thinking about Moundville culture. So the fruits of any article are temporary. The purpose of this brief article on Moundville is to provide basic information and a bibliography for those wanting to learn more or expand and update their knowledge.

The earliest pottery on the site dated to about 1050 A.D. Shortly thereafter, the Indians built the first mound, presumably as a burial mound for high-status people. Such earthen mounds had been built over hundreds of years. What made Moundville different than other older and contemporary mound sites was that the Moundvillians

Facing Page: This is the largest (68 feet high) of the Moundville chiefdom's 28 mounds, which were encompassed within 300 acres in west central Alabama. The recreated structure on top may have been a council house, the site of the chief's centralized power. (Courtesy Moundville Archaeological Park)

kept building mounds of various sizes and shapes and with different purposes. By 1300, Moundville had become the megalopolis of its day, probably as awe inspiring to visitors as New York City is to Americans from small rural communities.

Most settlements then consisted of a few houses, some gardens, less than a hundred people, and possibly a single mound. A 10-foot-tall palisade and the Black Warrior River to the north enclosed Moundville's 300 acres and 1,000 people. Within the enclosure were at least 26 mounds ranging from a few that were little more than knolls to immense edifices, one almost 60-feet high. Also within the enclosure was a central plaza and dozens of houses made of poles and thatch.

The arrangement of the mounds around the plaza implies order and planning, according to Vernon Knight, a University of Alabama archaeologist who has studied and published numerous articles about Moundville. In trying to interpret the plan, Knight uses what he thinks is a good analogy, a 1904 diagram by Chickasaw Josiah Mikey showing the house groups of a Chickasaw camp square arranged for an important council at some distant, though unknown time.

In the Mikey diagram, clans were arranged by rank around the rectangular campground divided bilaterally and centered on a council fire, symbolized in the traditional Chickasaw manner by a cross in a circle. The highest-ranking clans in each division were assigned positions on a north-south axis. Knight purports that the mounds arrayed around Moundville's plaza were also ranked kin groups.

Although Knight admits the analogy is not perfect, he does note that Moundville and the diagram share a rectangular plaza, bilateral symmetry on a north-south axis, a center reference point, arrangement of basic community segments by rank around the plaza, and ranking of the segments starting at center north. Accordingly, Knight speculates that the pairs of mounds around the periphery of the plaza represent a fixed rank ordering of local kin groups. He noted, "It was an attempt by an emergent nobility to make a newly transformed social order tangible, inviolable, immovable, sacred."

Archaeologists refer to Moundville as a paramount chiefdom, suggesting that power was concentrated in a chief and members of an elite class who controlled Moundville and some of the many smaller villages that were located nearby in the Black Warrior River valley, usually in riverbend areas to take advantage of the fertile farmlands. Moundville itself was developed in one of these areas undoubtedly for the same reason. No one knows why it mushroomed the way it did, becoming the center of political and religious activities. But it may have had to do with the ascendancy and maintenance of an especially charismatic and powerful family or group of leaders.

That could be why the pyramidal, flat-topped mounds grew to such heights. The larger ones must have taken generations to build. There is evidence that the chief lived in a structure on the top of the mound and that when he died, his survivors burned down and buried the remaining structure under fresh layers of dirt, carried by laborers in baskets. Such labor implies coercion and therefore different strata of Moundville society. Other laborers hunted, grew maize, squash, and beans, or crafted remarkable works of art. Supporting evidence for this elite and non-elite society is also derived from the burials found all around Moundville. Commoners typically were buried underneath their houses with little or no grave goods.

On the other hand, some of Moundville's lesser earthworks were used as mortuaries for the elite; prestige goods are present in most of these graves, sometimes adorning the human remains. These relics are identified with certain political or religious offices. Often, the chief conducted both civil affairs and highly ritualistic religious ceremonies inside his residence, barred from all but a handful of elite members. Moundville artisans fashioned prestige goods from marine shells, copper, and other minerals like mica and galena. Their artistic excellence with pottery and stoneware has made Moundville a primary site for the study and interpretation of Mississippian imagery. Other prestige goods were imported as tribute from smaller chiefdoms or as trade items from more substantial chiefdoms. These prestige goods from nearly the entire eastern part of the continent demonstrate that a vigorous system of trade existed. The ten-foot palisades indicate that warfare existed as well.

If 1200 to 1300 was the high watermark of the Moundville chiefdom, function and purpose seemed to change after that. Before 1400, the population seemed to have thinned out and the palisade was gone. These were the initial signs of what would be a century and a half of decline. Some of the mounds seemed to have been abandoned, and the mortuary rituals appear to have become less important. By 1500, few Moundvillians were left on site, and it was no longer a paramount chiefdom. Various theories seek to explain this decline. One for which there was plenty of evidence in many other Mississippian sites was that Moundville had simply outgrown the ability to feed its people. Contributing to this could have been successive years of unfavorable weather and/or a maize blight. Another explanation was profound mortality associated with the spread of infectious diseases via the de Soto expedition.

These last two theories have generated little support within the archaeological community in recent years. Virtually all agree that the decline was due to internal combustion of some sort, but there is no consensus on cause or causes.

This rendering by Chickasaw artist Joshua Hinson is an amalgam of symbols—serpents and eye in hand—commonly found on pottery and other material at the Moundville chiefdom. With no written language there is no way to know the symbols' meanings, but most are associated with war and death. (Media by Joshua Hinson, titled *Nunna Moundville Holba*— Looks like something from Moundville)

The Winter of Discontent
UNINVITED, UNWELCOME, DE SOTO AMONG THE CHICACAS

Just before sunrise, March 4, 1541.

Divided into many small groups, about three hundred Chicaca warriors crept silently through the savannahs to encircle and infiltrate the sleeping Spanish encampment—which until ten weeks before had been a Chicaca village. They were about to execute the attack that had been detailed during the previous several days. Throughout much of the winter, as warriors had been paying what were ostensibly social visits on the Spanish, but were actually reconnaissance missions, in which they noted everything about camp life that could enhance their opportunity for a successful attack.

Their target was a Spanish force of perhaps four hundred fifty to five hundred men and two women. Their leader was the conquistador Hernando de Soto. Although he believed in the moral righteousness of abusing and killing non-Christians, he knew or suspected that despite their overtures of friendliness, the Indians deeply resented his presence and he sensed they were "engaged in evil intrigue." Before he had retired on the evening of March 3, de Soto told his men: "Tonight is an Indian night. I will sleep armed and with my horse saddled." And he instructed an aide to "take extra precautions with the sentinels."[1]

Crouching, the Chicacas crept forward, wearing feathers and war paint and carrying their weapons and little pots of smoldering herbs. They paused on the outskirts of the camp, listening and looking for signs of danger. Had they walked into a trap? De Soto had wanted extra precautions. Where were the sentries? The night-time sounds of the savannah were ordinary except for the Spanish horses grunting and snorting. As they neared the houses on the periphery of the camp, they could hear the soldiers sleeping inside.[2]

A drum beat signaled the attack.

As a teenager, Hernando de Soto sailed to the Americas and soon gained notoriety and a fortune by enslaving Central American Indians for profit. Although he became wealthy, the power over the new Spanish lands was controlled by Francisco Pizarro. After several years, according to one historian, de Soto sailed back to Spain where King Charles I "did him the extreme honor of asking for a loan." For his part, de Soto wanted a royal commission to lead an expedition to the new world. Charles granted permission to explore Florida and conferred on de Soto the titles of governor of Cuba and Florida. He arrived in Cuba in 1538, deposited his new wife in Havana, and a few months later in 1539 set sail for Florida. De Soto was intent on fulfilling his missions of finding enormous caches of gold, extending Spanish hegemony, subduing and using whatever people appeared and building churches.[4]

De Soto's expedition was chronicled by three men who claimed to be eyewitnesses. Most subsequent publications dealing with the expedition are based largely on those narratives. The Spanish historian Oviedo copied part of a journal kept by de Soto's private secretary, Rodrigo Ranjel. Another journal is attributed to a Portugese soldier known only as "the Gentleman of Elvas." The third account was a report written for the king by an official Luys Hernandez de Biedma, whose main duty was to ensure that Charles got his share of the profits.[5]

Although the accounts encompass both personal and cultural biases, the narratives are neither uncritical of de Soto nor do they play down the misery of the soldiers. Furthermore, their descriptions of the same events often are similar. But the chroniclers recorded only what they observed and made few if any attempts to learn anything directly from or about the Chicacas themselves. That is regrettable to students of Chickasaw history, for despite a season of contact, little was recorded about the tribe in the sixteenth century. But, some historians have assessed the narratives rather than merely reporting them, judging them in context as well as content. Those historians are the main sources in this article.

Approximately 650 persons landed with de Soto on the western coast of Florida in 1539. Most were Spanish soldiers equipped with modern weapons, but the necessary auxiliaries, such as engineers and priests, and a few other nationalities and persons of other racial and ethnic origin were also present. Also included were dozens of horses for transportation and cavalry attack, hundreds of pigs (for pork) and numerous dogs trained in tracking and warfare. From mid-1539 through 1540, the expedition marched in a northerly direction, then westerly, cutting a swath through southeastern North America. De Soto and his men employed the same tactics and strategy on the Indians that had worked so well in South and Central America—deception followed by plundering, murdering, raping and enslaving.

Archeological evidence from the time suggests that the tribes of the Southeast did communicate and occasionally form alliances. Considering de Soto's notoriety, it is highly likely that word spread that what he wanted from Indians was directions to the gold, their food and women to serve as his men's sexual outlet. The Indians considered de Soto and his men to be barbarians. But the Indians conceded that the Spaniards' large numbers, mobility on horseback, relatively sophisticated weapons, equipment and military skills made outright attacks and pitched battles unfeasible. For their part, the Indians had no metal weapons, only clubs, lances and arrows tipped with stone or pieces of antler. They used their weapons to fight guerilla style.[6] Their best strategy was to avoid de Soto if possible. That is why the expedition found so many villages abandoned and bare of food.[7]

But some tribes could not avoid contact, and knowing what de Soto wanted most, they made up stories of gold and great wealth, always in the distance, away from their lands. De Soto assumed that the Indians were incapable of deception and that he was incapable of being had. He was wrong on both counts, which kept his expedition on a continuous wild-goose chase. During the second year, they arrived in the land of the great chief Tascalusa in present-day Alabama. De Soto issued his usual demands for Indians to carry his supplies and women. Although Tascalusa gave de Soto some men to serve as carriers, a violent incident involving the chief sparked a battle at the Indians' fortified town of Mabila. De Soto torched the town, which was encircled by a high wooden wall; hundreds of warriors were trapped inside of what became an inferno. According to Elvas, 2,500 Indians perished.[8]

The Spanish headed west, having lost about one hundred men to disease and battle. They were looking for the land of the Chicaca, which they understood had many fine fields of maize. They came upon a river, probably the Tombigbee, overflowing its bed. On the other side were Indians making threatening gestures.

An emissary of de Soto crossed the river and told the chief of the region that they could become the governor's friends if they would allow the expedition to cross in peace. The answer was unequivocal and emphatic; the emissary was executed on the spot in full view of the Spanish.[9]

De Soto ordered a piragua or barge to be made. It was big enough to accommodate thirty men and several mounted horsemen, and the crossing was made on December 17.

Elvas says the Indians showered the men with arrows, but as the barge landed and the cavalrymen prepared to charge, the Indians fled.[10] Where this landing was made is not known. Some students of de Soto's expedition believe it was in the vicinity of what is today Columbus, Mississippi. Others believe it was considerably more to the north, southeast of today's Tupelo, Mississippi. The Spanish marched to a Chicaca village of about twenty houses, arriving that same day to find it had been abandoned. Accounts of the village's name vary. Either it was a Chicaca village (with the name unknown to the Spanish) or it was named Chicaca by the former residents or the Spanish. Although the food store had been taken by the Indians, Elvas wrote that the reports of plentiful fields of maize were accurate. And since the weather had turned very cold and snowy, de Soto decided to winter at the village, which the Spanish augmented with several new structures for housing.[11]

According to the theory of some archaeologists, the Chicaca had recently abandoned several mid-size towns containing ceremonial mounds and were gradually migrating across the Tombigbee basin to the northwest. This transit, suggesting temporary shelters rather than a permanent home, makes it virtually impossible to pinpoint the location of the Chicaca village. The bitter cold and heavy snow recorded by the chroniclers during the winter of 1540-41 could mean that

the inhabitants were experiencing what climatologists believe was a so-called Little Ice Age in the northern hemisphere in the sixteenth and seventeenth centuries.[12]

When the Chicaca chiefs of the region realized that de Soto probably would not be departing until spring, they gathered to plot strategy.[13] How could they rid the barbarians from their land with the lowest loss of life? First, they would try to trick them into leaving. What brought the two sides together initially is not known. Either some Indians were kidnapped (a routine Spanish gambit) in a move to compel the *cacique* (chief) to meet with de Soto or the *cacique* came of his own accord. At any rate, the *cacique* offered de Soto

Cutting his bloody swath from Florida westward, de Soto first encountered the Chicaca at this river. As his reputation had preceded him, the Chicaca greeted his entrada with a hail of arrows.(Painting by Tom Phillips, titled First Encounter: De Soto Meets the Chickasaws. Courtesy of Chickasaw Nation) men to guide his expedition to the fabulous land he called Caluca.[14] When that ruse did not work, the *cacique* asked de Soto for help in putting down a rebellion at another village. The thinking was that if de Soto were agreeable, he would divide his force, thus making each part more vulnerable to a successful Indian attack. Some Chicaca accompanied de Soto and thirty soldiers to this village of Sacchuma, which of course was abandoned. The Indians, play-acting to the hilt, feigned anger and burned the village to the ground. Still, all of de Soto's forces remained vigilant, which kept the Chicaca from attacking.[15]

Because the chiefs could not agree on a new plan of attack, they thought it best to keep the Spanish in one place during the winter for two reasons. First, if they helped to feed and clothe the Spanish, they would not be so likely to bother the Chicaca in their camps. Second, by feigning friendship, they could observe the Spanish to learn the most effective ways to attack them in the spring if de Soto lived up to his reputation for making intolerable and outrageous demands prior to his departure.[16] Therefore, the *cacique* and two other chiefs Alimanu and Niculasa brought the Spanish food and clothing. During this time, the Chicaca were exhibiting remarkable restraint and patience considering the rage they must have been feeling. The invaders had expropriated their homes and much of their food supply at the beginning of a harsh winter. If the Spanish were miserable that winter, the Chicaca probably suffered even more. The tension in the Indian villages must have been palpable day after day.[17]

If the tension among the Chicaca and between the tribe and the Spanish was not already high enough, an incident that winter further imperiled the uneasy peace. Three Indians were apprehended for trying to steal a few of de Soto's prized hogs. Their motive, Elvas wrote, was an over fondness for pork. But it is much more likely, says historian David Duncan, that the three were "desperate for food." Two were executed. The third man's hands were cut off and he was returned to the *cacique* as a warning. No reprisals were made despite the fact that the Spanish had looted their food supply, imperiling the Chicaca in the dead of winter.[18]

Facing Page: A Chicaca firestorm engulfs Hernando de Soto and his Spanish expedition on March 4, 1541. The Spanish chroniclers wrote the first known account of the Chicaca, the ancestral Chickasaws, including this remarkable battle. (Painting by Tom Phillips, titled *Chickasaw Rout De Soto.* Courtesy of Chickasaw Nation)

By late February or early March, the snow was gone and the temperature was moderating. De Soto told the *cacique* that he intended to depart. Then, adhering to his usual practice, he demanded two hundred carriers and a supply of women. In his account of the expedition, Ranjel reported that the Indians "raised such a tumult among themselves that the Christians understood it" and extended the deadline to March 4.[19] On the night before the departure, de Soto mounted his horse and, riding among the Chicaca, found them "evilly disposed," and ordered increased vigilance. The Spanish camp gradually settled down for the expedition's last night there. But the Chicaca did not sleep. They were preparing for a massive predawn firestorm.

Even before the drum beat signaled the attack, the warriors had set fire to part of the village. The woven herbs smoldering in pots that they carried with them had only to be waved overhead to burst into flame. Some warriors touched their flaming weapons to the straw roofs, while others, having attached bits of the herbs to the points of arrows, shot them to ignite houses in the distance. In virtually no time the Spanish were caught in a fiery conflagration. Despite de Soto's pronouncement that he would sleep armed and with his saddled horse nearby, he and his soldiers had retired that evening "without precautions and unarmed."[20] The only explanation for the failure of the sentries to spot the advancing Chicaca was provided by de Soto's private secretary, Ranjel: "The Master of the Camp put on the morning watch three horsemen, the most useless ... in the army."[21] But why were the Spanish not prepared for an attack they believed was coming? The most likely reason was arrogance, manifested in the belief that they could not be defeated by Indians.

Roused from sleep by smoke and drumbeats, de Soto threw a saddle on his horse, mounted, and, with lance in hand, managed to mortally wound a Chicaca. But since the saddle was not cinched tightly enough, the force of the blow loosened the saddle and propelled him backward onto the ground. That Chicaca was the only Indian to die during the battle, so great was the confusion and panic among the Spanish. Ranjel and Elvas both wrote that the "Christians," unarmed and gasping for breath, tried to escape through gaps in the fire. Many were cut down at those points by bowmen.

The cacophony of shrieking animals and screaming humans, along with the nauseating smells of burning flesh, contributed to a chaotic rout. Francisca de Hinestrosa, one of the expedition's two women, left her husband's side and ran back into a flaming house to retrieve her pearls. The fire quickly engulfed the structure and she was consumed inside.[22] She was one of twelve to fourteen (the accounts vary) of the enemy to die during the battle; many more were wounded or burned and probably died later. In addition, fifty-seven horses and some four hundred pigs (of five hundred) died during the battle. Furthermore, fire destroyed most of their military gear, weapons and clothing.[23] Many of the survivors were left literally naked, Elvas observed.

Bad as it was for the Spanish, it could have been much worse. The chroniclers all agreed that the Chicaca could have wiped out the entire expedition. But for some reason the attack was cut short. Biedma called it "a great mystery of God."[24] In one account, it is alleged that the Chicaca did such a good job of creating confusion that they became enveloped in it, perhaps mistaking horses' frantic efforts to escape the flames for attacking lancers. But according to historian Mary Ann Wells, extermination "was not normal Chicaca strategy. The Indians seemed only to want the Spaniards to understand how unappreciated their continued demands were and at the same time to deliver an avenging assault to speed the Europeans' departure."[25]

The village was utterly destroyed. The Spanish salvaged what little they could from the ashes of their camp, and de Soto ordered a move to two or three miles away to another abandoned Chicaca village on an open plain. There they tended to the wounded and the business of rejuvenating themselves into a semblance of an expedition. Again, the chroniclers noted that had the Chicaca attacked at this time, not a man would have survived. But in keeping with the overall Chicaca strategy of minimizing their own losses, the Chicaca probably believed that the Spanish had been critically crippled and would have no choice but to move on.

But when they did not, the Chicaca attacked on March 15, again just before dawn.[26] This attack was not nearly as sophisticated as the first one. For one thing, de Soto's sentries, soldiers and cavalrymen were ready, and during the battle there were deaths and casualties on both sides.[27] For another, the Chicaca probably had a very limited objective—to demonstrate emphatically to de Soto that he must leave their land.

Within days, the Spanish moved out for good, forever weakened and demoralized, according to Elvas. Now, instead of searching for gold and riches, they were trying to find a water route to what would be called the Gulf of Mexico and their best chance of escape. De Soto would not make it back; he died of some infectious disease near the banks of the Mississippi River in May 1542.

The English Come to Call

The first and last white men known to have visited the Chickasaws in the 1500s were the Spanish serving under Hernando de Soto. Succeeding European groups in the seventeenth and early eighteenth centuries were primarily concerned with converting the Indian "infidels" to Catholicism. The Franciscan order established missions in Florida, and in addition to religious instruction, the missionaries also taught Indians the virtues of agriculture, peaceful coexistence and mutual interdependence with their new European "allies."

While the Indians did not always appreciate the efforts of the missionaries, and periodically staged violent uprisings, three Spanish mission districts remained intact until the latter part of the seventeenth century, when English traders came to call. They were as cold-blooded and calculating as the human species gets. They knew exactly what they wanted, and their goal was much more exact and measurable than the murky, unquantifiable aim of soul saving. As the Spanish were learning, or should have been learning from the periodic uprisings, they could never be sure whether the Indians were truly embracing Catholicism and therefore could be counted on as real allies.

Despite Spanish attempts to keep the English from settling a coastal colony on what Spain considered its own land, the English managed to establish Charles Town in 1670, which was protected from Indian attack by an extensive and fortified palisade. From the first, the goal of the English was profit, and their business was Indian trade. Although Europeans would buy deerskins and animal pelts, the most substantial profits were to be made in the slave trade. Slave labor was needed particularly on the sugarcane plantations of Barbados in the British West Indies.

But if the Indians of Carolina far outnumbered the colonists at Charles Town, how could the English traders hope to capture and enslave large numbers of Indians? Their plan was based on the experience of traders operating earlier in the seventeenth century in the colony of Virginia. They made several diplomatic mistakes and were nearly wiped out by the Indians of the Powhatan Confederacy in 1622 and again in 1644. But the English eventually subdued the Powhatans through military conquest and unwittingly by spreading deadly infectious diseases.

The Lords Proprietors of Carolina hoped that similar mistakes would be avoided in that colony, which was given to them by King Charles II. For example, antagonizing tribes might be avoided by making slave trading illegal. But because they governed from London, the proprietors lacked sufficient control over the colonists. Colonial officials had their own ideas about running Carolina. To start with, they gave the job of developing Indian trade to an experienced, ambitious, tough-minded, intelligent surgeon named Henry Woodward.

Woodward bided his time trading English goods for deerskins and beaver pelts, but there is no doubt that trade in slaves was his eventual goal. Indian slavery could be very profitable and tended to eliminate dangerous rivals (the Indians) by removing them to New England or the West Indies. Woodward had learned while living with Indians in Florida that slavery had long been a by-product of intertribal warfare. While trading with the Westoes, a tribe armed with

When the Chickasaws and English met for the first time in the late seventeenth century, both nations knew what they wanted from the other. Their reputations had preceded them so neither side could be disappointed. (Media by Joshua Hinson, titled *Hattak-Naahollo-Ut-Minti*—The white men are coming.)

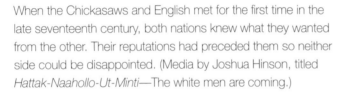

guns from the Virginians, Woodward encouraged these more lethal warriors to raid other tribes for young slaves. He would trade English goods, including more guns and ammunition, for slaves and deerskins. He made similar agreements with the Yuchis and Chiluques. By 1680 Woodward had turned things completely around: warfare had become a by-product of slave raids.

Also by then, Woodward and other English traders were pushing inland, trading with tribes west of Carolina. No document has yet been found to indicate when or how the Charles Town traders first came into contact with the Chickasaws. In a letter Woodward wrote in 1674 while visiting the Westoes, he quotes an unnamed source, saying that the "Cussetaws [Cusitaws], Checsaws [Chickasaws] and Chiokees [Keyokees] were intended to come downe and fight the Westoes."

We know from French accounts that the Chickasaws were ranging far and wide from their villages in northeastern Mississippi. And the tribe might have had good reason to fight the Westoes, given a possible ethnic link between the latter and the Iroquois. It was the Iroquois, equipped with guns, who had been raiding small villages of Southeastern tribes to capture Indians and incorporate them into their tribes to bolster their dwindling population.

Captain Thomas Nairne, the Carolina Indian agent who spent a few days with the Chickasaws in 1708, wrote: "Formerly when the Iroquois troubled these parts they drove the Chickasaws out of their Towns and made great Havock of them." "Formerly" is frustratingly imprecise, but since one may reasonably infer that the Chickasaws did not have guns to defend themselves, Nairne's reference could date back to the 1670s. Nairne further notes that the Chickasaws at some unspecified later time had been "furnished with Gunes and [the Iroquois] found so warm a reception, that they thought fitt never to return since."

It is even possible that a delegation of Chickasaw might have sought out the English to offer a trade agreement beneficial to the Indians. Nairne provided some evidence about the date of the first meeting when he wrote that Woodward "about 20 years agoe made peace with the Ochesees [Lower Creeks] and Tallaposies [Upper Creeks] these people then haveing Freindship with the Chicasaws he sent two of his men hither, who brought them aquainted with the English. "About" 20 years ago? We know that Dr. Woodward visited the Creek tribes in 1685. If Nairne's declaration is correct, this would be the earliest record of English contact with the Chickasaws.

One of the traders who might have been present at the first meetings was Thomas Welch, the companion of Thomas Nairne when he visited the Chickasaws in 1708. Welch is known to have cut a new way from Carolina to the Chickasaw Nation through the wilderness in 1698, called the Upper Trading Path and established himself as the premier English trader with the tribe.

No one has found a record of either meeting, most likely because none was ever made. The vast majority of traders had precious few talents or positive character traits, save bravery. Unlike the well-educated exception, Dr. Woodward, they were crude and illiterate. Second, it would be indiscreet to document meetings involving slave trading since the Lords Proprietors of Carolina had made it illegal.

Whenever and wherever the Chickasaws and English met, both sides knew what they wanted. This is contrary to the conventional view still perpetuated on schoolchildren in too many history courses, that the Europeans maintained control by dazzling the natives with trade goods. This is not to say that the Chickasaws were uninterested in the goods but that they probably had seen the English offerings through their previous contact with tribes to the east. From the Chickasaws the English wanted slaves and deerskins, both of which the

Chickasaws had been taking in their natural order of things for many years. Guns would greatly facilitate these tasks and eventually transform the Chickasaws from subsistence farmers to commercial hunters and warriors.

Since the early meetings were presumably unreported, we may never know if there were dissenters among the Chickasaw elders. In a tribe containing seers and mystics, it is almost inconceivable that some of them would not have warned of the harm or destruction that would befall the tribe for dealing with such dishonorable men.

Furthermore, there were reports that tribes to the east had been almost annihilated by the Westoes. Was this not evidence that the English should be avoided? On the contrary, these reports were a powerful argument that allying with the English was a key not only to survival but also to prosperity. Moreover, if the Chickasaws spurned the English offer, would not the English traders turn south and arm their traditional enemy, the Choctaws?

The tribe was likely governed in the 1680s and 1690s by consensus, as described by Thomas Nairne in 1708: "Plato nor no other writter of Politicks even of the most republican principles, could never contrive a Government where the equallity of mankind is more Justly observed than here among the savages." So quite possibly after a period of hot debate,

in which the English rifles might have been called the key to tribal salvation or destruction, a consensus was achieved to do business with the English. The traders demonstrated the deadly power of the guns, and an array of convenience and novelty products was rolled out, including cotton and woolen garments, hoes, axes, pots, kettles, glass beads, brass wire and ornamental bells.

After the English had departed, leaving a supply of these goods with the tribal members, there must have been a full range of emotion, from jubilation to discomfort to foreboding to fear. But if a consensus existed about how to deal with the English, there would very likely have been a feeling of unanimity among the members that the life of the tribe would never again be the same. Unlike de Soto, these white men would come again, and they would be only the first.

La Salle at Chickasaw Bluffs

Spanish chroniclers noted that the tattered Hernando de Soto expedition left Chickasaw lands (referred to as Chicaca) in 1541. After examining those accounts, including physical descriptions of where the tribe lived and archaeological evidence, historians and archaeologists have concluded that the home of the Chickasaws probably was located south of Lee County, perhaps as far south as modern-day Columbus or West Point, Mississippi.

No one knows how much longer the tribe lived in this region, but it is known that by 1700 most Chickasaws lived in the area of Lee County that would later be developed as Tupelo, and still later be famously identified as the birthplace of Elvis Presley.

Following 1541, the next documented encounter with Chickasaws occurred 141 years later. In February 1682, French explorer Robert Cavelier de La Salle sailed down the Mississippi and talked with some Chickasaw hunters near the bluffs overlooking the Mississippi River at a site that would become Memphis, Tennessee.

La Salle's purpose on the Mississippi was to explore and claim the lower Mississippi River Valley for France, which he did on April 9, 1682. Famed Chickasaw painter Tom Phillips depicted the ceremony in a large oil painting that he completed for the Chickasaw Nation in 1996. But in his painting, Chickasaws are shown passing by the scene of the French ceremony in their canoes on the way to trade. In the narrative that Phillips wrote to accompany the painting, he noted that the Indians that La Salle met along the Mississippi assured him he could travel in safety to the mouth of the river. They misunderstood his intent. Phillips said, "The Indians would surely have been furious if they had understood what he [La Salle] was actually doing that day in 1682 on the banks of their river."

To fortify France's claim and exploit the Indian trade west of the river, La Salle planned to establish a string of forts down to the river's mouth. The first such fort, Prudhomme, was erected on Chickasaw Bluffs near present-day Memphis.

While La Salle was recovering from illness at the fort, his troops captured two Chickasaws and brought them to him for questioning. According to a chronicler named Minet, the Frenchman captured the Indians by trickery. He demonstrably threw his gun to the ground, then when the Chickasaws drew near, he "pulled out a pistol from behind his back and took them by force" to La Salle. It is interesting to note that by this account the Chickasaws knew enough about guns to fear them so either they had had previous contact with colonists or with Indians with such firearms experience.

This comes as no surprise to some scholars who have examined seventeenth century French and English accounts of contact with Indians. John O' Hear, an archaeologist at Mississippi State University, believes that the Chickasaw may have sought out the English instead of the other way around. During the latter part of the 1600s, parties of Iroquois, armed with English rifles, were raiding Southeastern tribes. If well-armed Iroquois warriors wrecked havoc on some Chickasaw villages, O'Hear believes it is logical to assume that the Chickasaws "would have done whatever was necessary to protect themselves." He started thinking about this possibility more seriously after part of a metal ax dating to the mid-1600s was excavated in 1996 from an early eighteenth century Chickasaw village site in Tupelo.

The Chickasaws told La Salle that their villages were not far away. Two accounts affirm that the Chickasaws said that their villages were one and a half days away. Two other accounts stated the villages were two days distant. One of the French sources said the Indians generally consider ten to twelve leagues (thirty to thirty-six miles) to be a day's travel. La Salle hoped to visit the Chickasaw villages because he assumed that one of his men who had been missing for several days may have been captured by Chickasaws. If such was the case, he wanted to bargain with them to gain the man's release.

Whether La Salle or some of his men or both actually went looking for the villages is not clear. Five of the eight accounts of the expedition indicate that he or his men did try to find the villages. But if they did, they were not successful. It is quite unlikely that the same Chickasaws who were captured by the French would have led them to their villages. According to some accounts, La Salle and his men traveled two days and were then told by the Chickasaws that their village was another three to four days away. Probably sensing that he might be on a wild-goose chase, La Salle returned to the fort. Soon, his missing man turned up whereupon La Salle led his expedition away, having no more contact with the Chickasaws.

Since La Salle did not visit the villages, it is impossible to determine where they were located. But because there are no fewer than eight different accounts of La Salle's Mississippi River expedition, a few clues exist.

In the early 1980s, John Stubbs Jr., a Harvard University graduate student in archaeology, used the brief accounts of La Salle's meeting with the Chickasaws to make an educated guess at the location of their villages. The Mississippi Department of Archives and History (MDAH) hired Stubbs in 1981 to conduct a survey of eighteenth century Chickasaw sites in the Tupelo, Mississippi, area. The impetus came from charges that as the city of Tupelo expanded, Indian graves were being destroyed by heavy equipment and plundered by people looking for valuable burial goods. Hiring Stubbs was the state's attempt to stop or decrease the destruction. By no means would the survey stop development, but at least theoretically archaeologists could excavate the sites before the road graders moved in. (See Surveying Chickasaw Sites.)

Stubbs was recruited primarily by MDAH employee Dr. Patricia Galloway, who had written a number of published articles detailing contact between colonialists and

Southeastern Indians. At the time, Galloway was editing a book titled *La Salle and His Legacy* and Stubbs contributed an article, speculating on the location of the Chickasaw villages in 1682.

By multiplying ten leagues per day times the smallest distance estimate, four and one-half days from Chickasaw Bluffs to the villages, Stubbs placed the sites just south of Tupelo, where settlements were known to be located after 1700. When the Chickasaws arrived is not known.

In this display of temerity and arrogance, La Salle in 1680 claims the land on the east bank of the Mississippi for France while the Chickasaws who have resided on that land for eons sail by wondering what the ceremony signifies. (Painting by Tom Phillips, titled Chickasaw Bluffs Trade Fair. Courtesy of Chickasaw Nation)

If the villages were five or six days away, as other sources stated, then Stubbs believed that the villages likely would be farther south in Clay County. He found this plausible because the Frenchman Tonti, who had been with La Salle in 1682, seemed "to indicate a more southern location [than Tupelo]". And, Stubbs cited MDAH survey work in Clay County that "verified the presence of Chickasaw settlements in the area." (Some archaeologists who have studied the de Soto expedition route believe that they encountered the Chickasaws in Clay County near present-day West Point.)

As for the means that the Chickasaws used to get to and from Chickasaw Bluffs, Stubbs believes that while the Yazoo River doesn't link the Bluffs to their villages, the river's winding course runs at least close to either Tupelo or Clay County. He also cited Galloway's finding that in later years the Yazoo "provided good accessibility to the Chickasaw...."

No matter where the tribe was headquartered in 1682, the record of the chroniclers of the La Salle expedition demonstrates that the Chickasaws conducted business far and wide. At Chickasaw Bluffs, they were 120 to 150 miles northwest of their villages. And in the record of La Salle's expedition, it is implied that the Chickasaws had a friendly relationship with the Natchez located more than 200 miles to the southwest. The case for such an alliance is strengthened by the fact that in 1731 the Chickasaws offered refuge to the Natchez fleeing the French.

Stubbs concludes that the records effectively demonstrate that the Chickasaws, at this very early point in recorded history, had a remarkable "freedom of movement." And by the early 1700s, the Chickasaws were controlling part of the Mississippi River, severely restricting French commerce.

CHICKASAW LIVES

EIGHTEENTH CENTURY

Thomas Nairne Records the Chickasaws in 1708

Thomas Nairne was the first known person in history to record a detailed version of several notable elements of Chickasaw society. But it is important to remember that Nairne's letters that were discovered in the British Library in the 1980s were not written in his own hand. They were copied by someone who apparently was in a hurry; several words are misspelled while other words and phrases seem to have been omitted.

Furthermore, it can only be speculated about Nairne's sources of information. Certainly, he witnessed some things himself when he was visiting the Chickasaws for four or five days, but he does not say which ones. He also had unidentified Chickasaw informants and possibly some non-Chickasaw sources, such as English traders. Probably his traveling companion, Thomas Welch, who had traded with the Chickasaws since at least 1698, was a source of information. Even with these caveats in mind and considering the problems in language translations, scholars have given these manuscripts good reviews. As ethnohistorian Patricia Galloway has written, "I think Nairne's self-interest...assured that his attempt at accuracy was sincere and there are good reasons to believe that the goal of accuracy was largely achieved."

Nairne's account of his visit to the Chickasaws is contained in three letters dated April 12, 13 and 15. The excerpts below cover aspects of Chickasaw family life. The spelling, grammar, and punctuation have not been altered. The bracketed words and italicized sentences have been added for clarification. Some readers may be offended by Nairne's references to Indian people as "savages." While Nairne thought his own culture was superior, he did not believe that the Chickasaws were literally savages. The word

was part of the vernacular of the time, denoting aboriginal people and did not necessarily include a value judgment. Furthermore, it is evident in his letters that he was trying to understand Chickasaw culture, not disparage it.

Nairne wrote all three letters at Hollachatroe, which he identified as the Chickasaw's principal town. Several excerpts from Nairne's letters follow. They touch on the tribe's matrilineal nature; inter-clan relations; Chickasaw women's virtues; male-female roles; wedding etiquette; and marriage information, including related matters of polygamy, adultery and divorce. Nairne even writes about mothers-in-law.

The Chicasaw Customes relateing to woman are singulare and much diferent from the other Savages. They are far from allowing them these scandelous libertys, which are usual Else wher. They bring them up with more Decency and reservedness, so that modesty becomes habituall to them...This people are all togather for Impaling [impeding] even their young wenches, or at lest the watchfull Eye of their Aunts and mothers, carfully avoid makeing themselves cheap by being common. When any of the English Traders tempt the vertue of a young Chicasaw ladie with a present, they usually reject it, with contempt....

Among all the savages, it is Accounted the greatest crime in the world, for a man to marry or Lye with a woman of the same name [clan] tho never so remote or come from another Country. It's very scandelous for them to be so much as privately together. The same avertion we have to the worst sort of Incest they have to that.

A Girles Father has not the least hand or concern in matching her, he is not so much as of the same fameily. The mothers Brother does all, and to him a suiter makes his applaycation, if he gives concent, the bussiness is done, for his Interest is so great with his sister and her Children, that they seldom go against, what is resolved on.

After the unckles concent is procured the spark sends his Freind with a pound or 2 of small beads, these he Delivers to the Mother. She sends for her Brothers and sons and hold a consultation in from whether it shall be a match or not. If it be agreed upon, the beads are devided among the Girles nighest famell relations who are ordered to provide good store of Bread and other Vitualls against such a Day, then sett. Of this they send the man notice, who against the Day, invites his relations. Upon the time apointed, the Bride comes with a Dish of vitualls, and her Troop of Famell kindred, following in the same order. When they have eat and discoursed untill weary, the Bride and her she freinds Depart, to her house, but the Bridsgroom does not follow till Night.

Though by the above account the woman seems to have little or no say in the matter, Nairne also provides this:

The Beautys are so engrossed, by the men of Action, by great Warriors and expert hunters that ordinary Fellows who are sloathfull and unfortunate, are obliged to take up with very mean stuff. These shabroons [ragamuffins] are the only refuge of the Ladys something in years, or who have for their Ill humor, been dismised by better husbands. Thus indulgent nature always provides som releife even for the most unhappy.

The Savages reckon all their fameiles from the mothers side, and have not the least regard who is their father thus if a woman be of the Tygar or Turky fameily, her Childeren are all so too. It seems to be done with the greatest Judgment in the world thus reckoning kindred from the womans side...For this reason the Chiefs sisters son alwaies succeeds and never his own. The Indians call their Uncles and aunts, father and mothers their Cuzons both of the first and second remove, Brothers and Sisters.

Although the Chickasaw culture was matrilineal, as Nairne notes, the husband, also by custom, seemed to have the upper hand in the marriage.

The Chicasaws keep their wives, in good order, and within due bounds.... Its rare to see a man among them subject to Pettycoat Government, look on themselves too brave Martiall men far enough

Facing Page: Thomas Nairne spent a week observing and talking with Chickasaws in 1708, and his written accounts have been invaluable in our understanding of Chickasaw culture early in the contact period with Europeans. (Artwork by Gary White Deer. Courtesy of Chickasaw Nation)

above that they scorn so much as occasionaly to court a woman but alway's send their Freind.

Poligamy is such in fashion among the Chicasaws, the men of note have all 3 or 4 wives a peice, they ar so used to this custom they would never endure to be other wayes. They alledge it's the only convenient way of marriage, and the properest methode to keep a woman in a pleasant humor....

It is among this people, the prerogative of the masculine sex to divorce their wives. The woman are not allowed the same privelage, and dare not upon any Account Leave their husbands, yet when a Lady chances to be very uneasie, she'll by sullen pouts or other methods of Female Management order matters so that her husband will dismiss her and then she is at liberty, but if he don't make publick proclamation that he has freely let her goe, no other dare venture to take her without runing the risque of their lives from his relations.

The Chicasaws are very Jealous of their woman. Its reckoned the greatest afront In the world for one man to lay his hand on anothers wives, and married woman never dance with any man, except their husbands brother or his Freind.* If a Chicasaw Lady intends to Cuckold her husband, she must use the utmost conduct and discration, for upon the least Discovery Death Certainly Ensues, both to her and the gallant for the husband and his kindred seldom ever put up an afront of that nature, so that adultry here is scarce ever comited.

As to the Domestick way of liveing of the Chicasaws...The

men apply themselves to the warr and hunting, supply their Houses plentifully with meat, the woman plant and howe the Corn. It's reckoned beneath a man to touch a howe or bring a litle wood to the fire, and the Ochesees [Lower Creeks] are suficently rediculed among them for their Indulgence to the fair sex, but especially such Chicasaws as have Ochesees wives, never scap being well rallied by others of their Country men, who occasionally ramble that way. What say they have you been obedient to your wife and mother in Law this morning. Pray go cary home some wood they'le be out of Humor Else.

Among the Chicasaws the mother in Law, seldom or ever discourse with her daughters husband, it's reckoned imodest, but his wives breatherin have the same Freindship, with him as his own have. This was a custom so Deferent from the Talapoosies [Upper Creeks], wher the mothers in Law rule all the fameily, that nothing can be more. All the reason the Chicasaws give for it that its their paternall custom. Some crafty fellow I suppose haveing been teised with the impertinances of his Mother in Law, introduced this usage. When a mans wives disagree it does not in the least trouble him he only threatens to Cashier them all if they continue to disturb his repose.

The Grand mothers usually name the Childeren are often from some accident happening to the parents about the time they wer born, this if a man go abroad to the wars when his wife is with Child, he or the other will give it a name betokening his success.

The girles names are usually Flowar, Blosam, Doe, prety faun, or the like, the mens are Valiant , strong, fortunate, hunter, Enemy etc. They're no longer called by these names then they have Done some Military Actions, upon which they have a ware name and that is still changed to a more honorable, as they perform greater feats.

*Friendship is very special and is described in one of Nairne's letters not included here.

Eighteenth Century Deerskin Maps Chickasaw Diplomacy

The 1720s through the 1730s was a complicated, dangerous time-span for the Chickasaws. Broadly speaking, most of them were allied with the English of the Carolina and Georgia colonies (the latter after 1733). The enemy was considered by most tribal leaders to be the French and their Indian allies.

We have learned this from the reports and letters written by English and French officials. Admittedly one-sided and full of inaccuracies and misinterpretations, these communications were virtually the only records of these relations and activities. It would be well more than a century later before Chickasaws began having their side of any story in writing.

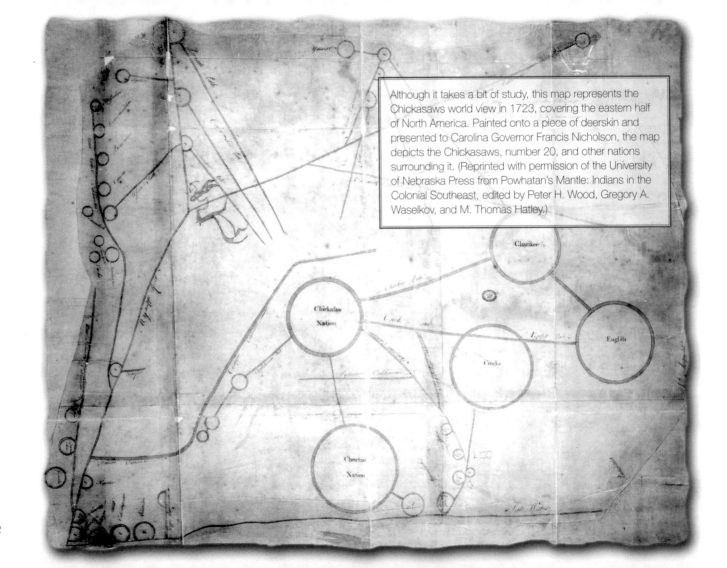

Although it takes a bit of study, this map represents the Chickasaws world view in 1723, covering the eastern half of North America. Painted onto a piece of deerskin and presented to Carolina Governor Francis Nicholson, the map depicts the Chickasaws, number 20, and other nations surrounding it. (Reprinted with permission of the University of Nebraska Press from Powhatan's Mantle: Indians in the Colonial Southeast, edited by Peter H. Wood, Gregory A. Waselkov, and M. Thomas Hatley.)

But there were instances when Chickasaw artists and diplomats did convey information to Europeans through drawings. Often, these were traced in the dirt or drawn with charcoal on the back of tree bark.

On special occasions or in special circumstances, maps that were intended to be preserved were painted on deerskin. One that was painted from the Chickasaw perspective survived long enough to have been reproduced on paper and a copy of it appears with this article. It was made following critical battles during troubled and tumultuous years in the history of the Chickasaw Nation. The map is the closest thing we probably will ever have to communication from the Chickasaw people who were struggling to hold their nation together.

Although the map was almost surely drawn by Chickasaws, the recipients wrote the explanation of the content. They were colonial officials who probably put their own spin on the commentary that was provided by the Indians. The map was drawn about 1723, and the recipient most likely was Carolina Governor Francis Nicholson.

In his article, "Indian Maps of the Colonial Southeast," Gregory Waselkov notes that the Chickasaws who had relocated to Savannah, just 100 miles south of Charles Town, met with Governor Nicholson and exchanged presents. The map probably was among the gifts, Waselkov writes. This was the only known meeting between Nicholson and Chickasaws that took place in 1723.

Carolina officials, doubting that the Chickasaw could survive the constant attacks of the French allied Indians, offered the tribe the opportunity to move lock, stock, and barrel to the Savannah River area. The English would provide necessities if the Chickasaws would agree to act as a defensive buffer between the Carolina colony and tribes unfriendly to the English.

The offer must have been taken seriously, especially since it came after the Choctaw apparently administered a stunning amount of death and destruction to the Chickasaws. On February 1, 1723, the governor of the French colony, Jean Baptiste Le Moyne d'Bienville, wrote that he had motivated or provoked the Choctaws "this winter" to destroy "entirely three villages of this fierce and warlike nation [Chickasaw]." He also wrote that the Choctaw had "brought in about four hundred scalps and taken one hundred prisoners." There is archaeological evidence that these villages were located on a ridge that runs along Coonewah Creek in southwestern Lee County.

No European-made artifacts found in those locations are believed to be dated later than the 1720s, which suggests that the village locations were abandoned about that time. It is known that the Chickasaws also had begun consolidating their houses and villages for better defense. Although the great majority of the Chickasaws turned down Carolina's offer, about eighty Chickasaws led by a chief known as Squirrel King accepted the offer and departed for the Savannah River area near modern-day Augusta, Georgia.

It is possible that any Chickasaw who led this group would have been known as Squirrel King. For as Carolina Indian agent Thomas Nairne wrote in a 1708 letter, *fane mingo* (squirrel king) was a title conferred on a Chickasaw who was skilled in the art of inter-tribal or white-Indian relations.

Although the map was probably presented to Nicholson by Squirrel King when the Chickasaw contingent arrived at Fort Moore, there is no hint about who sketched the map, for a major part of the story depicted on the map vividly illustrated the threat to the Chickasaws who remained in their homeland.

The map showed the Chickasaws in what is now northeastern Mississippi nearly surrounded by several tribes allied with the French. These ranged from the greatest threat, the numerous Choctaw to the south, to several small tribes arrayed in every direction except east. That the east was still open was especially significant because the path to Carolina lay in that direction.

The 1723 map contained sixty locations mainly representing tribes, trails, and rivers. Each of the locations is numbered on the map. Chickasaws (20) are located in the middle of the map (another reason it is thought to be Chickasaw made). This circle is linked by a line to an even larger circle (22) representing the Choctaw. Two bolder lines link the Chickasaws to the Cherokees (21) and the English colony of Carolina (24). The line running to Carolina goes through the top half of another larger circle, 23, representing the Creeks.

Two other lines originate from the Chickasaw circle, one is probably an Indian trail called the Natchez Trace (41) heading southwest to the Chakchiuma , Koroa, and Yazoo tribes. The other line probably represents the Tombigbee River (39) which empties into Mobile Bay, a location near a concentrated area of French-allied tribes, such as the Mobile (28), two Tohome villages (29) and (30) Apalachee villages (33) and three Choctaw villages (31). The dotted lines probably represent trails or tribal boundaries, Waselkov writes.

Another big group of French allied Indians—Natchez (13), Tunica (14), and Houmas (15) can be seen in the lower left-hand corner. They could be reached by the Chickasaw by sailing the Chickasaw River (42) and the Yazoo River (43). All tribes allied with the French have an F next to the circle. These would have been carefully noted so the English could not forget that the Chickasaws needed to be strongly fortified in order to play the key role in blunting French initiatives in the Lower Mississippi Valley.

The annotations were provided by the English but the

Chickasaw presumably explained every symbol on the map. That might explain why some of the words are not recognizable to today's historians or Chickasaw speakers. For example, the word denoting river, *oakhinnau*, is unfamiliar. Shaterrau (39) is apparently the name given for today's Tombigbee River. Either the English spelling didn't capture a phonetic pronunciation recognizable to the Chickasaws or the Chickasaw words have not survived to modern times. Sauhau (1) and Vossullau (2) are unknown names, but from their placement on the map, they were evidently small tribes west of the Mississippi River. Noe India (25) likewise is unknown, but is linked to the Choctaw.

Known tribes, also west of the Mississippi, included three Caddoan (12), two tribes (11) and (10) on the Red River (46) and the Quapaws (19) located at the mouth of the Arkansas River(48). Also on the map are bands of Apache (5), Wichitas (4), and probably the Comanche (3).

To the northwest of the Chickasaw are three paths leading to French-allied tribes, the Peoria (50), Cahokia (51), and Kaskaskia (52). By the latter path is a simple drawing of an armed warrior leading a horse. Waselkov speculates that the drawing symbolizes a Chickasaw attack on the Kaskaskias.

Waselkov notes that the mapmaker's knowledge was extraordinary. The map covers approximately 700,000 square miles and ranges from Florida, Pensacola (35) and St. Augustine (36) to New York (58) on the east and from southeastern Texas (12) to Kansas (3) on the west. Such a large expanse also suggests the far-flung mobility of Chickasaws. This mobility, in part, helped them survive against great odds. Mobility also was manifested in small groups traveling to Cherokee and Creek towns located on or near the two main trading routes to Charles Town, the capital of Carolina. Historian Wendy St. Jean notes that some Chickasaws even settled in those towns primarily to insure that the trading routes would remain open.

Even so, the Chickasaws' firearm suppliers in Charles Town faced an arduous and dangerous journey of more than 700 miles. The map shows that the Chickasaw were almost surrounded by hostile tribes being fed supplies and encouragement by the French. Under similar circumstances, many small tribes had been decimated by colonial led and inspired campaigns. Moreover, a significant number of Chickasaws had left the homeland for the Savannah River area.

So the tribe in 1723 was in dire straits, a condition that was portrayed graphically on the map. Nearly three centuries later to those who understand the map's symbols and the context of the time, the map still conveys not only the message, but the sense of urgency.

Note: Gregory Waselkov's article appears in *Powhatan's Mantle: Indians in the Colonial Southeast*. Permission to use the 1723 map was granted by the University of Nebraska Press, the publisher of *Powhatan's Mantle*.

The French-Chickasaw War of 1736
PART ONE

It was May 26, 1736. From the three villages in the southern part of their nation, the Chickasaws looked down over the prairie to where the French forces had bivouacked. Poised though the French army was, there was no consensus among the Indians that the French would attack these three villages.

There were no Natchez in these villages, and according to the captured French war plans, the French intended to first attack the Natchez whose village was just adjacent to the Chickasaw villages two or three miles to the north.

Ever since the Natchez and French had traded massacres in 1729 and 1730, respectively, they had been deadly enemies. The French army had nearly wiped out the Natchez; most of the Natchez survivors fled north to the Chickasaws who provided asylum.

Subsequently, as a condition to beginning any serious talks with the Chickasaw, the French insisted that the tribe first hand over these refugee Natchez for punishment. What the French may have failed to realize was that the Chickasaw and Natchez had a long-standing alliance. That would explain why so many of the surviving Natchez fled not to the Choctaws, who were much closer, but to the Chickasaws. Perhaps the French also failed to understand that the Chickasaw's tradition of hospitality, in and of itself, would preclude the Chickasaws from complying with the French demand.

The French commander Jean Baptiste Le Moyne d'Bienville should have known better. Bienville was serving his third term as the governor of France's vast colony Louisiana, and in that capacity, he had been dealing with the Chickasaw on and off since 1704. Actually, the Chickasaws had been the bane of Bienville's existence for most of his long military and diplomatic career in Louisiana. Through guile, resourcefulness and intellect, Bienville, without adequate resources, had been trying to develop Louisiana into a viable French colony. To achieve this goal, he needed to foil the English, the leading colonial competitor in the Southeast. This depended on the ability to forge a strong alliance with the Choctaws and Chickasaws to stop the English from making further inroads into the interior. He needed to lure the Chickasaws away from the English traders. Or at least the tribe had to be pacified. Bienville had the advantage of being much closer to the tribes than the English. But France could never even approximate the quality or quantity of the English trade goods. So during the first third of the eighteenth century, the French relations with the Chickasaws alternated between promises (mostly unfulfilled) and threats.

As he looked up toward the Chickasaw villages, Bienville almost surely knew that the Natchez were not in these three villages. The papers containing his war plans against the Natchez and Chickasaw had been found on the body of Pierre D'Artaguette, the commander of the French army, at a village the French called Ogoula Tchetoka (A-gool-a chee-toka), following the battle two months previously. The plans, based on various intelligence sources, probably would have indicated the Natchez's correct location. Or if not, the Choctaw guides certainly knew the Natchez's location. So the Chickasaws must have been wondering why the French were massing nearby because

they were still a few miles southwest of the Natchez's village on the northeast part of the larger prairie.

Possibly, Bienville had gotten word that the northern French and Indian army had been defeated and that his original battle plans may have been intercepted. That would have necessitated a change of plans. Or the sighting of hundreds of Choctaws off in the distance could also have been an important factor. Warriors from these three Chickasaw villages probably had been slave raiding the northern and eastern Choctaw villages intermittently since before 1700. (These three were the closest villages to the Choctaw Nation.) While the French wanted to avenge their national pride by annihilating the Natchez, many of these Choctaws had their own scores to settle with the Chickasaw raiders.

Inside their heavily fortified villages, the Chickasaw warriors, seeing no cannons, were probably confident that

Governor of Louisiana on and off since 1704, Bienville had been both a skillful diplomat and later the architect of a plan to exterminate the Chickasaws. By 1736, he was charged to carry out the plan with the aid of his Choctaw allies. The execution was a disaster for the colony. (Photo courtesy Chickasaw Multimedia) the French army could not dislodge them. Their fortifications combined Chickasaw and English design and experience and would be impervious to any attack except one bolstered by powerful and accurate cannon fire. Furthermore, the Chickasaws, under the war chief Mingo Ouma, had routed the French-led army that attacked Ogoula Tchetoka. Of the 145 French and 326 Indians (Iroquois, Arkansas, Illinois and Miami), more than half were killed and many were captured. French leader Pierre D'Artaguette (Dart-ah-get) and most of his officers were either killed during the battle or even worse for them were captured and burned at the stake. This included a Jesuit missionary Father Senat who was said to have been calmly, yet resolutely singing a hymn as he died in the flames. As a war chief, Mingo Ouma already was well known and respected. He would continue as the tribe's great war chief throughout much of the eighteenth century.

The Chickasaws waited for the French and their uneasy allies the Choctaws to make their move. Among the Chickasaws may have been Imayatabe, a chief of one of the villages most famously known as Ackia. (Chickasaw speakers today have various spellings for it. Pauline Brown spells it Hikeah, which means to stand. Joanne Ellis thinks it may have been Hikki'ya, meaning to stand back or to be left standing. One French official spelled it Ahahikeia. Since there is no spelling consensus, Ackia will be used here.) Imayatabe had made repeated attempts through the 1730s to forge an alliance with the French. They gave him the last name, Leborgne, meaning the "one-eyed man." The French also called him the "Great Chief of the Chickasaws." Traditionally, the great chief was always a peace chief, and because Imayatabe was allying with the French, historians have presumed he was a peace chief. But as a peace chief, he would not be so much pro-French as he would be anti-English because the English promoted continuous slave raiding, which kept the tribe more or less at war. Or it could be that Imayatabe Leborgne hoped that the tribe would benefit from the trade of both nations, but since the balance always seemed to be tipping the English way, he supported the French.

Although peace chiefs were forbidden from spilling blood and were obligated to support peace treaties, it is doubtful at this precarious moment in Chickasaw history that Imayatabe was smoking the pipes of peace. But he probably was responsible for sending out two peace emissaries to Bienville.

Bienville's scouts had returned with no word of the French army under the Illinois territory commander, D'Artaguette. It was evident to Bienville that his army would have to strike the Chickasaws alone. In the inexplicable absence of D'Artaguette's army, there would be no pincer attack (D'Artaguette from the north, Bienville from the south), which Bienville believed would trap the Chickasaws inside their villages where they would be destroyed. Now, the complexion and risks of an attack would be markedly different.

Only a few months before in a letter to his superior in France, Bienville wrote that in view of the formidable Chickasaw fortifications and superior numbers to the French, any attack against them without more equipment, supplies and soldiers would fail, if not end in disaster. Since the King agreed with Bienville (or the other way around) that the key to Louisiana's success was the destruction of the Chickasaws, Bienville was given a few more troops to supplement his army but not the four companies he requested. The cannon he wanted to soften up the Chickasaw fortifications and wreak havoc among the warriors had not arrived.

Bienville's army was an amazing amalgam of French and Swiss soldiers and various groups of others. There was a company of boatmen, forty-five black slaves commanded by a free black man, various Indians (probably mercenaries) and a company of volunteers from New Orleans. In this latter group were said to be merchants along for an excursion. It could be that to get his numbers up, Bienville had deliberately exaggerated the ease with which the campaign would be conducted. One writer said Bienville's campaign was regarded by many in New Orleans as a sort of picnic outing.

Looking across the prairie, the reality was somewhat different, despite what Bienville might have told the citizens and what the Choctaws had told him. As it was, he was facing three Chickasaw villages that formed a triangle on the prairie ridge top. The villages—Apeony, Chukafalaya and Ackia—were separated by a forest between two to three miles in length from a larger prairie where a contingent of Chickasaws were living in perhaps as many as seven villages. The Natchez refugees lived in two villages also on the large prairie. Bienville's intelligence reports indicated that each of the Chickasaw villages had a palisaded fort and several fortified houses outside the walls. These fortifications were protected by rows of thick stakes embedded in the ground, and the walls of the fortified cabins were terraced with earthen embankments to make the structures fire resistant. The cabins, as Bienville called them, contained loopholes for the muskets and were situated so that an advancing enemy would inevitably be caught in a crossfire.

The Choctaw great chief told Bienville he wanted to attack Chukafalaya first. Warriors from Chukafalaya, he said, had caused the Choctaws more trouble than any other village, and it was there that his son and uncle had been killed in battle.

To manipulate the French to that end, the Choctaw guides had led the army not to the Natchez village as they had agreed to do. But by taking a round about route, they wound up on the small prairie across from Chukafalaya, Ackia and Apeony. Then, in another maneuver to get their way, Choctaws had killed and scalped two Chickasaw peace emissaries referred to previously. Their scalps were presented to an abashed Bienville. The scalps didn't fluster him so much as the Choctaws did by aggressively trying to seize control of the situation.

Still, Bienville resisted. The King had ordered him to attack the Natchez. Another formal talk was held with the Choctaw, during which Bienville learned that a majority of his own officers favored an immediate attack from where they were. Furthermore, the Choctaws threatened to pull out if they didn't get the provisions they said they needed without delay. They

Not all Chickasaws were anti-French. One chief, Imayatabe, had attempted repeatedly to make peace with the French. It is possible that Imayatabe's goal was to achieve a diplomatic balance between the English and French. He even tried to prevent the battle at Ackia by sending peace emissaries holding white feathers to the French. Some Choctaws shot them dead. (Photo courtesy Chickasaw Multimedia)

said they knew the three villages contained much more food and supplies than the Natchez camp. They also assured him that the Chickasaw villages would not offer much resistance. As Bienville was about to learn, it was an easy claim for the Choctaws to make. The Choctaw promised Bienville that they would join him in an attack on the Natchez as soon as they had destroyed these slave-raiding Chickasaws.

Bienville looked through his telescope. He saw an English flag flying above one of the villages. He couldn't see behind the palisades, but he was sure that some Englishmen must be inside discussing the impending French attack. He told his officers not to attack that village. In 1736, France and England were not at war, and Bienville apparently thought it would be unethical or illegal to attack the English while the two nations were at peace, however briefly and cynically arranged. Although he didn't say so, the village was probably Chukafalaya; otherwise, he would have no reason not to comply with the Choctaws who had their sights on it. He told his troops they would be attacking the village called Ackia. Though Bienville didn't mention it in his journal, in all probability the Chickasaws inside the palisaded fort had begun to sing a war song.

This might have reminded some of the Choctaws about a sorry event that occurred in 1734. Diron D'Artaguette,

brother of the late Pierre and commander of the Mobile fort, led a large force of Choctaws (perhaps a thousand) on an unauthorized expedition against an unnamed Chickasaw village. Prior to the attack, the warriors inside had begun to sing. This apparently so unnerved the Choctaws that despite their vast numerical superiority, they were not able to take the village and retreated in confusion. And now as Bienville, however reluctantly, was giving the order to attack, the 600 Choctaw sequestered themselves in the rear as their clients (in a sense) the French marched forward, drums beating and flags flying.

*Bienville is the only known recorder of events associated with the Battle of Ackia. Other soldiers in his army are thought to have written accounts but if so those notes have not been located.

The French-Chickasaw War of 1736
PART TWO

At 2 p.m., Bienville gave the signal and the French forces began moving forward. They had spent nearly four hours camped at the edge of the prairie near the base of the hill below the three Chickasaw villages known as Apeony, Chukafalaya and Ackia. But now the leading edge of some 275 troops began marching uphill, both literally and figuratively—right into the teeth of the Chickasaws' heavily fortified defense.

The Chickasaws must have felt relieved when the attack began with drumbeats, not cannons blasting with twenty-pound balls of explosives raining down on their fortifications and heads. Of course, if the French had had the means to destroy the reinforced houses and stockade fort from long distance, they would have attacked hours before. Evidently, they used that time to argue about whether or not to attack any of these three villages.

Finally, they had decided, however reluctantly, to attack the village they thought was Ackia. It was the greatest distance away from the fort flying the British flag. Bienville was giving the British inside the walls of that fort time to clear away since Britain and France were not then technically at war. (Actually, the three villages were contiguous, and it would have been difficult for outsiders to recognize boundaries since there were no signs. Even if the village the French attacked was Ackia, warriors from all three villages would respond.) One final factor in the decision to attack might have been the report from the Choctaws that they had seen large numbers of Chickasaws from the Large Prairie villages to the north pouring into the vicinity. This probably made the battle inevitable.

As the army approached the outlying houses, the Chickasaws inside commenced firing. The French returned fire, but those Chickasaws were well concealed and protected in their houses behind two or three thicknesses of stockade walls and in some cases earthen embankments. In lieu of the only other method of attack that made sense under the circumstances, knocking down the Chickasaw fortifications with cannonballs and mortars, the French moved within musket range of the well-placed, reinforced houses. The front row of grenadiers were protected by a single, supposedly musket-proof shield called a mantelet. Since it was only named but not described by Bienville, this mantelet might have been made from any of several materials. But to minimize their weight over the long distance that they were carried from Mobile, the mantelet was probably made of woven rope instead of wood or metal. Moreover, if the French could have transported additional weight, the soldiers would have been wearing extra protection such as breastplates and helmets.

The French plan for the attack's first phase was to get close enough to lob grenades over the wall into the fort. Then, with the Chickasaws' defenses reduced and softened up, the Indians probably would scatter in alarm. One problem with this plan was that the mantelet protecting the grenadiers was held in place by unarmed, exposed and extremely reluctant black slaves. When Chickasaw marksmen picked off two of those slaves, the other bearers immediately threw down the mantelet and ran off, leaving the grenadiers vulnerable to deadly crossfires of lead coming from the Chickasaw houses.

The warriors stood in a four-foot-deep trench, dug just inside the perimeter of the walls, and fired their muskets through loopholes cut a bit above ground level. Before any of the grenadiers could get close enough to hurl their explosives, the well-protected Chickasaws continued to fire away. The French fell like matchsticks.

The only advantage that the French enjoyed at this point would not be realized for years. This advantage was that the only accounts of the Battle of Ackia would be written by the French, most notably their commander, Bienville. His account and an anonymously written shorter narrative of the battle included names and personal information about the French.

On the other hand, none of the Chickasaws were

Behind the palisade wall of their heavily fortified village, the Chickasaws cut down the advancing French-led army on May 26, 1736. The battle had far-ranging consequences for both sides but especially the French colony of Louisiana. (Artwork by Tom Phillips, titled Battle of Ackia. Courtesy of Chickasaw Nation)

identified, though Bienville knew many of them by name. As a result, in most accounts the French would be identified by historians such as Charles Gayarre and B.F. Riley as the protagonists while the nameless, faceless Chickasaws would be the antagonists. Although Imayatabe was not named in Bienville's narrative, he was recognized as the chief of Ackia in early 1730's French correspondence. Presumably he was there on May 26. Moreover, as a leader who worked to achieve and maintain trade relations with the French, it is likely that he was the one who had sent peace envoys out to the French earlier that day. They were greeted by hostile Choctaws, allies of Bienville bent on insuring that the French would attack and hopefully defeat the Chickasaws at these three southernmost villages. Two of the envoys were killed and scalped by the Choctaws.

The French suffered numerous casualties in their charge toward the fort, but their superior numbers in the outlying area enabled them to capture three fortified houses. Bienville did not report whether the Chickasaws inside the houses fled or were killed. The French also set fire to several smaller houses.

The price the French paid for gaining ground was frightful. The field commander, Chevalier de Noyan, a nephew of Bienville, apparently was unaware of the magnitude of the losses. As he and some junior officers crouched behind the fortified house nearest the fort, Noyan was thinking that the fort could be breeched. On the verge of giving the order to charge, he looked around and probably was stunned by what he saw. Instead of seeing troops moving quickly forward to join him, he saw what must have looked like a slaughter-house of dead and wounded French soldiers. He also observed that the troops who had survived relatively unscathed were cowering behind Chickasaw houses.

What distinguished Noyan's crouching from their cowering was fear. Noyan and the officers were prudently taking cover. But the panic of the soldiers immobilized them; they were too terrified to even run. Afterwards, Bienville emphasized the cowardice and low quality and stature of the soldiers in a report to Lord Maurepas, the minister in Paris in charge of Louisiana. He said the great majority were less than five feet tall and that most of the soldiers had received lashes for various infractions.

On the other side, the Chickasaw war chiefs must have discussed what to do next. They seemed to have a big advantage. Should they press it by sending warriors to finish off the French troops that were pinned down? Such mopping up probably would not take long, overwhelming the few

French troops with many warriors. But there would be some Chickasaw casualties. The chiefs waited for Bienville's next move. This decision suggests that the Chickasaws, not the British, were directing the defense of their villages. Some historians have written accounts implying that the Englishmen inside were in charge.

Meanwhile, French rearguard officers ordered their troops to advance into the battlefield. They refused. The officers alternately threatened dire punishments and offered battlefield promotions and even money, all to no avail. Bienville called this cowardice. But to the soldiers who had seen their compatriots mowed down by well-protected and concealed Chickasaws, moving forward into a shooting gallery may have seemed insanely dangerous.

Still, French honor and prestige were at stake. Something had to be done. Something was done, but not what Bienville wanted. The Chickasaws unleashed another hail of gunfire, and Noyan and other officers were wounded. It wasn't hard to imagine Chickasaw marksmen lined up with the unsuspecting officers in their sites, firing simultaneously. Bleeding from multiple wounds, Noyan ordered his aide to tell Bienville that he needed immediate reinforcements. The aide had scarcely turned to go when he was shot dead. This was the exclamation point in a very desperate situation.

The troops suddenly realized that they were completely vulnerable; death may have been only seconds away. Some were panicky; others were so immobilized they appeared to be in shock. Somehow, Noyan needed to get word to Bienville—reinforcements or retreat?—or all of the officers would perish. But by then the governor could see for himself that a retreat had to be sounded. He ordered an officer named Beauchamp forward with eighty men to protect the retreat and bring back the wounded and dead.

Bienville wrote that while this rescue mission was occurring, the Chickasaws "would not dare to charge them." He was implying that the Chickasaws did not have the courage, but the truth was that by staying behind their fortifications, they could continue to pick off the rescuers without risking a single Chickasaw life. In popular accounts of Ackia, historians made much of this effort, by detailing stories of French valor and heroism in contrast with the barbarism of the Chickasaw. In one such episode, Grondel, a Swiss officer, had been wounded and left to die near the walls of the Chickasaw fort. When Beauchamp's men arrived on the scene, a group of five attempted to rescue him. They were all killed or wounded in the process. Then, some Indians emerged from the fort to finish off Grondel and mutilate his corpse in some public fashion. But before they could reach

Grondel, one French soldier staggered through the hail of bullets, picked up the Swiss officer and raced back to cover. While this rescue was gallant, the historians conveniently forgot to remind the readers who had been attacking whom.

At this point in the battle, increasingly dense smoke, via musket volleys and the house fires set by the French, was probably making it hard to see the enemy. Still, as Beauchamp's soldiers ran forward, many were shot. Charles Gayarre's 1903 account of this part of the battle reported more about him, his fantasies and his fears than it did about the battle: "The Chickasaws, inside the fort and cabins, firing through loopholes, were uttering such appalling whoops and shouts, such blood-freezing shrieks and fiendish yells, that we would have thought that thousands of demons were rioting in one of their favorite haunts in Pandemonium."

Beauchamp's soldiers reached the pinned down officers, and apparently firing to provide cover, they helped some to escape. At this juncture, the Choctaws bestirred themselves. When they had arrived on the scene that morning, some had jeered and taunted the Chickasaws, firing their muskets toward the villages in a traditional show of contempt. Then, they retired to the bottom of the rise where they remained out of sight and action until Beauchamp's men were retreating. Suddenly, an unknown number of Choctaws charged across the prairie toward the fortifications, muskets blazing in a wild attack that seemed to make even less sense than the French attack. Twenty-two Choctaws were killed or wounded, and the rest beat a hasty retreat.

One interpretation of this charge across the plain was that it was a way of showing disrespect for the badly mauled French. Another was that the pro-French Choctaw chief, Alibamon Mingo had either been persuaded or had volunteered to help cover the retreat. Still another reason was the Choctaw hatred for these Chickasaws and their powerful need to uphold the tradition of blood revenge obliged them to do something when they realized that their stand-ins, the French, were being badly defeated.

With the French and Choctaws in full retreat, the Chickasaw war chiefs again may have considered pursuing them. Though such action ran counter to Southeastern Indian battle strategy, just two months before the Chickasaws went in hot pursuit after the retreating French following the battle of Ogoula Tchetoka. Many of the French were killed or captured and later killed. Likely one or more war chiefs advocated another hot pursuit to apply a Chickasaw *coup de grace*. However, two factors made Ackia different. First, routing the French enabled the Chickasaws to capture much needed French armaments and provisions. This was needed more then than now. A Choctaw chief who visited the Chickasaw villages in early 1737 told the French that he found no shortage of firepower and that each village was well stocked with English weapons. Second, the war chiefs could not be sure that the nearly 600 Choctaws would continue to retreat. They were capable of fighting back, which could prove costly to the Chickasaws.

So, with the sun dipping lower on the horizon by 4 p.m., the last shots were fired at the retreating French. No one estimated the number of Chickasaw casualties, though they were probably quite minimal, which was crucial to a tribe whose population had been decreased by warfare and diseases brought by Europeans. Furthermore, Ackia undoubtedly enhanced the tribe's value in the eyes of the British. The battle probably weakened the already diminished pro-French faction of the tribe. And it demonstrated to Choctaw leaders, particularly Red Shoe who was at Ackia, that the French were weak and unreliable allies. A few years later, the Choctaws would be engulfed in a civil war between the pro-French and pro-British factions of the tribe.

No matter how Bienville massaged the message to Maurepas, Ackia had been a terrible, crippling defeat. He reported twenty-four killed and fifty-two wounded. However, French officers had estimated sixty to seventy casualties before Beauchamp's troops arrived. Whatever the actual number, it is certain that Bienville's officer corps had been decimated. These losses were critical in that they were virtually irreplaceable. The absence of an officer corps further weakened an already fragile, undisciplined and needy colony. Though Bienville and the French army would return three years later, his much ballyhooed battle to exterminate the Chickasaws never took place. Therefore, Ackia marked the beginning of the end for the French empire's plan to link its northern territories to the southeastern colony of Louisiana.

Overleaf: With the sun low on the horizon, the French retreated toward the river that had borne them on their disastrous mission. While the battle had negative ramifications for both the Chickasaws and the French, the latter lost a substantial number of its officer corps, from which the colony never recovered. (Photo courtesy Chickasaw Multimedia)

1750s: A Decade of Crisis at Chokkilissa

The letter, expressed by Chickasaw head men in April 1754, stated their plight clearly to England's colonial governor of Carolina: *"It's true some Years ago we did not mind how many our Enemies were, but that is not our case at Present, our Number being reduced to a Handful of Men, and thereby we are rendered uncapable of keeping our Ground without a Continuance of your friendly Assistance, we not being able to hunt nor are we free from the Hands of our Enemies even in our Towns, so that it is impossible for us to kill Dear to buy Cloathing for ourselves, our Wives, and Children, or even to purchase Amunition."*

The head men conveyed that the traders understandably could not extend further credit. Yet, without more guns and ammunition, *"we must either stand and be shott, or defend the Enemies' Bullets with our Hatchets as we have nothing else... we may now say our Lives is in your Power to save or to let the Enemy have their Desire off us."*

Another factor in the critical state of the Chickasaws was that their population had decreased due to disease, the casualties of warfare and "a great many of our People has left us." This was particularly so of the young people who had chosen "to live in peace" rather than to "stay here where they are in Danger every Day." Although not mentioned in this letter, small groups of Chickasaws had been settling among the Creeks and Cherokees, allies of the English, in order to help keep the trading paths open with the English colonies. About this time, an English official wrote that the Chickasaw Nation contained no more than 350 men, down from a reported 700 warriors in 1708.

Nevertheless, the headmen and warriors ended their letter by saying that they would defend their land and liberty to the last.

If the letter reflected a grim scene and future for the Chickasaws, their predicament was actually worse still. Even if Governor James Glen were to grant the Chickasaws' request for more ammunition and guns immediately, the armaments were probably months away from being delivered, because of the great distance and difficulty of the overland route from Carolina or Georgia. Moreover, the arms might not even make it to the Chickasaws. In recent years, Choctaws and other French allied tribes increasingly had been ambushing English supply trains bound for the Chickasaw Nation.

Frequent raids on Chickasaw settlements and hunting camps usually resulted in Chickasaw casualties while forcing the warriors to expend their dwindling supply of ammunition. The French and their Indian allies were waging a war of attrition against the Chickasaws. Eventually, the relatively few Chickasaw survivors would not be able to defend their homeland at Chokkilissa, and they would either die trying or join other tribes.

Facing Page: In this vivid scene, Tom Phillips shows the intensity of Chickasaw warriors going about the business of controlling French traffic on the Mississippi River in the 1740s and 1750s. They managed this despite a dwindling population living more than one hundred miles away in seven villages heavily fortified against frequent French-inspired attacks. Their villages were encompassed in a three to four-square mile area called Chokkilissa.(Painting by Tom Phillips. Courtesy of Chickasaw Nation)

The French governors of Louisiana had been trying to subjugate or exterminate the Chickasaws since the 1730s. In the latter part of that decade, relatively large French and Indian armies attacked but failed to drive the Chickasaws from their homeland in what is now the Tupelo, Mississippi, area. The last large military operation against the Chickasaws came in August 1742 when about 1,600 Choctaws and a few French, in retaliation for war-related casualties, targeted Ogoula Tchetoka for two successive days. But this operation was more a provocation than an attack. When the French forces had struck Ogoula Tchetoka in 1736, the Chickasaws initially held firm inside their heavily fortified village and then came pouring out to rout the enemy. This time, the Choctaw objective wasn't to breech the palisaded walls, but to incite the Chickasaws to attack and then be overwhelmed by superior numbers. Accordingly, the Choctaws staying at a safe distance probably hurled more insults than lead. When the Chickasaws did not bite, the "battle" ended with only a few casualties suffered on both sides.

Another reason for the Choctaw operation to come when it did could have been the reports that some Chickasaws seeking English protection recently had migrated to Carolina and that many others were considering following in their wake. Instead of fighting dispirited Chickasaws, the Choctaws found that one or more Chickasaw war chiefs (probably Mingo Ouma and Paya Mattaha) had rallied the warriors to defend their nation. Furthermore, the Chickasaws and their Carolina and Georgia trading partners wanted to lure many of the Choctaw towns out of the French trading orbit and into the much more reliable and attractive English partnership. They had a receptive audience in two western Choctaw leaders Red Shoe and Fanemingo Tchaa.

Other chiefs, most notably Alibamon Mingo, remained pro-French. Conflict soon developed among Choctaw chiefs, factions, and towns over whether to have trading alliances with the English or the French. Even though the French and Choctaws had been allies since 1700, French trade goods, never plentiful, had become scarce and were poor quality. English commodities were superior in number and quality and were cheaper. English traders began trading predominately with western Choctaw towns. James Adair, thirty-seven, had taken up business with trader John Campbell and residence with the Chickasaws at the Chokkilissa homeland settlement in 1744.

With the support of two Chickasaw chiefs Pastabe and Pahemingo-Amalahta, Adair and Campbell ventured, with numerous Chickasaw escorts into western Choctaw towns whose residents wanted trade goods and perhaps had Chickasaw kinship connections. Believing that the Carolina governor had promised him a monopoly in the Choctaw trade, Adair conspired with Red Shoe to plot a rebellion against the French that contributed to the Choctaw Civil War of 1747-49.

The roots of the Choctaw civil war were more complicated than that. Although the Chickasaws and their English trading partners were egging on the Choctaw pro-English factions whenever possible, these were relatively peaceful years for the Chickasaws.

Nevertheless, during the war, the French offered rewards for the heads of rebellious chiefs (meaning anybody not pro-French) and bounties for scalps of Chickasaws. By early 1749, the chiefs of all pro-English Choctaw villages were reported to be dead, including Red Shoe in 1747 and Fanemingo Tchaa in 1748. But before the war ended, French records reveal that the Chickasaws absorbed some fleeing Choctaws and Chakchiumas into their villages. Even more Choctaws would have fled to the Chickasaws if Louisiana Governor Pierre Vaudreuil had not granted pardons to those Choctaws he considered rebellious. But he warned that those who joined forces with the Chickasaws would be dealt with harshly.

When the Choctaw Civil War ended in 1749-50, the French insisted that both factions of Choctaws renew continuous attacks against the Chickasaws, for Louisiana's worst-case scenario would be a Chickasaw-Choctaw peace. In an optimistic report to the French king in 1751, it was noted that "so few of them [Chickasaws] remain that the Choctaws will soon succeed in destroying them...."

Only the word "soon" made the report overly optimistic. No one battle or probably even several would destroy the Chickasaws. The number of attacking warriors depended on the season and the resources available from the French. In addition to the Choctaws, the French induced their northern tribal allies to attack the Chickasaws as well. (Some, like the Arkansas, Miami and Kickapoo, didn't need much, if any, inducement because they had been long-time enemies of the Chickasaw.) Nobody executed frontal attacks against the well-entrenched Chickasaw in their homeland, which since about 1740 consisted of about seven villages within the settlement known by them as Chokkilissa, and by the British as Big Town. Instead, the French alliance isolated and cut them off by burning outlying houses; by killing and capturing men, women and children; by intercepting trade goods; by picking off members of hunting parties; by destroying crops; and by killing or capturing as many horses as possible to hamper trade.

The reports from English and French sources during the 1750s are inconsistent and sometimes contradictory. On the one hand, the Chickasaws often seemed to be completely cut off in their villages; on the other, Chickasaw hunting parties seem to abound. The main reason for these mixed reports is that the traders were not tribal insiders; they could only report what they had seen and were told by chiefs dictating what they wanted English colonial officials to know.

Though they seemed to be virtually surrounded by enemies, the Chickasaws from 1752-54 were able to restrict France's use of the Mississippi River, a crucial supply route from New France in the north to Louisiana in the south.

Yet, English traders like John Buckles assumed considerable risks to get gifts and trade goods through to the Chickasaws and would not attempt to do so without a substantial number of Indian (usually some combination of Chickasaw, Creek and Cherokee) escorts. It was certainly in the best interest of the Choctaws to capture these supply trains, and both tribes operated in deadly earnest. These were kill or be killed situations, and attempting to even the score was a powerful motivator. In a 1752 report, it was recounted that after two Choctaws killed two men and a woman, the Chickasaw survivors pursued them, eventually killing four, capturing two and burning them alive. The captured and wounded Choctaws were scalped and disemboweled. The Chickasaws who had recently lost friends to the Choctaws painted themselves with their victim's blood.

In light of past Chickasaw immigration to the east, the traders gave the chiefs lectures on staying the course, which they didn't need. In fact, the chiefs in 1754 asked Carolina Governor James Glen to send the Chickasaw chief Squirrel King's warriors back to the homeland to help defend it. (Years before, Squirrel King and about eighty Chickasaws had accepted Carolina's invitation to settle near Savannah.) One French intelligence report noted that the Chickasaws would have been broken up without the support of the Cherokees and Shawnees, some having married into the tribe (it is speculated in the report) to receive English gifts.

Chickasaw mortality reports during the early 1750s support the tribe's pleas to the English for as much assistance as possible. In 1753, thirty-one Chickasaws were killed in battle, and several more were captured or wounded in the prior eighteen months. In a tribe as small as the Chickasaws, those were significant numbers. In a 1754 report, trader Buckles wrote that twenty-eight had died during the last year, seventeen of whom were killed by Choctaws.

Finally, Governor Louis Kerlerec of Louisiana wrote in December 1754 that he "had been assured that they [the Chickasaws] were on the eve of abandoning their villages and of drawing near the English territory."

Today, Kerlerec's observation appears to have been wishful thinking. But in late 1754, he may have thought that his intelligence reports were accurate, although there was no telling what was in the hearts and minds of the Chickasaws defending their homeland. Nevertheless, available documentation establishes the Chickasaws were in mortal danger over the next four years. According to a 1755 report by Carolina official Edmond Atkin, the Chickasaws had 350 men in seven villages within a circumference of ten miles, while the Choctaws had 3,600 men in some fifty-two villages.

The Choctaw advantage appeared to be substantial, yet the Chickasaw homeland fortifications throughout Chokkilissa verged on impregnable. Atkin wrote that a fort and ditch protected each village. Certainly, the French forces or Choctaw warriors had never breeched the fortified villages. Another layer of protection was provided by swamps that bordered the villages on three sides. To those who would look in vain for those swamps today, Tupelo resident Steve Cook says the swamps were courtesy of a huge population of beavers whose dams had flooded every stream in the area. Cook gained this insight from an examination of some 1834 survey maps and notes and a reading of Thomas Nairne, writing in 1708 of the "multitudes of Beavor Dams."

One more factor in the Chickasaw's favor was that while some English pack trains never got through, enough supplies arrived to keep the muskets firing (and the Chickasaws dependent on the English). For example, in 1756 Carolina records show that the colony supplied the tribe with 75 guns, 600 pounds of powder, 1,200 pounds of musket balls, and 4,000 gun flints. A year later, the colony provided another large supply of arms. In emergencies, English traders gave away ammunition to their Indian allies, such was the Chickasaws' strategic importance to the English colonies.

Meanwhile, Louisiana, never having been adequately supplied by the French crown, was in "utter destitution" in 1756, according to its governor, Kerlerec. Soldiers were deserting, and the colony's Indian allies were restive, to say the least. A year later, the governor wrote that he had not even heard from France since mid-1755. The governor wrote that the warehouses were empty and the Choctaws needed "everything." Fighting colonial insurgencies in India and Africa and the French and Indian War in 1754 against England in the north, France was too overextended to help. Moreover, an English naval blockade prevented many ships from reaching the French colony. Clearly, Louisiana's survival had to have a higher priority in Paris.

But with all their problems, both tribes continued their war of sorts, often raiding each other's hunting camps or the outskirts of a village. These two entries from English trader John Buckles' 1757-58 journal are representative.

> *June 24th: A small Gang of Chactas* [Choctaws] *came into the Nation in the night, killed a fellow and wounded a Child as they were asleep on a Corn House Scaffold.*

> *15th December: The Chactaws killed a Chickersaw as he was going out a hunting and carryed off a Woman and two Children. The 16th the Chickersaws pursued them... killed five and redeemed said Woman and Children.*

The anxiety among the Chickasaws in the villages within Chokkilissa must have risen during the late 1750s. Not only were they in crisis but they also probably lacked the intelligence reports that would have assured them that the French could not supply their Indian allies and save Louisiana. Moreover, when the British captured Quebec from the French in 1759 and Montreal in 1760, Kerlerec must have known that France would consider Louisiana expendable. The die was cast. Choctaw raids tapered off and virtually ceased.

Until 1763, when the Treaty of Paris ended hostilities, England and France continued their war, but not in the Mississippi River Valley. France ultimately relinquished virtually all of its North American holdings. Unlike some other small tribes caught up in the competition between England and France for dominance in the Mississippi River Valley, the Chickasaws had survived. But the changes in the tribe's culture had been profound and were irreversible.

Living in one of the villages of Chokkilissa at this time was trader James Colbert, who would play a pivotal role in the next era of the tribe's history. He had come to the nation as a Carolina trader and by 1740 was a resident trading agent learning to speak Chickasaw. By 1758, when the Choctaws and Chickasaws were finally at peace, Colbert began trading with the Choctaws. Three years later as a British officer, Captain Colbert led eleven Chickasaw warriors to the aid of a British fort under siege by the Cherokees. Most importantly, Colbert married a Chickasaw woman who two years later gave birth to their son, William. James would marry two other Chickasaw women and would father seven more children. The family would become a dynasty of Chickasaw leadership that would extend far into the nineteenth century.

Hearts and Minds of the Chickasaws in the 1780s

In the 1780s, the Chickasaws were split into roughly two factions. They were distinguished mainly by their two well-known, charismatic leaders and the imperialist nations they supported. One faction, led by Piomingo, supported the Americans; the other, led by Ugulaycabe, generally backed the Spanish. The Chickasaw King, Mingatuska, repeatedly changed his support from one side to the other.

This may have been a tactic on his part to keep his chiefs and both suitor nations off balance. Or he may have been indecisive, or vain, or corrupt. Not enough is yet known about Mingatuska to understand his motivations.

At any rate, both factions seemed to do as they pleased. Ugulaycabe (the modern Chickasaw pronunciation is Oo-goo-LA-ka-bee) signed a treaty of alliance with Spain at Mobile in 1784. Piomingo signed a similar treaty with the United States at Hopewell, South Carolina, in 1786.

These commitments to powers competing for control over the lower Mississippi Valley might have led the Chickasaws to war with the United States or Spain, or to a civil war. But the tribe benefited from the attention of both in terms of military hardware and supplies. Spain's plan was to use the Indian nations of the South as a buffer between Spain's Louisiana Territory and the American settlements. During the 1780s and 1790s, the Spanish governor held several meetings with the Chickasaws, Choctaws, Cherokees and Creeks, proclaiming that Spain was the Indians' protector. Ugulaycabe was invited periodically to New Orleans, where the Spanish officials wined, dined and bribed him with an annual sum of $500.

The Americans conducted similar acts of "diplomacy." American agent William Davenport in 1786 distributed gifts and medals to Piomingo and the other tribal leaders. President George Washington had dispensed military commissions to Piomingo, William Colbert and several head warriors.

It was clear that neither Spain nor America wanted to go to war over the Lower Mississippi Valley, and both sides were content to continue courting the Southern Indians. Even though Piomingo remained staunchly pro-American, Spain was more attentive to Chickasaw needs. Spain's special Chickasaw agent, Captain Juan de la Villebeuvre, lived with the tribe. America's Chickasaw agent, James Robertson, lived in Nashville and refused to move south. He was replaced in 1797 for that very reason.

Still, war was possible largely because of the actions of one man: Alexander McGillivray, a mixed-blood Creek chief. His motivation for signing an alliance agreement with Spain in 1784 had been his hatred for Americans. His enmity was derived, in part, from America's support of Georgia's encroachment onto Creek lands. With Spanish arms, he attacked white settlements on the eastern edge of the Creek Nation and checked Georgian expansion.

McGillivray was most active in lining up the other Southern tribes to make an alliance with Spain. He regarded the Chickasaws as the most problematic tribe because of Piomingo's unswerving friendship with the Americans. Ugulaycabe's group supplied clandestine reports to McGillvray about Piomingo's activities and those of American agents and traders in the Chickasaw Nation.

In 1787, McGillivray demanded that the Chickasaws

expel American agents. When the Chickasaws did not comply, McGillivray began sending or leading raiding parties into the Chickasaw Nation to harass and occasionally kill Americans or Chickasaws not supporting the Spanish. One Chickasaw killed by Creek raiders in 1789 was Piomingo's nephew, who was carrying a message from Piomingo to President Washington.

Simultaneously, McGillivray, aware that the Chickasaw king was angry at the Americans for ignoring him in favor of Piomingo, attempted to whip up intra-tribal hostility. In response to Creek incursions, Piomingo visited New York and Philadelphia, requesting military assistance and trade goods. McGillivray's warriors had been intercepting American trade goods intended for Chickasaws. Only Spanish goods were getting through. Piomingo told the Americans that the trade goods were indispensable and that the Chickasaws would wind up fighting the Creeks or joining the Spanish alliance.

Meanwhile, President Washington in 1790 invited McGillivray to come to New York to negotiate an agreement between his faction of Creeks and the United States. Profession of "justice" aside, Washington issued the invitation because he knew the United States was facing an Indian war in the Northwest and he did not want to be facing hostilities on two fronts. For agreeing to give up some land to Georgia, McGillivray received a promise of federal protection and the right to evict whites from their land. He also received $1,200 and a commission as a brigadier general in the U.S. Army. When he arrived back home, he promptly revealed the details of the treaty to the Spanish governor, Miro, and accepted a $2,000 annuity from Spain.

The Americans were unresponsive to Chickasaw requests for aid until 1791, when Piomingo and fifty warriors volunteered to help the young American Republic put down the Indian uprisings in the Northwest. Finally, U.S. officials realized that Piomingo's faction would be useful in combating the Spanish and Creeks. President Washington lavished gifts on Piomingo and invited him to Philadelphia for a personal meeting.

The next year the Americans invited delegates of many Southern tribes (including the Creeks) to Nashville to sign a peace treaty. William Blount, a superintendent of Indian Affairs, uttered a sentence that would have lived in infamy if so many other government officials had not said the same thing. He told the Indians that while Spain would demand land cessions, "we shall not; we wish you to enjoy your lands and be as happy as we ourselves are... the United States have land enough."

In 1792, McGillivray signed another treaty with Spain, guaranteeing all Creek lands that the tribe possessed and the support to defend those lands. The chief's annual annuity was increased to $3,500. The Creeks guaranteed to Spain the territory of Spain in Louisiana and west Florida.

Creek raids on the Chickasaws increased, and in February 1793, a raiding party killed a Chickasaw hunter and then made an example of him by hacking and mangling his body. Piomingo convened his followers who voted to retaliate on the Creeks. Simultaneously, the chief requested American aid. This time the federal government promptly shipped a large supply of arms by armed boats to Piomingo's warriors at Chickasaw Bluffs (now Memphis, Tennessee). Now, well equipped and highly

Piomingo was a staunch ally of the Americans in competition with Spain and the Creeks for control of the Lower Mississippi Valley in the 1780s and 1790s. This magnificent sculpture of Piomingo is ensconced in front of City Hall in Tupelo, Mississippi. The location is just a few miles from Piomingo's home in Long Town, where Chickasaw warriors repulsed a large Creek attack in 1795. (Sculpture by William N. Beckwith, Taylor, MS. Photo provided by Mr. Beckwith.)

motivated, they drove the Creeks out of their nation. It probably helped that McGillivray had died. While visiting the trader William Panton in Pensacola in February 1793, McGillivray, only 34 years of age, succumbed at a time when he was suffering mentally and physically from gout and exhaustion. He told Panton he was "approaching to a despondency" over the prospects of a general alliance against the Americans.

Spain changed tactics; officials tried to bribe Piomingo. Unsuccessful, Spain obtained authorization from the Ugulaycabe faction to build a palisaded fort in the Nation at Chickasaw Bluffs, garrisoned with 150 men and supplied by the trading firm of Panton and Leslie. Then many of Ugulaycabe's followers established a settlement nearby for protection against Piomingo's warriors seeking retribution.

But Piomingo's warriors were by then attacking Creek settlements. In 1795, the Creeks counter-attacked, sending an estimated 1,000 warriors across the Tombigbee River. Their objective was to subdue Long Town, Piomingo's headquarters. Blessed by excellent reconnaissance, the Chickasaws hid in the woods near the Long Town stockade. When the Creeks attacked, the Chickasaws came screaming out of the woods at the unsuspecting Creeks who fled willy-nilly. Approximately forty Creeks and five Chickasaws were killed, according to Malcolm McGee, a Chickasaw interpreter.

Actually, McGee was not present. He and a delegation of Chickasaws were on a mission to protest to American officials Creek aggressions and the building of the Spanish fort at Chickasaw Bluffs. They first stopped in Nashville to register their complaints with General James Robertson and to ask him to equip them for the trip to Philadelphia to see the president.

Blount had asked Robertson to "turn them back if you can." Robertson tried his best but wound up outfitting them for the trip. Washington received the delegation on August 22, 1795. It consisted of McGee, Major William Colbert, John Brown the Younger and Captain William McGillivray, who like Colbert had received his commission from Washington. They asked Washington when he would be sending an army against the Creeks, as General Robertson had told them was in the offing.

Washington said his man was wrong: "It was never the design of the U.S. to interfere in the disputes of the Indian Nations among one another unless as friends to both parties, to reconcile them. If I were to grant you the aid of my warriors...the consequence would be a general war between the United States and the whole Creek Nation. But the power of making such a war belongs to Congress exclusively. I have no authority to begin such a war without their consent."

But, the president told the delegation that his friendship for the Chickasaws "will not permit me to let them suffer from the want of provisions," and Governor Blount "will receive my orders on this subject."

Washington called the building of the fort on Chickasaw Bluffs an "unwarranted aggression as well against the United States, as the Chickasaws to whom the land there belongs. I shall send talks, and do what else shall appear to me proper to induce the Spanish King, or his Governor, to remove their people from that Station, and to make no more encroachments on your lands."

Washington diplomatically directed Spanish governor Gayoso of Natchez to remove the fort. Though the president may have been persuasive, it is also true that Spain had recognized the futility of its plan to create and maintain an Indian confederation loyal to the Spanish. As a result, the United States and Spain signed the Treaty of San Lorenzo, which recognized the United States title to all of the southwestern lands north of 31 degrees latitude and west to the Mississippi River—in short, all of the land that Spain had sought to use as a buffer between its own territory and the United States.

CHICKASAW LIVES

NINETEENTH CENTURY

Forced Removal of the Chickasaws
An Epic Tragedy

Thomas Jefferson's version of Manifest Destiny was logical and orderly. He hoped the frontier would move westward at a regular pace with few, if any, costly wars because the original residents, the Indians, would either be civilized and brought into American society or be bought off and removed. As the first step toward achieving this, he told the Indians, through Meriwether Lewis and others that American trading posts were to be established in their country that offered them jobs and secure income if they would take furs instead of scalps. President Jefferson told them he wanted a mutually beneficial relationship based on commerce.

But Jefferson knew that such a relationship could not last long because the game animals were a non-renewable resource. What he had not anticipated was how quickly the hunt would be over, because increasing numbers of white intruders were also hunting on the Indians' land. Furthermore, Jefferson's plan was "to exchange lands which they [the Indians] have to spare and we want for necessaries, which we have to spare and they want." American traders were to extend credit to the Indians so that they would soon be deeply in debt. At that point the Indians "become willing to lop them off by a cession of lands."[1]

This is precisely what happened with the Chickasaws who ceded land in 1805, 1816 and 1818. Before 1805, the Chickasaws controlled millions of acres in what is now western Kentucky, and western Tennessee, northern Mississippi, and northwestern Alabama. After 1818, they retained only about 495,000 acres in northern Mississippi and northwest Alabama and were, according to historian Arrell Gibson, "easy marks for the final pressure which would appropriate all that remained of their eastern homeland and would cast the nation into the trans-Mississippi wilderness."[2]

Indeed. In the instructions to the Americans who negotiated the 1818 land cession with the Chickasaws was the following: "The president (James Monroe) is very anxious to remove the Indians on this side to the west of the Mississippi; and if the Chickasaw could be brought to an exchange of territory, it would be preferred."[3] An exchange did not happen in 1818 nor in 1826, when commissioners representing President John Quincy Adams tried to negotiate a removal treaty with the Chickasaws. In answering the government's arguments for removal, the tribal representatives said the Chickasaws preferred to remain in their historic homeland because they doubted that a more suitable land could be found. And there was another compelling reason: if the government could not protect the tribe in the East, it would only be a matter of time before the government would be unable [or unwilling] to protect the tribe in the West.[4] Enticements to explore lands west of the Mississippi at government expense and threats that the federal government might develop a sharper edge in future dealings with the tribe did not move the unyielding Chickasaws.

In 1827, the tribe was visited by Thomas McKenney, commissioner of Indian Affairs. Instead of using threats and bribes, as previous commissioners had, McKenney displayed an enlightened, respectful and friendly approach. He told his friend Levi Colbert and the other leaders that it was just as important to think about the future as the past. Removing to the West, though a painful and costly step, would in

McKenney's opinion "relieve them from the ...increasing causes [white incursion] that had operated to render them miserable where they were." [5]

McKenney persuaded the leaders to at least look at lands west of the Mississippi. This was the first time that the tribe had not refused flatly to discuss removal, and it proved to be a turning point in relations with the federal government. After Congress appropriated the expense money, a Chickasaw party of twelve, including Levi Colbert and other mixed bloods and some full bloods, explored parts of present-day, east-central Oklahoma in 1828. They reported that the land was not nearly equivalent to their eastern homeland and recommended against moving. [6]

But in 1829 and 1830, Mississippi and Alabama extended its laws over the Chickasaw Nation. When the tribe appealed to President Andrew Jackson, under whose command they once fought the Creeks in 1813-14, he said he was powerless to intervene. Either the Chickasaws could move west or be subject to state laws and extinction as a tribe. [7] The die was cast. Since the federal government would not enforce its obligations under the 1786 Treaty of Hopewell, the leaders of the tribe felt they had no choice but to negotiate a removal agreement with the best possible terms.

Over the next six years, the tribe signed treaties with federal negotiators three times, most famously at Franklin, Tennessee, and Pontotoc, Mississippi, and explored without success potential new homes to the west. During this time, the Chickasaw agent Benjamin Reynolds wrote that "whiskey traders, pedlars and all types of intruders were entering the country and doing injury to the Chickasaws." [8] Apparently, he did not realize that the state governments and federal government in reality were supporting the whiskey traders and intruders. Furthermore, since Chickasaw reservations could be sold under certain limitations by Chickasaws, a host of white speculators appeared bearing money and whiskey, and a great deal of land swindling took place. As historian Guy Braden wrote, `The stench of the pool of corruption into which the Chickasaws were sinking, no doubt, had a sobering effect on the majority of the Chickasaw leaders and gave them a new desire to leave for the West." [9]

Between 1833 and 1837, Chickasaw parties spent much time exploring the trans-Mississippi territory. The Chickasaws found land in east Texas acceptable but the federal government rejected their finding and refused to discuss the matter further. While the Choctaws would permit the Chickasaws to settle with them on their land, they were unwilling to sell a portion of it to the Chickasaws. [10] For their part, the Chickasaws were unwilling to subsume their national identity.

Finally, in January 1837 at Doaksville near Fort Towson in the Choctaw Nation, the Chickasaw leaders agreed to pay the Choctaws $530,000 for the right to settle on about five thousand square miles in what was the western portion of that tribe's vast estate. The Chickasaw leaders wisely asked the president not to deliver them into the hands of selfish contractors and made pertinent suggestions about steamboat transportation and the purchase of supplies. A few years earlier, the Chickasaws had witnessed the suffering and hardships of the Choctaws as they removed to the West and resolved not to follow in that tribe's path. But the Chickasaws were not always masters of their fate.

The Chickasaws would not refer to their removal to the West as the "trail of tears." But that did not imply that tears were not shed along the way, that death and tragedy did not stalk many within the tribe, or that the elders and full bloods were not heartsick at leaving the home of their ancestors.

The federal government named A.M.M. Upshaw as superintendent of the Chickasaw removal. He outlined the travel route prescribed by the commissioner of Indian affairs: from Pontotoc to Memphis, "thence down the Mississippi River and up the Arkansas to the mouth of the Canadian in steamboats, and then by land to the west portion of the Choctaw tract where the Chickasaws were to be located."[11] Upshaw expected the first thousand tribal members to gather in June. However, by mid-June only about four hundred Chickasaws had assembled at the first staging center. Some could not bring themselves to leave their homes; others were victimized by whiskey peddlers. According to Upshaw, fifty to one hundred Indians were drunk each day. Moreover, a chief named McGilvery decided to oppose removal and most members of his district would not leave their homes.[12] One incident just prior to the first removal seemed to symbolize the dispirited state of the tribe. Emubby, a famed warrior and advisor to the chiefs, was murdered in front of several witnesses by a white man in cold blood. Traditionally, Chickasaw revenge was a clan duty, and the government agents expected trouble. But there was no retribution; the Chickasaws continued to prepare for a June departure.

The initial group of some 450 to 500 Chickasaws pulled out of their settlements in late June, heading for Memphis. According to John Millard, conductor for this first group, the Indians "traveled with slaves, herds of cows and horses, and wagons crammed with their possessions and farm implements."[13] They arrived in Memphis, ironically,

on July 4, the birth date of American Independence. They were described as "handsome in appearance, being nearly all mounted, and, with few exceptions, well dressed in their national costume." They were said to be traveling "in good order" and "not a drunken Indian was seen in the company; and the whole after traveling eight miles crossed the Mississippi on the same day."[14]

The conductor, Millard, kept a daily journal of the passage .[15] Between July 4 and July 25, he chronicled their difficult, 135-mile trek between Memphis and Little Rock. On the 7th, "we were compelled from the severity of the rain to stop [early] and camp for the night." The next day their road ran out after five miles, and they "found the swamp nearly impossible." Two wagons were abandoned in the swamp. Due to "the inclement weather" and bad roads, their progress was slow and extremely fatiguing. On the 12th, exhausted and repairing their wagons, they did not move at all. On the 16th, they were joined by an additional thirty-nine

Facing Page: Although it has been said that the Chickasaws suffered less in their removal to Indian Territory than other tribes, look at the faces of the family as they bury one of their own. (Painting by Tom Phillips, titled Chickasaw Removal. Courtesy of Chickasaw Nation)

Chickasaws, bringing the total to about five hundred. On the 18th, they spent the day crossing a river, and Millard reports "some few [Chickasaws] sick."

They continued to Little Rock, where Chief Sealy announced that they would not be traveling by steamboat, as had been arranged, to Fort Coffee, Indian Territory. Before his death, Emubby had told them to go the Red River route, southwesterly toward Fort Towson in the Choctaw territory. Millard warned them against such a course, noting that the trip by steamer was far shorter and easier and warning about the "impossibility of procuring food on any but the Fort Coffee road." After meeting in council again, the Chickasaw leaders announced that some 150 elderly and sick would go by steamer to Fort Coffee. They reached Fort Coffee five days later on August 1 with only one loss of life; a woman fell overboard and drowned. More than three hundred others under Chief Samuel Sealy, however, set off overland with their horses.[16]

The Chickasaws suffered greatly while going overland during August, pausing every day to bury those who had died from disease. They also stopped to hunt, recover their horses from thieves, and deal with white traders who sold whiskey to the Indians at every stop. These delays greatly aggravated the removal officials, so they threatened to call for troops who would compel the Chickasaws "to march at the point of the bayonet."[17] The death rate climbed. From an occasional death at the beginning of the journey, four or five were dying daily near the end.[18] Most of these were babies who died from diarrhea and the elderly including the tribe's great war chief Tishomingo. The site of his grave is unknown. The heartsick survivors arrived at Fort Towson on September 5, suffering from exhaustion, illness and malnutrition.

Meanwhile, reportedly 4,000 Chickasaws were gathering at Memphis, and the federal officials hoped to avoid the problems and delays of the first group. The Chickasaw chiefs and removal officials agreed that the tribe would travel by steamboat, and a deal was made to employ Simeon Buckner to ferry the tribe from Memphis to Fort Coffee. Just before Buckner's steamboats docked in Memphis, the Chickasaws learned that a steamboat carrying Creeks to their new western home had exploded, killing 300. As a result of the report, more than 1.500 Chickasaws refused to go by boat. Upshaw railed at them, threatening to withhold their rations, but the leaders pointed out that he could not withhold rations because the tribe had paid for its own emigration expenses. Upshaw gave in and assigned removal personnel to accompany the land-bound Chickasaws.[19]

It took four days for all the Chickasaws who refused to travel by boat to cross the Mississippi River. According to Upshaw, they had "an immense quantity of baggage and four or five thousand ponies. I have used all the influence that I had to get them to sell off their horses, but they would...part with their lives as part with a horse."[20]

Afterward, writing from an "Arkansaw swamp," a white adventurer described a Chickasaw encampment:

I do no think that I have ever been a witness of so remarkable a scene as was formed by this immense column of moving Indians...with the train of Govt. waggons, the multitude of horses; it is said three to each Indian & besides at least six dogs and cats to an Indian. They were all most comfortably clad—the men in complete Indian dress with showy shawls tied in turban fashion round their heads—dashing about on their horses, like Arabs, many of them presenting the finest countenance and figures that I ever saw.

"The women also very decently clothed like white women, in calico gowns—but much tidier and better put on than common white-people—and how beautifully they managed their horses, how proud & calm & erect they sat

in full gallop. It was a striking scene at night—when the multitudes of fires kindled, showed to advantage the whole face of the country covered with the white tents and white covered waggons.... Then you would hear the whoops of Indians calling their family party together to receive their rations, from another quarter a wild song from the negroes preparing the corn, with the strange chorus that the rest would join in ... this would set a thousand hounds baying & curs yelping—& then the fires would catch tall dead trees & rushing to the tops throw a strong glare over all this moving scene ....[21]

How many Chickasaws Buckner did transport in the steamboats is not known, but an 1842 investigation by the U.S. House Committee on Public Expenditures found that the number could not have exceeded three thousand. Despite scant and unreliable documentation, the record shows that Buckner received the outrageous sum of approximately $146,000. The congressional committee found that the government (or the Chickasaws, who were really paying the costs) could have bought four steamships and transported the tribe for an estimated $92,000, some $54,000 less than Buckner was paid. Of the $146,000, Buckner charged and was paid some $37,700 for the Chickasaws who refused to

go by steamship but instead went overland. Furthermore, he charged and received some $54,500 for transporting 1,000 tons of baggage. Simple computation done by members of the congressional committee showed that the total tonnage could not have exceeded forty-five tons. Apparently Buckner had charged for transporting the Chickasaws' livestock that had been driven overland.[22]

Heavy rains in Arkansas were advantageous to those traveling by boat and a major impediment to those land-bound emigrants. Boat travelers reached Fort Coffee within eight days. Those going overland took four to six weeks and were confronted by heat, mud, swamps, unclean rations and diseases. One observer wrote that "money could not compensate for the loss of what I have seen" the Indians endure on their trek.[23]

And yet almost from the beginning of the emigration, Chickasaw leaders had charged contractors with fraud of one kind or another. The rations were rotten, not delivered, or not properly weighed. Despite the fact that the Chickasaws were paying their own removal expense, their complaints were ignored or otherwise not addressed by federal officials. When the charges—primarily from Chickasaw chiefs, but also from the Cherokees and other tribes—did not abate in number or volume, the U.S. War Department ordered Major Ethan Allen Hitchcock to conduct an investigation of the removal of five southeastern tribes—Chickasaw, Seminole, Choctaw, Cherokee and Creek. Arriving in December 1841, Hitchcock spent three months in Indian Territory, carrying out a vigorous and exhaustive inquiry, uncovering numerous instances of bribery, perjury and forgery. His report with one hundred exhibits was filed with the Secretary of War J.C. Spencer in the spring of 1842.[24]

The report was sent to a U.S. Treasury official who, upon examining it, in effect agreed with the Chickasaws that Harrison and Glasgow, whom the government had awarded the contract to provide rations to the tribe, had delivered rations that were inferior in quality, insufficient in quantity and irregular and fraudulent in issue. He wrote that "it is apparent that the Indians were wronged, and that the Government officers did not guard their interests. But as to whether the government should sue Harrison and Glasgow, he thought the evidence insufficient as to time, quantities and sums.[25]

Members of Congress immediately asked the U.S. secretary of war to make the report public. The secretary refused. Hitchcock strongly suspected a cover up to protect important members of the administration of John Tyler who might be charged "with felonious acts."[26] In a resolution adopted by the U.S. House of Representatives, the secretary was called upon to provide the full report to the House. Apparently at the direction of President Tyler, Spencer refused on the grounds that it would not serve the public interest and that those alleged to have committed fraud should first have an opportunity to answer the charges .[27]

Members of Congress reiterated their demands, but before long, the report was said to have been lost in the files of the War Department. Since it was the only copy, members could do nothing but fume. Historian Arrell Gibson noted that subsequently Congress determined that removal had cost the Chickasaws some $1.5 million.[28] How much of that was fraud, no one was prepared to say. The removal treaty had stipulated that the Chickasaws would pay the costs of removal from the $3.3 million the tribe had in federal trust from the sale of their Southeastern lands prior to 1839. Tribal leaders asked that their removal superintendent purchase provisions for them as required as they moved along the route. The cost of provisions was estimated to be a little more than $100,000.

However, Washington officials purchased several hundred thousands of dollars of pork and flour for Chickasaws and Creeks and in anticipation of the Indians arrival had these provisions sent by boats in the summer 1837 to Fort Gibson and Fort Coffee. When the Chickasaws were not ready to sail as early as anticipated and when many of the tribal members decided to go overland, the provisions that had already been delivered began to spoil.[29] In a statement to the House Indian Affairs Committee in 1843, Hitchcock laid the blame not with the tribe but with federal officials. Contrary to the tribe's wishes, the superintendent had not been empowered to furnish their supplies. As a result, Hitchcock determined that "$200,000 worth of spoiled rations had been sold to the Chickasaws." Furthermore, he found evidence (though this was never made public) that the tribe was charged $700,000 for rations that were never delivered.[30]

In addition to Hitchcock's statement, several witnesses and participants also made statements to Hitchcock that were included in House Report 271 and illustrated various types of fraud. Richard McClure testified that during the trip west with two hundred others in the winter of 1837-38, the only corn that was delivered was rotten. All of his horses died, and he had to buy provisions at greatly inflated prices to keep himself alive. Alfred Hume described one instance in May 1839 in which Harrison and Glasgow agents shorted the Chickasaws in their beef entitlements by at least one-third. R.J. Humphrey was owed two months of back rations and during that time had to "take my family into the buffalo country for subsistence." When the rations arrived at the depot, he was refused his back rations.

Sloan Love arrived with one hundred other Chickasaws at Fort Coffee on December 5, 1837. They were issued damaged pork, flour and corn. "The pork was so bad that Doctor Walker told me that, if the emigrants continued to use it, it would kill them all off. It gave those who ate it a diarrhea, and it was always my opinion that many of our poor people died in consequence of it." William R. Guy, a white man and the issuing commissary for the Chickasaws on the Boggy River, wrote to superintendent Upshaw, "I am here starving with the Chickasaws, by gross mismanagement on the part of contractors," which, he added, "is one failure after another without end. I begin to think we shall have to starve to death or abandon the country."[31]

Despite such testimonials, anecdotal and circumstantial evidence that the Chickasaws were substantially defrauded, and even government officials' admission that the charges of fraud were generally correct, no redress from the government was made until 1887, a half century after the Chickasaw removal began. The Court of Claims awarded the tribe $140,884.17 for "moneys improperly disbursed" from the Chickasaw trust fund.[32]

Notwithstanding Upshaw's estimate that only "18 or 20 families" remained in the East after 1838, a federal census in Mississippi revealed that more than five hundred Chickasaws were still to be relocated.[33] Traveling in small groups, most of them crossed the great river throughout the 1840s. Grant Foreman wrote that nearly a thousand Chickasaws "travelled to their new home without assistance or direction by the government." Among these were one group of Chickasaws and their slaves led and financed by George Colbert and another party of 171 led by Pitman Colbert.[34] By 1850, the emigration was complete.[35] According to the government's list, 4,914 Chickasaws and 1,156 slaves were removed.

Severe distress and adversity affected the Chickasaws once they arrived at their new home. In September 1838, several headmen petitioned the federal government for emergency aid. Among them were James Colbert, Isaac Alberson, Sloan Love, Colonel Greenwood, George Colbert and James Perry. They wrote:

Many of our people have died and the general drought through the Ovnclian country has been particularly felt through ours; for these reasons together with the fact that many of our people arrived too late to make a crop, makes it our duty to apply for further subsistence.[36]

Captain G.P. Kingsbury, assistant agent for removal, reported in December from Fort Towson that the Chickasaws were without food. Some were "almost starving." Two months later, Captain William Armstrong stated that "immediate action" was required "to save them from starvation." To the Commissioner of Indian Affairs, he wrote:

The Chickasaws settled on Blue and Boggy (streams) are in danger of great suffering; there is neither cattle nor hogs in the country; a small drove of forty or fifty hogs was driven in while I was on Blue which commanded the enormous price of twenty five cents a pound, but few of the Indians have money, and if they had they are one hundred twenty miles from the line; such was their pressing wants that they hung around me, stating their situation, and without either corn or beef, they must starve... [Their] petition set forth their wants; without the provisions but few could have remained at their new homes, they would have come into the settlements and abandoned their homes.[37]

Aside from food shortages, disease contributed to more than 500 deaths and threats from unsettled tribes heaped even more misery on an already debilitated and dispirited people. Furthermore, being uprooted from their homes, exploited by speculators and agents, and resettling in an unfriendly and alien land fragmented Chickasaw society.

The History of the Chickasaws' Great Seal

At some point, probably in 1855 or 1856, Chickasaw leaders or a committee of some kind convened to design a Great Seal. Since no record of this meeting could be found, we infer that the planners decided to honor the tribe's last great war chief, Tishomingo, who died on the Trail of Tears in 1837. An article on the Chickasaw Seal by the noted Oklahoma historian Muriel Wright was published in 1940. She wrote that "the figure of the warrior ... commemorated the courageous Chickasaw of old times, represented in the person and character of Chief Tishomingo."[1]

No details of how the Chickasaws' first Great Seal was developed and designed are known to exist. But the work must have been done during the first Constitutional Convention in 1856. Interestingly, the language did not identify the warrior as Chief Tishomingo. (Photo courtesy of Chickasaw Council House Museum)

She had been researching the seals of the Five Civilized Tribes so that the seals could be reproduced on banners at a special Flag Day event that was sponsored by the Alabama Department of Archives and History in June 1940. The idea was to present flags from all the nations that had once held dominion over Alabama land. Since the tribes had not adopted official flags, banners depicting each tribal seal were presented.[2]

In her 1940 article, Wright described the Chickasaw Seal, interpreted some of its elements, but cited no sources. She wrote, "The two arrows in the warrior's hand represented his guard over the two ancient phratries or tribal divisions, in which all Chickasaw clan and house names originated. These two phratries were called respectively, *Koi* and *Ishpani* in the native language. In the ancient tribal organization, the hereditary ruler or chief of the Chickasaws was selected from the *Ishpani* division."[3]

She continued: "In historical records, the Chickasaws were referred to as a nation noted for intrepid warriors, unconquered in battle. *According to old tribal lore* [my emphasis], the bow and the shield in the Great Seal represented the insignia of the Chickasaw warrior, by right of his descent from the 'House of Warriors.' This organization was sometimes called the 'Tiger Clan' (i.e. *Koi* Clan or Division), which counted its members from more than one Indian tribe long before the Europeans came to the shores of America."

What are we to make of this reference to "old tribal lore?" Did Wright find this reference in the tribal records? Or was this interpretation passed through the generations in the traditional way through oral history? Since there is no account in the tribal records, we will probably never know. In her article and in other accounts, there is an interesting and intriguing reference to the first mention of the Seal in the 1856 Constitution. She writes that the Constitution and laws were sent to Louisiana to be printed. "Strangely, the person with whom the documents were entrusted lost them en route and they were never found." The process was repeated later, at an unspecified time.[4] After the Civil War, another Constitution was promulgated, and new documents were adopted for the official Seal in 1867. According to both Wright and historian W. David Baird, the Seal was affixed to the papers of Governor Cyrus Harris during his term from 1872 to 1874.[5]

Wright, the editor of *The Chronicles of Oklahoma* and daughter of former Choctaw chief Allen Wright, was a member of the Oklahoma committee that participated in planning the Alabama event. The Chickasaw members were Floyd Maytubby, governor, and Mrs. Jessie E. Moore. A.M.

An updated Great Seal was embellished in a watercolor painting by an Oklahoma City architect. He had received guidance from Muriel Wright, a Choctaw and editor of the *Chronicles of Oklahoma*. All symbols and colors are explained in the Chickasaw Nation Code, enacted in 1994. (Photo courtesy of Chickasaw Council House Museum)

Landman, superintendent of the Five Civilized Tribes Agency in Muskogee, supplied original impressions of the seals, and Ms. Wright supplied "copies of the Indian laws and other data" to Guy C. Reid, an Oklahoma City architect who "donated paintings of each of the seals from his drawings enlarged to scale and hand done in water color."[6]

Are we to understand that the original Seal was embellished through a collaboration of Muriel Wright and Guy Reid? The Seal, looking much as it does today, was reproduced in black and white in that 1940 issue of *The Chronicles*. At some point, the colors and other symbols depicted on the Seal were explained and were eventually included in Appendix 1 of the Chickasaw Nation Code enacted by the Legislature in 1994.

Among the points are: The outer rim of the Seal is gold and represents the purity of the Chickasaw people. The inner rim is light purple and represents the people's honor. The head feathers represent the four directions of the earth. The band crossing over the warrior's left shoulder is known as the Warrior's Mantle and was made of swan feathers. The quiver, made of deerskin, represents the hunting prowess of the Chickasaw warrior as well as his willingness to defend his people. The bow, also representing the hunting prowess of the Chickasaw people, was made of hickory. Knee straps were made of deer hide and were a form of Chickasaw medicine; they were thought to bring fleetness to the wearer. The shield, also made of deer hide, signifies the protection of the warriors for all Chickasaw people. The Mississippi River is in the background. It was crossed at some indefinite time when the Chickasaws made their way to their new home in the East. The trees and plants pictured are indigenous to the area near the Mississippi River and serve to remind the people of their original homelands.[7]

The origin of these interpretations is not known. But it is possible that Muriel Wright, through her extensive knowledge of Chickasaw history and culture, took it upon herself to interpret the elements depicted on the original Seal and directed Guy Reid to draw in additional elements such as the Warrior's mantle and shield, the river and plants, all of which she also interpreted.[8]

Since that time, the Seal has been either unaltered or slightly altered depending upon who has the better memory. Gary Childers, who has worked for the Chickasaw Nation since the late 1970s, said he remembers that while Overton James was still governor, some people remarked that the warrior (on the Seal) should be drawn more professionally. "As I recall it, Governor James asked Ted Key [an artist and official with the Chickasaw Housing Authority] to touch the warrior up some." Contacted in his Washington office where he works in Indian housing for the U.S. Department of Housing and Urban Development, Key said that his friend Childers "must have been dreaming." Former Governor James could not remember his directive but said that he was not happy with the appearance of the warrior and that "it is possible" that Key or someone else might have done a more professional job improving the appearance of the seal without changing anything substantive.[9]

In the opinion of (now former) Chickasaw Nation Chief Judge Wilson Seawright, any subsequent change in the Official Seal of the Nation would have to be approved by the Chickasaw Legislature. Seawright said that in the past the Legislature has dealt only with the use of the seal, not its appearance.[10]

Design aside, papers of the governor were affixed with the official Chickasaw Seal since after the Civil War. In her research, Muriel Wright said that the papers of Governor Cyrus Harris were affixed with the Seal as early as 1872. There is a well-known and popular story about the Seal that, if true, means that a device of some kind for leaving an imprint of the Seal existed even earlier than that. In February 1864, Union forces invaded the Chickasaw Nation. As a result, the tribal governor Winchester Colbert fled to Texas for several months.[11] According to the story, Colbert carried with him the Seal, and upon returning the next year, he brought the Seal with him. Some people have heard that the device Colbert is alleged to have carried with him was the same one that is in the custody of Governor Bill Anoatubby.[12]

While that may be so, there is probably no way to be certain. What is known is that the Great Seal that was affixed to copies of some official papers before statehood was made with a rubber stamp. One of these is held by the tribe.[13] Undoubtedly there were others, some official and some counterfeit. Swindlers knew that committing fraud was easier if papers such as contracts, agreements or laws included the Seal because, by definition, the Seal authenticated the contents of the paper. Those entrusted with the Seal, therefore, ran the risk of having it stolen. According to Kelley Lunsford, when her great grandfather Martin Van Buren Cheadle was secretary of the Chickasaw Nation and carried the seal in his saddlebags as he made his official rounds, his wife worried constantly that he would be waylaid for the Seal.[14]

Sometime after Oklahoma statehood, the official seals of the Five Tribes were taken into the custody of the Bureau of Indian Affairs (BIA). We do not know when, but we do know that the seals were kept at the BIA headquarters in Muskogee for many, many years. In the mid-1980s, Zane Browning, superintendent of the BIA agency in Ardmore, saw the devices in a walk-in safe in the Realty Department.

They had been used by BIA realty employees to stamp papers transferring land. Browning asked if they were still being used and was told no. "Then, I asked could I take the Chickasaw Seal back to the tribe and was told I'd have to put the request in writing. I did and nothing happened. But to make a long story short, after repeated requests by phone and mail, I was able to obtain the Seal when I was in Muskogee and simply signed for it. The man I got it from didn't know the history of those stamping devices, but they all looked the same. I took the one with the Chickasaw Seal back to Ada and presented it to the Nation at a meeting of the Legislature, I think it was."[15]

The stamping device certainly looks very old, but there are no identifying marks. It is made from cast iron, is painted black with fading gold leaf designs and operates by means of a handle protruding from the top. Press the handle down, and the metal jaws of the device close on a circular piece of gold foil paper, leaving an imprint of the Seal.

It is immaterial whether it is the Civil War stamping device and whether Muriel Wright added any elements to the Seal. The Seal that we have today is official because the Legislature has proclaimed it to be so. Generations of Chickasaws who have known little or nothing about the Seal and its history have nonetheless been proud of the Great Seal because it has been and is the symbol of a people with a long and proud history.

The Paradox of Sulphur Springs

"The Great Spirit took a tomahawk and struck a rock causing water to flow in abundance. Water seeped into earth and extracted health-giving properties of great powers, coming up in springs. The waters had a peculiar taste and odor, as they ran over dark stones, turning them white. Sick Indians bathed and drank to get well. Old ones drank and became young."[1]

Located near the center of the land that became the Chickasaw Nation in 1855—midway between the higher land and the bases of the valleys—are outcroppings of hard, pebbly limestone, interspersed with layers of other rock strata. The water, emanating from this topography of uncommon beauty, flowed from about thirty fresh and mineral springs. They are manifested in steep and rugged slopes, terraces and cliffs—all clothed in many places with trees and vines.

Fresh-water springs originate upland but flow down a declining grade in a series of natural low falls and rapids and over dams constructed by the streams' deposited sediments. Above the falls are placid pools, and the dams are covered with mosses and ferns. The mineral springs, of which there are about twenty of various gaseous compositions, arise from beds of limestone conglomerate or out of one of the creek beds.[2]

> As a sanctuary on a vast prairie, the land of the spring waters had drawn people for ages. Artifacts of a prehistoric people have been found along the clear creeks. Until the early nineteenth century, Indian tribes of the southern plains regularly visited the area. When the southeastern tribes were removed to Indian Territory, Chickasaw families settled in the area after 1839. They used the springs and creeks to water their livestock. The Indians still called the area Buffalo Suck, but by mid-century, the great herds of bison had been virtually exterminated.[3]

During the next thirty years, families and small groups of Chickasaws and Choctaws camped by the streams in the hot summer months. After the Civil War, a few cattlemen and traders wandered through the area, but none settled on a permanent basis. Because the few Chickasaws and Choctaws living in the area were not commercial farmers, the land resembled its primeval state.

That was about to change. The white adventurers and settlers who began invading the Chickasaw Nation in the 1880s and 1890s believed that nature's resources existed to be used. So in and around the springs, they began cutting down trees, plowing up the grasslands and building a town— Sulphur Springs.[4]

The Chickasaws were not oblivious to this development, but their attention was focused on the bigger picture of their survival as a tribe. The Dawes Commission was present to carve up their nation, and the Curtis Act of 1898 largely emasculated the Chickasaw and Choctaw tribal governments. The tribes realized it was fruitless to resist, but there were many details to work out between the tribes (the Chickasaws and Choctaws jointly owned their land) and the federal government. Among issues were determining tribal membership, land allotments, town sites and unalloted lands, including those containing vast deposits of coal and asphalt.

By the turn of the century, despoiling the land of the springs—in the name of advancing civilization—was in full swing. Acres of trees had been cut down, the inhabitants of Sulphur Springs were polluting the streams and entrepreneurs of one stripe or another were trying to corner the mineral-water-for-health markets.[5] Although the town residents and developers owned the buildings and businesses, the Chickasaws and Choctaws still owned the land, which would be the key to its preservation.

As recently as 1878, no one lived permanently at the springs. But that year a former mail carrier named Noah Lael established a cattle ranch there and married Lucy Harris, the 16-year-old daughter of Chickasaw Governor Cyrus Harris. Lael built a four-room house near the present-day park headquarters. A son of former Governor B.F. Overton lived in the house in 1881, but the Laels sold their spread, which they called the "Sulphur Springs Place," in 1882. The new owner was Perry Froman, another intermarried citizen and cattleman who maintained the four-mile square ranch until the allotment period began.[6]

In her book, *Murray County*, Opal Hartsell Brown traced the comings and goings in the area through contemporary newspaper accounts and eyewitnesses interviewed by WPA workers in 1937-38 for the Indian-Pioneer Papers Collection. Accordingly, Brown noted that the Seven Sisters Dance Hall was built over Gum Springs in about 1888; grass thereabouts was said to be eight to ten feet high. There was a blacksmith shop, a store and one house in 1890. In 1893, there was one store and thirty tents. By the summer 1894, people were attempting to capitalize on the area's natural resources. "Plenty of hotel accommodations" were advertised, and the area was called "a Mecca for recreation lovers, camp meetings and picnics. People from as faraway as New York was [sic] there recently." A year later, readers of the *Davis Advertiser* learned that "thousands of people go to Sulphur Springs" and that transportation to the "great health mecca and summer resort" would be available from every stable (fifty cents one way)."[7]

The source of these ads likely was the Sulphur Springs Improvement Company, which was formed and led by Colonel R.A. Sneed of Pauls Valley. The company paid $2,500 to rancher Froman for 547 acres that encompassed the existing town, including Pavilion Springs. A surveyor divided up the land into lots, and each developer took lots in proportion to the money he had invested. But when the company in 1895 asked the real owner of the land, the Chickasaw Nation, for a charter, tribal Governor Palmer Mosely refused the request. He said that the springs were public property and should be

As recently as 1878 no one lived permanently at the springs. But throughout the 1890s and without the permission of the tribal land owners, the town of Sulphur Springs evolved. This is a snapshot of part of the town in 1902, with more than one thousand residents and a dance hall built over Pavilion Springs. (Photo courtesy of the National Park Service, Chickasaw National Recreation Area)

enjoyed by everyone. He was not opposed to building a hotel and improving the grounds, as the company proposed to do, as long as the public got the benefit. Their plan, he noted, would exclude the poor, who could not afford to buy lots. The company dropped plans to build a hotel.[8]

Nevertheless, the pace of developing Sulphur Springs picked up, and in 1896 the town (population 200) organized a municipal government. The business district of various stores, a bank and a hotel assumed the shape of a T. By 1900, the city

of about 1,200 people enjoyed two newspapers, telephone service, two schools and enough hotels and boarding houses to accommodate another thousand people. In the center of town was Pavilion Springs, over which there was a dance hall.

Still, residents wanted a post office. The one established in 1895 operated only irregularly. In one account, businessman Sneed offered to travel to Washington to secure a promise for a post office if townspeople would pay his expenses. They did and he made the trip. Upon his return, Sneed announced a qualified success. While he extracted no promise of a post office, things did look good, he allowed, for the establishment of a park. There was one proviso, however: the town would have to move.

The citizens of Sulphur Springs could not believe their ears. It was reported that "feelings for a time ran high" against "the betrayer" Sneed and, in their opinion, this preposterous idea. Why, a park, they pointed out, would kill any chance they had to develop a major health resort.[9] Even if the story about Sneed in Washington was apocryphal, the idea of creating a park was gaining support. In his history of Platt Park, former park superintendent Perry Brown wrote that the tribes probably had the original idea. With land allotments looming and Sulphur Springs thriving, the Chickasaws must have felt that eventually they would be excluded from using the springs. By 1900, there was some commercial use of the waters.[10]

Furthermore, J. George Wright, the Indian inspector in Muskogee had recommended to Secretary of Interior Ethan A. Hitchcock that the springs be reserved for a park if the Chickasaws and Choctaws were agreeable. Without bringing the matter to the attention of the tribes, Hitchcock dispatched Joseph A. Taff of the U.S. Geological Survey and a team of surveyors to the springs, and they worked from March into July 1901. Taff recommended the establishment of a national park.[11]

Still, the federal government recognized that the springs belonged to the Chickasaws and Choctaws, and any initiative to set the land aside for a park would have to be discussed with them. The acting Interior secretary Thomas Ryan said as much to the Indian inspector in a letter regarding queries about a park from citizens of Sulphur Springs. The citizens were Eugene E. White, a Sulphur attorney and president of the Sulphur Springs Railroad Company, and T. R. Cook, president of the Dennis Flynn Republican Club.[12] These developers had a different philosophy about the springs than their predecessors. They figured that since they could not control the land about the springs, it would be in their interest and the community's to upgrade and preserve the land as a national park.

White spoke about the matter with Chickasaw Governor Douglas Johnston and addressed the tribal Legislature on October 31, 1901. White said the Legislature advised him to ask the Dawes Commission to submit a proposition to the Chickasaw commissioners, who were negotiating a Supplementary Agreement dealing with the final disposition of the tribe's land.[13] White then met with acting Dawes Commission chairman Tams Bixby, who suggested that White furnish a draft of the provision to the Dawes Commission. White sent a proposal to the Dawes Commission and commissioners of both tribes negotiating with the Dawes Commission. He was chagrined, however, to learn that the tribal representatives did not think the matter of a park was of enough national importance to include in the negotiations. Perhaps it could be inserted later as a bargaining chip or means of compromise.[14]

White appealed to the Indian inspector J. George Wright to educate his boss, the interior secretary, on the importance of the park proposal. He wrote that if a park were not set aside the springs would be included in lots that would be sold to the highest bidder, "and the springs will thereby pass into private control and monopoly, to the irreparable injury of the town and all persons, whether white or Indian … who may ever wish to have the benefit of these excellent curative waters."[15]

In December, the Dawes Commission notified White that his proposal had been misplaced or lost. After collecting himself, he reproduced from memory a draft of the three-page legal-sized proposition. In this version, a permanent reserve consisting of all the springs but not to exceed eight hundred acres would be set apart from the town, the name of which would be changed from Sulphur to Chickasaw Springs to "commemorate the national existence of the Chickasaw Nation." Money from the sale of town lots would be used to pay the current residents for improvements (most often buildings erected) and the Chickasaw and Choctaw tribes $2,893—a rate of $10 per acre. How White came up with 289.3 acres is not explained. The last section of his "Item for Supplemental Agreement" permitted the secretary of interior to lease "reasonable portions of the said reserve for bath house sites and other proper purposes." The income derived would be applied to the care and improvement of the reserve.[16]

Inspector Wright emphatically endorsed the importance of establishing a reserve, and in submitting his version of an amendment on March 3, he recommended to the interior secretary that Congress add it to the agreement. Much of Wright's proposed amendment was lifted verbatim from attorney Eugene White's version, but no amount was specified to be paid the tribes (only that they would be paid the full appraised value of the park). There was also no mention of changing the name Sulphur to Chickasaw Springs.[17]

Later that month at Atoka, the two tribes readily agreed to the establishment of a government reservation called Sulphur Springs Reservation. To say it was even a minor part of the tribes-U.S. government negotiations leading to the signing of the Supplementary Agreement on March 21 would be an exaggeration. It was of little moment indeed compared to the immense financial significance attached to the citizenship litigation, the proposed sale of hundreds of thousands of acres of coal and asphalt holdings and other larger issues. Nevertheless, after Congress ratified the agreement on July 1, the tribes voted their consent in separate elections on September 25, 1902.[18]

According to Section 64, the tribes ceded to the United States a tract of land not more than 640 acres selected by the secretary of interior but had to include all of the springs in the area. The government also could reserve additional land adjacent to the springs in order to protect them. The

tribes would be paid $20 an acre by the federal government, which would also appraise and pay for buildings and other improvements that had to be removed from the reservation. At the tribes' insistence, a promise that all people would have free access to the springs for all time was added to the agreement by the government.[19]

In February 1903, the appraisement of buildings and other improvements in Sulphur Springs was placed at some $87,400. Indian Inspector Frank C. Churchill concluded his lengthy report on the matter by noting that most people thought they were not paid enough, but with only two or three exceptions, no serious complaints were presented. Then, he wrote: "The taking of the homes of such a large number of people, most of who are possessed of small means, must be looked upon as a rather serious matter."[20]

The federal government paid the tribes $12,586.60 on January 15, 1903. In accordance with their historic land agreement, the Chickasaws received $3,146.65 and the more numerous Choctaws got $9,439.95.[21] Churchill, who was in charge of the transition period, announced that everyone had to leave the reservation as soon as practicable after they had received payment for their improvements from the government. Despite howls of protest, many people started buying lots south of the reservation, and several businesses

sprang up on a new Main Street. In 1903 and 1904, many of the buildings of Sulphur Springs were dismantled and moved off the reservation to the new town of Sulphur. This included homes, cafes, grocery stores, the post office, hotels and even the dance pavilions.[22]

To protect the integrity of the reserve, a congressional appropriation in 1904 enabled an additional 218 acres to be purchased, so the Sulphur Springs Reserve then totaled nearly 850 acres. This time the Chickasaws and Choctaws were paid $60 an acre or approximately $13,000. In June 1906, Congress authorized the secretary of the interior to change the name Sulphur Springs Reservation to Platt National Park. The late Henry Orville Platt, a U.S. senator from Connecticut and long-time member of the Committee on Indian Affairs, apparently had played some role in the creation of the Sulphur Springs Reservation.[23]

Platt National Park was the seventh national park established and administered by the U.S. government. For seventy years, the springs that had been part of the Chickasaw Nation were part of Platt National Park. But with the revitalization of the tribe, which in the early 1970s was headquartered in Sulphur, Governor Overton James launched a successful campaign to change the name of the park to the Chickasaw National Recreation Area.

The Trails To Atoka

One hundred years ago official representatives of the Chickasaws, Choctaws and federal government met in Atoka and, after much negotiations, agreed that the Indian Nations would be divided among their members and that their governments would be extinguished by 1906.

The events leading to that momentous meeting, which marked the end of an era and the beginning of a new chapter in Chickasaw history, began in February 1893. In that month, a number of delegates representing the Five Civilized Tribes drafted a letter to their leaders warning of "grave dangers now threatening our political and property rights."

Following several intense meetings, the letter was signed by seventeen delegates including Chickasaws Overton Love, William Rennie and Tandy Walker.[1] There was nothing new in members of Congress introducing legislation designed to emasculate or destroy Indian Nations. But now, the delegates realized that the attacks were more concerted, that the Indians' friends and supporters were weaker and that the Supreme Court had ruled that Congress could abridge the Indians' political rights.[2]

In a report, members of the Senate Committee on Indian Affairs had written that "the anomalous condition of five separate independent Indian governments within the Government of the United States must soon ... cease." Conditions had changed, they had concluded. When these governments were established, they were remote and isolated. "Today they are surrounded by settled states and territories. White citizens, by the permission of the Indians themselves, have been admitted into their Territory, until now the white people ... outnumber the members of the tribes, and are rapidly increasing." It was alleged that the tribes no longer could protect their own citizens much less the increasing number of white settlers. Therefore, a stable and satisfactory government was said to be necessary for the protection of both classes.

After the Cherokee Outlet (now much of northwest Oklahoma excluding the Panhandle) was purchased from the Cherokees by the federal government, it refused the tribe's request to reiterate its former pledges of self-government. Furthermore, the delegates noted an amendment was added to the Cherokee Outlet Agreement, directing that a commission be sent to "negotiate with the five civilized nations for a change of their government and method of land holding to allotment and to a territorial government with a view of forming a state."

Late in 1893, members of the Dawes Commission arrived in the Indian Territory to do just that. They were not greeted warmly or enthusiastically and did little the first two years except meet tribal members here and there and write reports. They would negotiate with the tribes individually except the Chickasaw and Choctaw. Since the tribes owned land in common, the Dawes Commission proposed to negotiate with them jointly. To get the ball rolling, the Commission presented eight propositions for discussion. These involved how the government intended to allot the lands, while reserving mineral lands and town sites for sale. All money derived from the sales and owed to the tribes by the federal government, except that devoted to school purposes, would be distributed on a per capita basis to all tribal members. This included the promise to settle all tribal claims against the United States. Once the members were in possession of their allotments and the money owed was paid to them, the tribal governments would be extinguished, replaced by a territorial government.[3]

Members of both tribes were sharply divided on these issues. Generally, the full bloods and other traditionalists wanted to be left alone by the federal government. The progressives, consisting mainly of mixed bloods and intermarried citizens, thought that negotiating with the Dawes Commission, while distasteful, was essential to getting a more favorable settlement from the federal government. When the Commission presented its proposals in Tishomingo in February 1894, the Chickasaw delegation appointed by Governor Jonas Wolf consisted of (not surprisingly) twenty full bloods. Wolf was himself a full blood who spoke no English. After the morning session, the two groups were to meet again after lunch, but the Chickasaws packed up and went home. Henry L. Dawes, the chairman of the Commission, should not have been surprised. Previously, Governor Wolf had told the Legislature that allotment and statehood "should be strenuously opposed."[4]

His hand-picked successor, Governor-Elect Palmer S. Mosely, said that true to his campaign pledge he would refuse to treat (negotiate) with the Dawes Commission.[5] But by 1895, Mosely, realizing that he could not continue to ignore the Dawes Commission, recommended to the Legislature that a Chickasaw commission be appointed to meet with them to "learn their terms so that this may be submitted to our people for approval or rejection."[6] Members were duly appointed, but now the Dawes Commission was calling for Congress to intervene immediately and drastically in the affairs of the Indian nations. The Commission based its recommendation on charges that the Indian governments were "wholly corrupt, irresponsible, and unworthy to be longer trusted with the care and control of the money and other property of Indian citizens, much less their lives."

The Commission reported that the reason the Indian nations were not cooperating with them was because their leaders were personally benefiting from the status quo. The Commission charged that although the tribal lands were held in common, a relatively small group of mixed bloods and intermarried citizens were actually controlling much of the most lucrative tribal lands (mineral land and town sites) for their own personal gain. Furthermore, alluding to "statistics and incontrovertible evidence," the Commission reported that the courts of the Indian nations "have become powerless and paralyzed. Violence, robbery and murder have become almost of daily occurrence, and no effective measures of restraint or punishment are put forth by these governments and courts to suppress crime. A reign of terror exists."[7]

The 1895 report concluded: "There is no alternative left to the United States but to assume the responsibility for future conditions in this Territory." Were these reports true? To some extent, yes, although it was in the interest of the federal government—bent on extinguishing tribal governments—to bolster an impression of lawlessness and mayhem. According to the maxim: "The history of an oppressed people is hidden in the lies and the agreed-upon myth of its conquerors."

While the Chickasaws and other tribes had invited whites into their nations under their permit laws after the Civil War, a trickle of adventurers and settlers had become a flood of intruders, and the federal government for a generation had done little or nothing to remove them, despite their treaty obligations to do so. Meanwhile, the small tribal governments were ill-equipped to deal with conditions that were getting more and more out of hand. The Dawes Commission always emphasized the lack of protection of persons and property. But the commissioners were not there to offer constructive criticism; they were there to negotiate the termination of the Five Tribes.

In concert with the views of the Dawes Commission were reports from a U.S. Senate Committee that had investigated the Indian Territory in 1894 and the Indian reform delegates at the annual Lake Mohonk Conference in New York in 1895. The platform of the conference included, in part, the position that despite treaties, the federal government was under "a sacred obligation to exercise its sovereignty extending over the three hundred thousand whites and fifty thousand so-called Indians in the Indian Territory."[8]

Accordingly, on June 10, 1896 Congress passed a law directing the Dawes Commission to begin making out rolls of Indian citizens in preparation for land allotment. The Commission was to be the arbiter of the fate of thousands of applicants claiming to be tribal citizens. The law also stated that it was the duty of the United States to establish a government in Indian Territory that could protect the citizens. These were the mandates that the Dawes Commission needed to facilitate the abolition of the Five Tribes.[9]

In early 1896 at Tuskahoma, Choctaw leader Green McCurtain and others organized the Tuskahoma, a new political party. The purpose of the party was to make an agreement with the Dawes Commission and to serve as a vehicle for the election of McCurtain as principal chief. Their platform that spring included a provision calling for an equal division of the lands among all citizens by blood and intermarriage. Freedmen and their descendents were to receive forty acres each. McCurtain was nominated by the party to run for chief later that summer. He had three

opponents, whose dispositions to deal with the Dawes
Commission ran from cool to hostile.[10]

While Governor Mosely had appointed a commission to
meet for defensive purposes with the Dawes Commission,
he continued to avoid meeting personally with the Dawes
Commission. If one newspaper account is accurate, Mosely and
the Chickasaw Legislature invited the Commission to meet with
them in Ardmore, and then the Indian leaders failed to appear.
Only a few intermarried citizens greeted the Commission
members, who voiced their disgust at having been stood-
up by the leadership. According to the news story, the Dawes
Commission said it would not come again to visit the Chickasaws;
next time, the tribal leaders would have to come to them."[11]

The Chickasaws also held elections that summer; there
were two candidates for Governor, former Gov. Jonas Wolf
against Robert M. Harris, the progressive candidate. Like
Green McCurtain, Harris favored making an agreement
with the Dawes Commission but shunned being tagged

Choctaw Green McCurtain and others organized the Tuskahoma Party
in 1896 to make an allotment agreement with the Dawes Commission
and to get McCurtain elected chief. It worked, and this was the first
signal that the Choctaws were ready to deal with the United States on
the matter of land allotment. (Photo courtesy of Chickasaw Library)

as pro-Dawes Commission. Both candidates for governor contributed to a hotly contested campaign. As the *Atoka Indian Chieftain* maintained, the tribal elections had more to do with pro- or anti-allotment stands than with the candidates themselves. Like the majority of Indian Territory newspapers, the *Indian Chieftain* was pro-allotment: "Are 50,000 citizens of this territory able to bring to submission the 70 million citizens of the U.S.? It is a foolish dream of an idiot that supposes our treaties are an invulnerable shield to ward off the powerful and irresistible forces of the government. The fact that the government has proceeded so far in this matter without our consent proves conclusively that it has virtually abrogated the treaties. The time for dreaming and moralizing is past …"[12]

The progressive forces in both tribes triumphed. Harris defeated Wolf by a vote of 214 to 161. While McCurtain was elected chief by 169 votes, the other three candidates combined polled about a thousand votes more than the victor. Nevertheless, McCurtain's election was heralded by the newspapers as a victory for allotment.[13] The Indian agent at the Union Agency in Muskogee also wrote that the elections indicated "beyond doubt, that the Indian mind has undergone a change on this question. Hitherto, all the tribes have stood solid against allotment, and the victory achieved by McCurtain and Harris may be classed as a remarkable and significant one under the circumstances."[14]

In his first message to the Chickasaw Legislature in September 1896, Governor Harris acknowledged that the federal government had not honored the former treaties and wondered what value a new agreement would have with that government when "it suits the United States to call on us for some other change and concession of our property rights." Yet, he felt he had no choice but to recommend the appointment of a Chickasaw commission to meet with the Dawes Commission.[15] Harris thought the new commissioners should first meet with representatives of the Choctaws and other Indian nations. The Legislature agreed and appointed four prominent Chickasaw leaders—former Governor William L. Byrd, Richard McLish, M.V. Cheadle and Overton Love, chairman. The recommendations made and measures passed were matters of expediency, not enthusiastic support of the federal plan. The same was true of the Choctaws. Writing in the *Indian Citizen*, E.N. Wright stated that he believed that McCurtain's defeated opponents for chief would not try to "thwart the will of the people." He said it was critical, with the Choctaw Nation "hanging by a mere thread," to demonstrate that they are law-abiding people united in the "one great cause of saving our country if possible.[16]

Although "hanging by a mere thread" may have been hyperbole, it probably was not. There were sentiments on the federal government side and the Indian side reflecting the belief that this would be the last chance for the Chickasaws and Choctaws to negotiate the terms of their dissolution. Keeping attuned with the tribal situation, the Dawes Commission in October sent to both tribes propositions that were nearly identical with those extended in 1894. Then the Commission prepared to move to Fort Smith to carry on its citizenship work and the negotiations with the two tribes.

Meanwhile, representatives of the Five Tribes met in McAlester in November. They adopted a resolution recognizing that it was time to act and to act uniformly. Therefore, a program to govern the nations in their dealing with the federal government was outlined. Provisions included: the insistence that the federal government pay all claims arising from treaties; an equal division of the lands,

In discussing the impending allotment of Chickasaw lands by the Dawes Commission, Chickasaw Governor Robert M. Harris in 1896 wondered about the value of making a new agreement with the United States, which, "when it suits their purpose, ignores treaties with Indian nations." (Photo courtesy of Chickasaw Library)

the title of which would be held by the Indians until a new government might be organized; setting aside certain lands for investments for tribal education funds; and maintaining tribal governments for as long as possible. In addition, each tribal citizen should receive $500 to assist them in adjusting to the new order, a new state should not be created for at least twenty-five years and the nations were never to consent to single territorial existence or statehood with Oklahoma.[17]

The Chickasaws and Choctaws met with the Dawes Commission at Fort Smith in November 1896. After a week of making proposals and counter-proposals, it was learned that the Chickasaws had come without authority to negotiate. When the Dawes Commission refused to meet with them until they had the proper authority, the Chickasaw commissioners departed, saying they hoped to return with their Legislature's blessing. The problem probably stemmed from the Chickasaw Act of September 12, 1896, that set up the Commission. The act authorized the members to "meet and confer with the Dawes Commission in cases of citizenship and any other business that may come before them."[18] "Meet and confer" is certainly not the same as "negotiate and sign an agreement."

After the Chickasaws left, the Choctaws continued to negotiate in Fort Smith and later in Muskogee. On December 18, the two commissions signed a very detailed agreement, covering the transfer of title to tribal lands to the United States. The lands of both tribes would be held in trust by the government and subsequently parceled out in allotments to tribal citizens. Thus, after three years of persuasion buttressed by the threat of hostile legislation, the Dawes Commission made an agreement with the representatives of the first of the Five Tribes. But, if the Choctaws thought they had reached the agreement also on behalf of the Chickasaws, they were sadly mistaken. On January 15, the Chickasaw Legislature passed an act creating a commission of six, in addition to the two regular delegates, to visit Washington to officially protest congressional ratification of the agreement. Even though the two tribes had common goals, the Chickasaws considered themselves independent and would not allow the Choctaws to unilaterally usurp their authority. Furthermore, the same January 15 act gave the new commission power to negotiate an allotment agreement with the Dawes Commission, provided that the government would pay all the money due the tribe.[19]

The act also gave the tribe more power than under the terms of the Choctaw-U.S. agreement. Allotment would be carried out by a tribal commission, not the Dawes Commission. Freedmen would receive no allotments or share of Chickasaw assets, because they had never been adopted by the tribe. Town-site lots would be rented rather than sold. The proceeds as well as mineral royalties—beyond those needed for the educational system—would be used as the Legislature saw fit. Furthermore, the act specified that no agreement would be valid until the Chickasaw Legislature had ratified it and the Chickasaw people had approved it. Commission members were William L. Byrd, R.L. Boyd, S.B. Kemp, T.C. Walker, William M. Guy, Isaac O. Lewis, Richard McLish, Josiah Brown and Governor Harris (ex-officio.)[20]

After opponents of the Dawes-Choctaw agreement had had their say in Washington, the secretary of the interior submitted the agreement to Congress on January 27 for ratification. Chances for success were further weakened because of dissension within the ranks of the Choctaws. Even the great conciliator E.N. Wright had refused to sign the agreement.[21] When the Chickasaw commissioners got the chance to protest the agreement, they did so with considerable zeal. In addition to the provisions included in their Legislature's January 15 act, commissioners voiced more objections:

> We object to the agreement requiring all laws and ordinances passed by the Choctaws and Chickasaws to be approved by the president. We object to being regarded as a conquered province. We object to the proposition that all claims that the United States government may have against the two nations, and vice versa, be submitted to arbitration. [22]

The Chickasaw Commission incorporated both its objections to the Choctaw-U.S. agreement and its proposals to the Dawes Commission in a report dated February 12, 1897.[23] According to Chickasaw commissioner R.L. Boyd, the Commission put forward its proposals to counter a claim by *The Washington Post* that the Chickasaws were in town only to block any settlement before congressional adjournment. "In order to vindicate our position," Boyd said, "we decided to memorialize Congress, and did so on the lines laid down by the Chickasaw legislature ...."[24]

Senator James K. Jones of Arkansas presented the Chickasaw memorial to Congress on February 8. Congress adjourned without acting on the ratification of the agreement, but members attached to the Indian Appropriations bill an amendment that Governor Harris said "virtually destroys us as a nation." The offending provision required that all acts of the tribal legislatures be submitted for presidential approval. Because Harris believed that the appropriations bill would pass, he telegraphed a recommendation to the Legislature to modify the January 15 act "so that an agreement can be affected between the three parties on the best terms that can be made for the Chickasaw people." Time, he believed, was of the essence; any delay "would be dangerous."[25]

Congress did pass the appropriations bill, but outgoing President Grover Cleveland allowed the act to die through the pocket veto.[26] Nevertheless, the die was cast. The veto delayed, but in no way, stopped congressional determination to consummate national purpose in the Indian Territory. In March, new President William McKinley called a special session of Congress to deal with funding the Indian Service. During this time, the Chickasaws and Choctaws met individually and together to get prepared for meeting the Dawes Commission. Writing in his book, *The Chickasaws*, historian Arrell Gibson wrote that a compelling motivator for spurring the Chickasaw leaders on to the negotiation table was the fear that Congress might soon require that the tribe adopt freedmen and grant equal shares of the tribal estate to them. In light of the agreement that was made, however, Gibson appears to have been mistaken.[27]

Accepting Governor Harris's recommendation, the Chickasaw Legislature, despite the objections of many Chickasaw officials and citizens, passed an act on March 1, creating a new commission of eight members with full power to make an agreement on allotment.[28]The Legislature named the following men to the Commission: R.L. Boyd,

M.V. Cheadle, R.L. Murray, Holmes Colbert, William Perry, Amos Colbert, Isaac Lewis and, interestingly, that old foe of allotment, former Governor Palmer S. Mosely. Governor Harris was ex-officio chairman.

Beginning on March 24, they held preliminary conferences in Atoka with their Choctaw counterparts. Within three days, the commissioners had agreed on a set of joint proposals to be offered to the Dawes Commission. Alexander Montgomery and Frank Armstrong, two members of the Dawes Commission, were present on the last day of the tribal discussions.[29] Notices were printed in newspapers informing Chickasaw and Choctaw citizens that commissioners of the tribes and the federal government would be meeting in Atoka on April 1 to entertain presentations on a number of pertinent subjects, including statehood, town sites, farm leases, mineral interests and "the rights of colored people."[30]

The meeting began on April 1 with the election of Frank C. Armstrong of the Dawes Commission as chairman. Then the members settled in for more than a week to listen to individuals and vested interests have their say. On March 30, representatives of the town sites in the two nations had formed the Choctaw and Chickasaw Protective Association and had passed resolutions urging preference for occupants in the sale of lots and the right of any citizen occupying a homestead including a town site to purchase the site and dispose of it.[31] (After the issues were decided, the Protective Association became inactive. But as new issues or calls for grassroots action common to both tribes emerged later in the twentieth century, the Choctaw and Chickasaw Protective Association would reemerge.) Other interests represented at the hearings were farmers, railroads, lease holders (particularly mining companies)and the Presbyterian church.

After negotiations got underway among the Chickasaw, Choctaw and United States commissions, rumors began circulating that trouble was brewing. The newspapers printed them, apparently having no ethical position against running rumors. For example, it was reported with no attribution that the Chickasaw and Choctaw commissions could not agree on anything. Also, the Choctaw and Dawes commissions were said to have agreed upon all points. Fortunately, most of the newspapers in the Chickasaw and Choctaw nations were weeklies and could inflict only periodic damage.[32]

Finally, on April 23, it was announced that a very lengthy agreement had been reached by all three commissions. An Atoka attorney, Joseph Rails Jr., claimed in an interview conducted in the 1930s that the agreement had been signed in his law office. Rails said he typed the document and provided "a copy of said agreement to the newspapers." He added that

he had saved the typewriter as a keepsake.[33] Like it or not, everyone recognized the Atoka Agreement as momentous. The agreement was translated into the Indian languages and was published by D. A. Homer, the owner of the *Atoka Indian Citizen*.[34] Many newspapers in the Chickasaw and Choctaw Nations published the Atoka Agreement in its entirety, consuming two or more full news pages.

The framers got to the point quickly. The agreement's first provision stated that all of the Chickasaw and Choctaw lands "shall be allotted to the members of said tribes so as to give to each member of these tribes except for Choctaw freedmen [Chickasaw freedmen were not tribal members], so far as possible, a fair and equal share thereof, considering the character and fertility of the soil and location and value of the lands."[35] Unlike the agreement signed by the Choctaws in 1896, which would have issued deeds-in-trust to the federal government, the new agreement provided that the chief executives of the two nations should execute all patents and deliver them to the allottees. The allotments were to be non-taxable and inalienable [non-transferable] for twenty-one years.

Coal, asphalt, timber lands and town sites were reserved from allotment and were to be sold separately. The proceeds from the sales and all trust funds held by the government for the two tribes were to be paid to tribal members on a per capita basis. Mineral royalties were to be used to support schools. Choctaw freedmen and their descendants would each get forty-acre allotments but no share of the other tribal resources. The Indian governments were to terminate on March 4, 1906, and all tribal members would automatically become U.S. citizens.* Until then, all legislation passed by the Chickasaw or Choctaw legislatures had to be approved by the President.

Apparently in return for these concessions, the Chickasaw freedmen were omitted from consideration in the Atoka Agreement. After learning that they had been left out of the agreement, a group of Chickasaw freedmen asked the President and Congress either to provide allotments for them prior to the pact's ratification by Congress or to reject the agreement. To promote their interests, the freedmen retained two attorneys to work on a contingency basis.[36] Members of the Dawes Commission also objected to the absence of Chickasaw freedmen concessions in the agreement. The commissioners urged Congress to remedy this feature before the ratification vote.[37]

All members of the three commissions, except for three Chickasaws, signed the Atoka Agreement. Amos Colbert did not sign because he was reportedly ill; Palmer Mosely and M.V. Cheadle refused to sign the agreement.[38] Since a majority of the Chickasaw Commission did sign the agreement, it was considered approved. Nevertheless, this lack of unanimity among the Chickasaw commissioners was a harbinger of future trouble. As powerful and influential Chickasaws, Mosely and Cheadle had many followers who would be having their say during the agreement's ratification phase.

As early as April 29, it was reported that the sentiment around Ardmore favored the rejection of the agreement. Soon, numerous editorials and articles, both pro and con, on the agreement appeared throughout both Indian nations. The flames of controversy were fanned on May 12 with the release of a report issued by the Office of the Commissioner of Indian Affairs. The report stated first that the "diversity and magnitude of interests" in the two nations "make it almost impossible" to frame an agreement satisfactory to all. The report cited 11.3 million acres, inhabited by "14,560 Indians and 100,000, approximately, of whites and others engaged as they are in nearly every kind of business and industry." Then, in apparent contradiction of its initial finding, it was stated that "no objections to this agreement have been filed in this office; therefore, so far as known, it is satisfactory to those persons having interests in the country or who may in any manner be affected by it." With that, the Interior Department transmitted the agreement on May 18 to Congress for "consideration and ratification."[39] Whether or not objections had been filed with the Indian Affairs office, its bland,

spurious finding that the agreement was satisfactory to all further stirred up the opposition.

Former Choctaw chief candidate Jacob Jackson led a group of conservatives in advocating an emigration plan, under which they were to sell their land improvements and migrate to Mexico.[40] At a convention of some three hundred Indians in Antlers in November, the Choctaw-Chickasaw Union Party was founded. In December, the Union Party sent

Camps such as this one grew up around the field operations of the Dawes Commission. Despite the participation of the Commission in the deliberations of the Atoka Agreement in 1897, and the Commission's urging that the agreement be passed by the Choctaws and Chickasaws, Chickasaw voters rejected the lengthy, complicated document. (Photo courtesy of Chickasaw Library) a letter to the secretary of the interior stating its objections to the Atoka Agreement. The letter said the nine signers represented the "majority of the people of the Choctaw and Chickasaw tribes" in protesting the ratification of the agreement. The letter charged that the ratification was "procured by unscrupulous means" and that "a number of the Commissioners who were parties to the consummation of the aforesaid treaty have taken advantage of their position and have trafficked in our coal and asphalt, greatly to their own individual pecuniary interest and much to the detriment of the people." No names or substantiation were provided .[41]

Despite such organized opposition, the Tuskahoma Party gained the upper hand in the Tribal Council and under the leadership of Chief Green McCurtain the agreement was ratified by both Houses of Congress on November 4. Governor Harris reminded the Chickasaw Legislature on September 7 that if the Atoka Agreement were approved, tribal government could continue for eight more years. Otherwise, new federal legislation that would emasculate the tribe's judicial and legislative departments would go into effect on January 1.[42] The Legislature ratified the agreement on October 30 and provided for an election by the people to approve or reject the pact.

On December 1, Chickasaw voters rejected the agreement by a majority of 112.[43] A number of factors probably were responsible. The Atoka Agreement was a lengthy, complicated document, and the means of communicating its many provisions to tribal members was primitive. Misinformation and misunderstandings about the agreement were rife, and the implications of ratifying or not ratifying were probably not well understood. On the other hand, two groups of opponents saw things clearly enough. One group benefited economically from the status quo. Governor Harris blamed the defeat on the "pressure of out-side influences, by people whose personal and private interests were at stake .... "[44] The other group benefiting psychologically, emotionally and spiritually from the status quo, would never betray the trust of their ancestors by voting to terminate the Chickasaw Nation.

The Chickasaws could vote no, but they could not alter the inexorable tide of events. As the Dawes commissioners noted in an 1897 report, even if the agreement were not ratified, "great strides had been made in convincing the Indians of the change that was to be made."[45] Now the time for persuasion was over. There was no turning back. In less than five years, the forebodings of members of the Five Tribes' delegates meeting in 1893 had all been realized.

*Members of the Five Tribes were made U.S. Citizens by an act of Congress in 1901.

Alfalfa Bill's Work for the Tribe

While Tishomingo's population in 1898 was still only five hundred, it was the capital of a nation that was preparing for the allotment of its land and the dissolution of its business and political affairs. Thus, the little town on Pennington Creek was becoming a magnet for attorneys from surrounding states. One who arrived that spring was a young Texan named William H. Murray. Although he hit town with a prosperous appearance, wearing a Prince Albert coat and derby hat, he was broke. In his carpet bag, he carried a change of clothes, a copy of the U.S. Constitution and a world history book.[1]

Murray joined a law firm that was serving as advisors to Douglas Johnston in his Chickasaw gubernatorial campaign. Since Murray had a flair for politics, he soon became the secretary (manager) of the National Party, which had nominated Johnston.[2] Although the campaign brought the two men together frequently and Murray was seeing Johnston's niece, Mary Alice Hearrell, the two men were not well acquainted even after Johnston's election in August 1898. But one day shortly after the inaugural, Johnston sent his bodyguard, Ed Bradley, to fetch Murray to Johnston's home near Emet. Bradley told Murray, "The governor wants to see you at the mansion and wants you to remain overnight."[3]

Murray was flattered and happy to go. His legal career in Tishomingo was off to a slow start. With his customary directness, Murray asked why the governor wanted to see him.[4] Johnston said they would get to that later. After

This photograph of William H. Murray, second from left, seated, shows him with colleagues in Tishomingo about the time he started working for Douglas Johnston, a candidate for Chickasaw governor in 1898. Murray helped get Johnston elected, married his niece and drafted laws for the Chickasaw Legislature in its waning days. (Photo courtesy of Chickasaw Library) supper and a few hours of conversation having nothing to do with Chickasaw affairs, Murray's impatience was again showing.

As he would come to understand later in his relationship with Johnston, this was the governor's way of sizing up a man. Murray saw first hand many examples of those who didn't measure up to Johnston's standards. On one occasion, a U.S. senator asked Johnston to appoint a friend of his to be Chickasaw attorney. Johnston invited the man, Bill Murray and two other guests to dinner. Afterwards, Johnston told Murray that the man would not do. "That man couldn't spell the word faithfulness. He would be running around telling everybody he was running my office. I know what policies I want to lay down, I want a lawyer that will lay down the law to govern those policies."

At that initial meeting Governor Johnston finally showed Murray a letter from Secretary of Interior Ethan Allen Hitchcock. In a patronizing and sarcastic vein, the letter said, in part, "we are returning certain papers purporting to be laws. They are disapproved because they lack form, and are therefore void." (According to a provision of the Atoka Agreement signed and approved in 1898 by the Chickasaws, Choctaws, and the federal government, all tribal enactments had to have federal sanction.)

Johnston handed Murray the enactments in question and asked if he could write the laws. "I can write anything from a political platform to the constitution of a republic," Murray said without even glancing at the papers. "If I don't succeed, it won't cost you a cent." With no further mention of remuneration, Murray drafted the laws that in due course Hitchcock approved.[5] Murray's bill was $500, which Johnston considered reasonable because, by his reckoning, the tribe had been saved "many thousands of dollars."

For one thing, Murray had devised a plan, later enacted, to shift the target of tribal taxation from non-Chickasaw people to their livestock. Since this put the burden on those most able to pay (the big cattlemen who grazed thousands of head annually) the fee of twenty-five cents per head per year brought in substantial revenue (Murray says it was $375,000) and helped pay the Nation's debt of $300,000.[6]

Nevertheless, Johnston told Murray that because the Legislature was used to paying a draftsman $4 a day for the service, presenting the lawmakers with a bill of $500 would not be politically palatable. Johnston offered to pay Murray himself, but Murray refused to accept the governor's check. Johnston overcame the embarrassing impasse. In return for Murray continuing to draft bills and to do other legal work for the tribe, Johnston began referring cases of persons who Johnston believed should be included on the tribal roll but had to go to court to prove their citizenship. Murray suggested and Johnston agreed to a contingency fee of 25 percent of the value of the land. To put this in perspective, other lawyers had been charging and getting 50 percent.[7]

Murray started this work in 1899, the same year he married Johnston's niece Mary Alice Hearrell. To discourage intermarriages and hold down the number of opportunists angling for a share of the tribal estate, the Legislature was considering a bill to raise the marriage license fee from $50 to $1,000 for whites wanting to marry a tribal member. Although Murray was not an opportunist and was very much in love with Mary Alice, he was also not above mentioning to two Chickasaw legislators that he wished the Legislature would hold off passing the bill until the September session, for Murray was to marry Mary Alice in July. According to Murray, no more was said about it, the bill did not pass, and Murray paid $50. In September, the bill raising the fee to $1,000 passed unanimously.[8]

Bill Murray began practicing criminal law, defending tribal members in the federal territorial courts. In his memoirs, Murray wrote that the judges were dictatorial and often prejudiced against Indians. He began referring to them as the "inferior courts."[9]

For work on fifteen such cases, the tribe paid him $800 in 1901. He earned most of his income, however, on contingency. By 1902, his income for legal services was nearly $5,000, far more than earned by most small-town lawyers. Governor Johnston's salary at the time was $1,500.

The Symbol on the Hill:
A HISTORY OF THE CHICKASAW CAPITOL BUILDING OF 1898

Chickasaws started arriving early that morning, November 17, 1898. They converged on Tishomingo from all over the Chickasaw Nation. Guests came from other nations within Indian Territory and even Texas to attend the momentous event scheduled for that evening.

According to the two existing newspaper accounts of that day, everyone in town seemed to be in a festive mood. Probably that impression is generally accurate. Many of the full bloods and other more traditional minded Chickasaws who voted against the Atoka Agreement may have stayed away.

Furthermore, the object of the gathering was a source of tribal pride and the most conspicuous sight in town. On the hill, a little north and west of the main street, was the striking and splendid new tribal Capitol Building, a two-story, granite-block building with an arched roof featuring ornate gables and supporting a lofty, rather narrow and ornamental cupola. A traveler's first sight of the capital city coming from almost any direction would be the silver cupola glimmering in the sun, materializing above the trees.

The people arrived on foot and by one of several modes of horse-powered conveyance: covered wagon, buckboard, surrey and horseback. Although gas-powered automobiles initially had been offered for sale in the United States two years before,[1] it is doubtful that few if any had appeared in Tishomingo by 1898. In an Ardmore newspaper account of the day in which the reporter described the scene, automobiles were not mentioned .[2] If no autos were present, it was just as well. The area, trapped in a drought, was already dusty enough without automobiles kicking up even more dust from the unpaved streets.

Furthermore and not coincidentally, Tishomingo had no rail service. By treaty following the Civil War, the Chickasaws and Choctaws were forced to accept the coming of railroads through their lands, but the Chickasaws were not obliged to permit trains to bring non-Indians right into their capital. Nevertheless, over the next thirty years trains would be one of the principal means of transporting thousands of white and black settlers (who paid taxes) and intruders (who avoided paying taxes) into the Chickasaw Nation. As a result of the tribal government being unable and the federal government being obliged but unwilling to control the emigrants, the abolition of the Chickasaw and Choctaw nations was in sight, prescribed in the Atoka Agreement of 1897.[3]

Some people in town that day may have wondered why the Chickasaws, in the shadow of their abolition as a tribe, had gone to the trouble and expense of erecting a new capitol building. There was no simple answer; many factors may have been involved:

- The old capitol building was so structurally unsound that it was no longer safe for occupancy.
- In advocating the construction of a new capitol building, Governor Robert M. Harris offered to sell the tribe the granite to construct the building from his quarry north of town. The Legislature agreed.
- Tribal officials had the assurance from federal officials that a federal district court would be housed in part of the new capitol building, so the tribe could reasonably expect that the building could and would be sold after 1906.

- Despite abundant written evidence to the contrary, some tribal members never believed that their government would be abolished completely.
- Last, but not least, the fact that the building was so well constructed of granite virtually guaranteed its durability. This meant that no matter who occupied the building after 1906, it could be a permanent monument to the Chickasaw Nation. For many Chickasaws, this reason alone justified constructing the building; getting it done was their moral imperative.

Unfortunately, because no records exist of the legislative discussions or debate involving the proposed new building, knowing what was on the minds of the decision-makers cannot be determined. If any significant opposition existed, it is not reflected in the available documentation .[4] Nevertheless, five committees met to plan the program for the dedication of the Capitol Building, and by November 17, all was in readiness.[5]

Constructed in 1898, the Chickasaw Capitol Building was the third and last built in Indian Territory. Before removal, Chickasaws met at a council house. The last such seat of government was located near Pontotoc, Mississippi.

Facing Page: The Chickasaw Capitol is pictured on the day it was dedicated, November 17, 1898. While most were in a celebratory mood, some questioned why the Chickasaw Nation went to such expense when the tribal government had already approved the terms for its abolition by 1906. (Photo courtesy of Chickasaw Library)

A large contingent of Chickasaws assembled there in 1816 to hear a message from President James Madison urging them to sell a part of their lands in Tennessee to the United States. After several days of negotiation with the U.S. delegation headed by General Andrew Jackson, the Chickasaws agreed to sell the land.[6] Following 1823, tribal members received their annual annuity payments from the federal government at the Council House. The last noteworthy event to take place there was the signing of the Treaty of Pontotoc in 1832, in which the tribe—bowing to pressure from the federal government and the state of Mississippi—agreed to remove to the west once suitable land had been found.[7]

The first structure referred to as the Council House in the new Chickasaw Nation was a twelve by twenty-four-foot log house constructed in either 1854 or 1855. According to an undocumented note in the files of the Chickasaw Council House Museum in Tishomingo, Charles W. Flint was paid $505 for his part in building the log Council House.[8] Clearly meant to be a temporary meeting place by the leaders of the new constitutional government at Good Spring (later Tishomingo), the log building was used for meetings only until a new, two-story brick capitol was constructed in 1858. The log building, which reportedly had been located adjacent to the location for the second Capitol, was moved off the

property, supposedly used to store livestock feed until it was rehabilitated in 1965, and eventually became the namesake exhibit inside the Council House Museum.[9]

After the Capitol was built, the National Bell was purchased and installed near the building. The iron bell, twenty-four inches high by three hundred pounds, was rung to summon tribal members to meetings.[10] Soon, however, the bell might have served as an alarm, announcing the commencement of hostilities between the North and South. Not long afterward, some hearing the bell may have detected a funereal quality, tolling the demise of Chickasaw government.

Sometime after the Peace Treaty was signed in April 1866, the tribal government, virtually broke, resumed functioning on a limited basis.[11] By the time the Chickasaw's economy was beginning to improve in the late 1870s, the condition of the brick Capitol Building had deteriorated. Governor Jonas Wolf told the Legislature in 1884 that without repair work, "[the building] certainly cannot stand much longer in its present condition."[12]

The Legislature passed an act on November 1, 1884, authorizing the repair, "both inside and out." Though the act included authorizing an appropriation for the repair, no amount was disclosed, and whether the money was, or ever became, available is not reflected in existing tribal records.

Over the next decade, the building's condition worsened, and in 1893 a report indicated that the building had been "condemned" as unsafe.[13] Since the article did not identify a source, the condemnation may have been a fiction, perhaps cooked up by proponents who wanted the seat of Chickasaw government moved from Tishomingo to Davis or Purcell.[14] Nevertheless, the news reports indicated that the building was unsafe for occupancy and that the time for major repairs had past. Complicating the Capitol Building issue still more was the fact that the Dawes Commission was making its initial visit involving its congressionally mandated mission of abolishing tribal government and the title to tribal lands. Viewed from today, it may have seemed pointless in 1893-94 to have even discussed erecting a new capitol. But such are the perils of drawing conclusions from a century-old perspective. From a present-day vantage point, it is known that the Dawes Commission succeeded. But in 1893 and later, many Chickasaw leaders were unwilling to concede anything. In fact, the tribal leadership refused to discuss allotment with the federal government's representatives.[15]

Even when Robert Harris, a man more conciliatory with the federal government, was elected governor in 1896, he recommended to the Legislature that a new capitol be built. To cynics, Harris may have been aiming to enrich himself

The tribe's first designated Capitol, erected of brick in 1858, two years following the Chickasaw Constitutional Convention and three years prior to the American Civil War. Some of its bricks were used in the construction of the 1898 Capitol. (Photo courtesy of Chickasaw Library)

further by selling the tribe the granite building material from his quarry. But the Legislature had no compunctions to deal with Harris; he owned the commodity of choice located just a few miles north of town. Moreover, an article in *The Daily Ardmoreite*, a newspaper that was no friend of the governor's, noted that "all the legislature seem to want a new capitol, but are rather at a loss to know how long present conditions will endure. They are willing to build the new building with an assurance that the same will be taken off their hands upon the advent of a new and separate government."[16]

A year later on November 8, 1897, Governor Harris signed a legislative act appropriating $15,000 to pay for the erection of the new Capitol Building in Tishomingo City. According to the act, Harris would appoint a three-person committee to assist him in contracting for and superintending the construction.[17] Harris appointed three men prominent in Chickasaw affairs: William Rennie, Charles D.Carter and

Facing Page: Posing mid-way in the construction of the granite Capitol are, left to right, Governor Robert M. Harris, Will Rennie and R.L. Murray. The granite came from a quarry owned by Gov. Harris. (Photo courtesy of Chickasaw Library)

R.L. Murray.[18] With Harris participating, it was, in effect, a four-man committee. They would be paid $4 per day. The act gave them the power to accept bids, to provide specifications and to dispose of the old Capitol Building "in any way they think best." Any revenue resulting from the disposal of the old Capitol would defray the cost of the new Capitol. The act gave the committee members the ultimate authority and power to construct a building. But photos of general contractor C.P. Shaeffer and Will Rennie holding up the "plans" of the Capitol Building only suggest a working relationship. The tribal records documenting the interaction between the committee members and the architect and general contractor apparently have been lost to history.

But before a contract could be signed, the tribe wanted to know if a federal district court would be located in Tishomingo. If so, changes would have to be made in the Capitol plans. In January 1898, Governor Harris and Attorney General R.L. Boyd were in Washington promoting the need for a court in Tishomingo.[19] Apparently they got the federal go-ahead, for a special session of the Legislature was held in February to consider Harris's recommendation that the original plans be altered to accommodate the court and to appropriate additional money for a larger capitol building.[20]

In March, it was reported in *The Daily Ardmoreite* that

Chickasaw authorities had been assured by federal officials that Tishomingo would be the home of a new federal district court when the Capitol Building was completed. The building "will be two stories high," constructed of "Chickasaw granite, steam heated and have all the latest improvements." It "will also have a senate chamber and assembly hall, together with six office rooms."[21]

The contract between the committee of four and general contractor C. P. Shaeffer was signed on April 7. Shaeffer, of Denison, Texas, would be paid $10,987, in increments for completing construction of the new Capitol on the site of the old Capitol by August 31, 1898. He would be responsible for supplying all materials and labor but would have free use of all raw building materials found on the public domain of the Chickasaw Nation. In addition, after the old Capitol Building was demolished, the building committee permitted Shaeffer to "use, barter or sell" its components as he saw fit.

The work would be inspected by project architect and superintendent J.A. Shannon to ensure that the specifications were met. Shaeffer was responsible ultimately for any work default or fraud. The contract stated that "time was of the essence." The reason for urgency was not given, although it may have been related to the bid by the tribe and Tishomingo to have a new federal district court housed in the building.

Though speedy construction was vital, rainy weather was recognized as a possible legitimate cause of delay.[22]

The demolition of the old building was nearly finished by April 27. Meanwhile, laborers were at work in Governor Harris's quarry, and the walls of the new building were expected to begin going up soon. Each granite block was said to weigh 175 pounds per square foot. Apparently, Shaeffer decided to use some of the old brick in the interior of the new building. According to a news story reported in 1992, a curator of the Council House Museum noted that "you can see them [the bricks] just inside the arch of the main entrance to the building and on the inside walls of the adjoining rooms."[23]

On April 28, it was announced that William H. (Bill) Murray had moved from Fort Worth to Tishomingo to begin working with the law firm of Treadwell, Murray and Lucas.[24] Soon thereafter, Murray would be retained by the National Party to help run the 1898 campaign of its candidate for governor, Douglas H. Johnston. As newcomer Bill Murray began watching the granite walls begin going up in May, even he, endowed with an elephantine ego, probably did not imagine making a major address at the new building's dedication seven months hence.

Johnston's opponent was tribal treasurer H. H. Burris, unanimous nominee of the Progressive Party. An Ardmore newspaper said Burris had conducted himself honorably in his duties and would make a formidable candidate.[25] The 1898 gubernatorial election offered voters a clear-cut choice. Burris campaigned largely on a policy of continued resistance to ending tribal affairs. Johnston, long-time superintendent of the Bloomfield Academy, believed he needed to work with, not against, the U.S. government to wind up tribal affairs as favorably as possible by the 1906 deadline. As the candidate of the special interest groups waiting to make a financial killing when the land and money started changing hands, Johnston undoubtedly had a much better financed campaign. Furthermore, Congress passed the Curtis Act on June 30, 1898, which, among other things, abolished tribal courts, made any action of the tribal government subject to approval by the federal government and provided for the abolition of the tribal government by March 4, 1906.[26] It was clear that further tribal resistance to the federal government would be futile if not harmful. Johnston defeated Burris in all four Chickasaw districts by a total of 255 to 117.[27] Several days later, the Chickasaws and Choctaws ratified the Curtis Act by a substantial majority.

To increase attendance, the Capitol Building's cornerstone was laid in a June ceremony held on the same day as the closing exercises of the Chickasaw boarding school, the Harley Institute. In the cornerstone ceremony, Judge Colbert A. Burris invoked the memory of two great men—George Washington, the father of his country, and Tishomingo, "the father of the Chickasaw Nation."[28]

The weekly construction reports that were contractually required are not among the existing tribal records. Consequently, progress cannot be traced, nor can it be determined if the August 31 deadline was met. One undated legislative act passed sometime between August 24 and November 17 appropriated $1,500 for "further development of the building and grounds." Included within the act was money for a "substantial wrought iron fence to surround the building." The *Purcell Register* used the fence as the means to criticize the entire building project: "As the tribe has no government, why should a fine building be built at tribal expenses?"[29] While it may have been true that tribal members had recently been asking that question, by late August the building must have been virtually complete. Why be critical after the fact? Perhaps Purcell, which had been in competition with Tishomingo for the site of the new Capitol Building and federal district court, was merely engaging in sour grapes.

Other provisions of the aforementioned act included lighting the building with an acetylene gas machine that powered thirty-two gas burners dispersed around the building and placing in the tower a "Seth Thomas clock with a dial at least three feet in diameter" and a "gong to strike the hours." Finally, the Chickasaw National Jail and jailer's house would be removed from the Capitol grounds and placed on an acre specifically provided for that purpose.[30] Seventy-seven years after the building was completed, the inside of the tower was described as "like looking up into an oil derrick. Heavy wooden braces criss-cross the top of the belfry and huge beams anchor the frame securely to the roof." Not surprisingly then, the tall cupola had survived everything Mother Nature could throw at it. The reporter who was touring the building in 1975 also reported finding "piles of boxes stuffed and overflowing with legal papers dating to 1902." She noted since no one knows what to do with them, "they have been relegated to the attic."[31]

It has been written many times that the 1898 Capitol Building cost $15,000.[32] That belief is probably based only on a reading of the Legislature's November 1897 appropriation of $15,000 for the construction of the building. But a look at the existing tribal records reveals that the Capitol project cost approximately twice that amount. Four warrants issued to Governor Harris alone totaled $15,000.[33] Unfortunately, the warrants only contain the notation "New capitol building" or "work on capitol building." The agreement paying general contractor Shaeffer almost $11,000 specified that he would provide all labor and material but that he would have free use of all building materials found in the Chickasaw Nation. According to a diary kept by Shaeffer's son (who worked for his father on the project) the work on the Capitol Building financially ruined the contractor. He wrote, "We had to haul buildling material from Denison or Durant by wagon and team. We quarried our own granite, burned our own lime, burned our own brick and hauled sand from the Pennington Creek. [Because of the great hauling] distances, bad roads and weather, we left there broke."[34]

In addition to the contractor's fee, the architect was paid $384.54. Harris was also paid $1,036 as chairman of the building committee, and warrants were also issued to the other committee members, including, R.L. Murray, $1,024; C.D. Carter, $1,028; and William Rennie, $980.[35] At $4 per day, they would have been credited with working approximately 250 days.

The man who had moved to Tishomingo in April to practice law says his help was solicited (probably by Governor Douglas Johnston) in planning the Capitol's dedication. Having attended the inauguration of a Texas governor, William H. Murray suggested the evening begin in a similar fashion with the Grand Promenade led by Governor Johnston. Since Johnston's wife was ill, he needed a partner. Murray suggested that the governor escort Murray's date,

Mary Alice Hearrall, who happened to be Johnston's niece and later Murray's wife.[36]

Actually, ex-Governor Harris and his wife led the promenade on that evening of November 17, 1898. Johnston was governor, but it was Harris's night, as the newspaper accounts attested. Since he had been most responsible for the construction of the new Capitol, Harris performed as the dedication's master of ceremonies and undoubtedly played a pivotal role in planning the event. He also donated the building's keystone, the central wedge-shaped stone in the arch over the doorway that locks both sides together. His name, "R.M. Harris," was carved into the keystone. This act may have been a source of an unfounded rumor that many people today still believe: that Harris donated the granite for the entire building.

In the mixture of reporting and editorializing that was typical of the day, the *Daily Ardmoreite* proclaimed the new Capitol "second to none" and threw bouquets to one and all. "Well may Architect Shannon wear turkey feathers in his hat and feel proud of the edifice on Capitol Hill." Approaching the building, the reporter wrote, presented a "fairy-like picture," as the Caucasian, full-blood Indian, bright Indian maidens and the more stolid mothers of the race," all moved toward the "rows of cedars between which are the arched portals illuminated by Chinese lanterns." As if reporting from inside a beautiful dream, the reporter floated from one scene to another, "not seeing one unpleasant feature in any part of the proceedings."[37]

The upstairs House chamber had been converted into a ballroom for the evening. The orchestra of a Professor Bower performed from an elevated stage at one end. Among the tunes played in the early evening were "Dixie" and "Hot Time in the Old Town." The room was decorated with a "profusion of Old Glory," and interspersed wreathes of evergreen. Supper was served downstairs in the Senate chamber, also decorated with American flags and "life-size pictures" of Harris and Johnston. There were three tables stretching from wall to wall, laden with "delicacies of the season."

One item on display at the banquet not mentioned in the newspaper accounts was recalled by Oscar White, a fifteen-year-old Chickasaw boy who was there. "I remember this ol' Indian boy named Marvin Burris from Stonewall, he always had a saying, `The goose hangs high.' Perhaps in honor of Burris's favorite saying," White recalled. "Somebody had got a hold of an old goose and hung it up from the ceiling."[38]

Before supper was served, emcee Harris made introductory remarks, and the new Capitol was dedicated by the Reverend Henry B. Smith of St. Phillip's Episcopal Church of Ardmore "in the name of the Holy Trinity."[39] Supper was served at 9 p.m., followed by a series of speeches that lasted until midnight. Among the speakers were tribal secretary C.D. Carter; legislative leader Martin Van Buren Cheadle; former governor William M. Guy; Holmes Colbert, former Chickasaw justice; I.0. Lewis; and Bill Murray, who presented a brief lecture on constitutional government. Acknowledging that Indians had been "cruelly treated," Murray exulted that their evolution, nurtured by the American Republic, had resulted in an "enlightened civilization."[40]

The tribal leaders who had planned the program would have agreed that the evening's festivities were emblematic of that enlightenment. Here were Chickasaws making long flowery speeches and singing and dancing till dawn, not in the traditional way of their ancestors but to American standards and tunes of the Gay Nineties. Such trappings suggest that the tribal leadership was poised for entry into American society. But land allotment, the prolonged thorny issues of citizenship, and the dissolution of tribal government were still in the future.

Throughout the long night, the Capitol glowed on its hill, illuminated from within by acetyline gas. In a Tishomingo otherwise entirely dark, the Capitol must have been a beautiful and inspiring sight, even to those Chickasaws gathered outside who for one reason or another did not feel welcome inside. Yet, it was their Capitol, too, and each person who looked at the shining symbol on the hill perhaps felt something different. However dissimilar their perspective or vision, they shared passion. More than one hundred years later, the sight of the Capitol Building still tugs at one's heart.

Facing Page: Aside from flowery speeches and Professor Bower's orchestra playing ragtime music, and a lecture on Constitutional government by Alfalfa Bill Murray, the dedication featured a supper and a ball. The tribal leadership seemed ready for entry into American society. (Photo courtesy of Chickasaw Library)

INVITATION COMMITTEE:

Gov. D. H. JOHNSTON, Chairman.

P. S. MOSELY.   RICHARD McLISH.   W. W. POYNER.
    M. V. CHEADLE.   H. H. BURRIS.   HOLMES COLBERT.

RECEPTION COMMITTEE:

R. M. HARRIS, Chairman.

L. C. BURRIS.   R. L. MURRAY.   A. TELLE,   L. N. TURMAN.
        J. S. MAYTUBBY.   NICK WOLFE.

ASSISTANTS :

MESDAMES R. M. HARRIS,   W. F. BRIDGES,   W. R. BLAKEMORE,
        L. C. BURRIS,   R. L. MURRAY,   R. L. REAM.

ARRANGEMENT COMMITTEE:

C. D. CARTER, Chairman.

J. WES. PARKER.   WM T WARD   WM. H. MURRAY.
        WM. RENNIE.   NICK MICKLE.   GEO. BURRIS.

FLOOR COMMITTEE:

MOSE CHIGLEY, Chairman.

W. R. BLAKEMORE.   W. F. BRIDGES.   S. C. TREADWELL.
    J. H. WILLIS.   MARVIN J BURRIS.   R. L. REAM.
        J. L. THOMPSON.   J. A. COLBERT.

REFRESHMENT COMMITTEE:

S. M. WHITE, Chairman.

A. T McKINNEY.   I. O. LEWIS,   T. B. McLISH.   C. H. BROWN.
    MESDAMES A. J. ADDINGTON,   WM. RENNIE,   L. N. TURMAN,
            W. W. VANNOY.

Ball and Banquet

DEDICATING

The New Chickasaw Capitol,

TISHOMINGO, IND. TER.,
NOVEMBER 17, 1898.

Press of Tishomingo Herald.

CHICKASAW LIVES

TWENTIETH CENTURY

Thousands of Fraudulent Citizenship Claimants Foiled

Congress ruled that the land of the nations making up Indian Territory would be parceled out as allotments to tribal members. Since the average allotment of 160 acres was valued at $5,000, thousands of non-Indians came forward claiming that they should be on the tribal rolls of one tribe or another. Federal courts ruled in favor of 2,500 claimants who the Chickasaw and Choctaw nations believed were frauds.

Both tribes appealed the citizenship cases, but the Supreme Court upheld the decisions of the lower courts. In 1899, the tribes employed the new law firm of Mansfield, McMurray, and Cornis, to work exclusively on citizenship matters. The firm persuaded the federal government to admit that mistakes had been made, but no remedy was forthcoming. McMurray saw a possible mechanism for remedy in the fact that the Atoka Agreement of 1897—to close out both tribal domains—was incomplete. Therefore, a supplementary agreement needed to be drafted and signed by both tribes and the federal government.

The Chickasaw and Choctaw nations agreed they wouldn't sign with the federal government any agreement that wouldn't provide for reconsideration of the disputed citizenship judgments. It was their bargaining chip; the government couldn't close out the tribes without new legislation.[1] After three years of negotiating, the Supplementary Agreement was signed by both tribes and the government in Washington, D.C., in March 1902.[2]

The key to the citizenship matters was a section of the Supplementary Agreement Act, skillfully inserted by lawyer Frank McMurray during a congressional hearing. It called for the establishment of a Choctaw-Chickasaw Citizenship Court, effective immediately upon passage of the act.[3]

The ratification of the Supplementary Agreement became the central issue in the 1902 Chickasaw elections for governor and the Legislature. That is why those elections, especially the one for governor, were crucial in the tribe's twentieth century history. Since Douglas Johnston was prohibited by the Chickasaw constitution from serving a third successive term, he wanted the nominee of the National Party to be a politically experienced man he could trust to campaign ardently and tirelessly for ratification of the Supplementary Agreement. Palmer S. Mosely measured up in every way. He had been elected Chickasaw governor in 1894, upsetting the favorite ex-governor William Byrd and serving a term beset with great turmoil, dirty tricks and the threat of armed rebellion.

Mosely had campaigned on resisting government intervention in tribal affairs, and in 1896 he refused to meet with the Dawes Commission. Mosely had come to understand that continued resistance would elicit harsher government terms. Coincidentally, his opponent in 1902 was William Byrd, the nominee of the Progressive Party, who opposed not only the Supplementary Agreement, but also the entire allotment system.

Byrd, a mixed-blood, generally represented the views of a large number of full-blood Indians, but Mosely, nominally

a full-blood Chickasaw, represented the opinions of most of the mixed bloods. The two sides ran a bitter campaign, and fights among citizens increased as the election date drew near. There were four polling places, one in each of the nation's counties. Voting was oral and not secret; the voter would call out his name and selection to the official who would simply mark it on a sheet of paper.

Both sides claimed victory, Byrd by eight votes and Mosely by nine votes. The Nationals claimed irregularities in the Pontotoc County voting. The initial announcement reported that Byrd carried the district by thirty votes. A few hours later, the election officials counted the returns eight different times and each time they announced a different vote! Apparently, the voting sheet was hard to decipher and was partially mutilated. The Legislature would meet the next month in September to canvass the vote and announce the winner. Governor Johnston announced, however, that Mosely had won and would be seated.[4]

Melven Cornish, was one-third of the law firm that devoted so much time, money and ingenuity to combating the legal challenges posed by thousands of persons fraudulently claiming membership of either the Choctaw or Chickasaw nations. (Photo courtesy of Chickasaw Library)

Meanwhile, he called for a meeting with his chief aides to plan strategy.[5] All present believed that if the list of voters were compared with the citizenship records of the Dawes Commission, several of the Pontotoc County votes for Byrd and the Progressive candidates would be ruled ineligible. But tribal attorney Melven Cornish noted that the "Pontotoc crowd" would be guarding the records and would not hand them over to the enemy. Another tribal attorney, William Murray, said he would get them. But even if illegal voters could be detected, Murray felt the Pontotoc judge was "unfriendly" and would probably not conduct a fair trial involving the dispute.

A few days later, Murray delivered to the Pontotoc judge a commission signed by Governor Johnston appointing this judge to a job of greater honor, responsibility and pay. Minutes later, Murray had the judge's resignation and was on his way to find George Colbert, who would be the new county judge.

Palmer S. Mosely served as a stand-in for Douglas Johnston, who was constitutionally prohibited from serving a third successive term as Chickasaw governor. Mosely was governor during the negotiating that led to the critically important 1902 Supplementary Agreement, which contained a provision establishing the Citizenship Court. (Photo courtesy of Chickasaw Library.)

Murray then visited the county clerk to tell him of the changes and, by the way, that he wanted the election records. The abashed clerk handed them over without question. Murray tucked them into his grippe and departed for Emet with Colbert to be sworn in by Governor Johnston. The new judge issued writs that were served upon every successful candidate in Pontotoc County, informing them that the election was being contested. When the list of voters was checked with the citizenship rolls, several illegal votes were found. While this was crucial, nothing was final, given the pervasive threats of violence.

The trial in the court of Judge Colbert was set for September 2, two days before the Legislature would meet. Murray argued the suit protesting the election. George Burris argued the Progressive side. At one point, a spectator physically attacked Murray. The attacker was then restrained by one of the U.S. Secret Service agents present to maintain order. The trial lasted all day. Incredibly, the Nationalists took Colbert to Tandy Walker's home for "safe keeping" and escorted him back to court the next morning.[6] To no one's surprise, Colbert did find voter fraud and declared the county's election illegal. This gave Mosely a safe margin of victory, but nothing was said about barring the newly elected Pontotoc County legislators. They were determined to be

seated at Tishomingo the next day and to carry on the fight to defeat the Supplementary Agreement.

The Pontotoc County legislators were forestalled on September 4, however, by the efforts of Ben Colbert, a Mosely supporter and U.S. marshal for the Southern District of Indian Territory. Colbert and twelve deputies simply barred them from the Capitol Building while the group inside, perfectly choreographed by Johnston, Murray, and Cornish, declared the election in Pontotoc County illegal and Palmer Mosely governor by a forty-four-vote margin. Then, the Legislature set the Supplementary Agreement ratification vote for September 25.[7]

When the news hit the street, the opposition seemed to wilt, according to one source. The "wilting" was almost undoubtedly due to the deployment of a large and professional contingent of peace officers, including Marshal Colbert's armed deputies, Indian Agent Blair Schoenfelt's Indian police, and several Secret Service agents. The ratification vote was not close: 2,140 for and 704 against.[8]

Prompted by the law firm of Mansfield, McMurray, and Cornish, the presidential appointments were made to the Citizenship Court, pending tribal ratification of the Supplementary Agreement. During this period, the firm employed several additional lawyers to help them begin to secure copies of all citizenship cases in the courts. Being obliged to trace the roots of a person's ancestry, the law firm examined records and took testimony in South Carolina, Virginia, Georgia, Tennessee, Alabama, Mississippi, Florida, Louisiana, Texas and Indian Territory. Simultaneously, opponents filed a suit attacking the constitutionality of the existence of the Citizenship Court. In November 1903, the U.S. Supreme Court upheld Congress's right to create the court, thus ending the last challenge to the authority of the Citizenship Court. Over two years, the Citizenship Court tried some 259 cases involving the citizenship of between 3,500 and 3,900 persons. Some 3,400 claims were denied.[9]

As a result, the two tribes were saved an estimated $15 million to $20 million; consequently, they had that much more in land and money to divide among those who were entitled to a share. Finally, one of the largest lawsuits in American history (to that time) was concluded successfully.

The last duty of the Citizenship Court, as provided by the Supplementary Agreement Act of 1902, was to determine the fee earned by the law firm. According to their contract with the two tribes, Mansfield, McMurray, and Cornish had earned about $1.5 million, but the secretary of the interior refused to recognize the contract.

He eventually consented to $250,000, but the attorneys turned down that offer. In December 1904 the court set a fee of $750,000. The firm accepted this amount and was paid in March 1905.[10]

Pursuing Justice
THE PROSECUTION AND PERSECUTION OF FIVE CHICKASAW NATION LEADERS IN 1905

The news that "prominent officials of the Chickasaw nation are said to be connected" to a massive amount of fraud appeared in many Indian Territory newspapers for the first time on June 22, 1905. Without naming names or going into much detail, the *Muskogee Phoenix* titillated its readers by reporting that "for several months it has been whispered that a scandal in official circles was brewing and that the storm center located in the Chickasaw Nation would develop into a sensation," and the newspaper promised its readers that "startling disclosures are probable every day."[1]

The next day a story in another Muskogee paper said several Chickasaw Nation officials, including Governor Douglas H. Johnston, had been indicted for fraud by a federal grand jury sitting in Ardmore. The fraud involved alleged forged warrants and the recirculation of non-cancelled but paid Chickasaw school warrants. The swindle may have totaled between $200,000 and $300,000, according to an article in the June 23 *Daily Ardmoreite*.

The grand jury issued four separate indictments on June 25, two or three days after these articles were published. A few days later, people learned that these premature stories were based on dispatches emanating not from Ardmore but from Washington, and were the handiwork of none other than Secretary of Interior Ethan Allen Hitchcock.[2]

Three indictments dealt with bank fraud involving the recirculation of the Chickasaw school warrants.[3] The fourth indictment charged Governor Johnston, ex-Governor Palmer S. Mosely, and the tribe's attorneys George Mansfield, J. Frank McMurray, and Melven Cornish with fraud in an unrelated case.

However, the Hitchcock-inspired stories wrongly identified Johnston, Mosely, and the three lawyers as parties in the school warrant fraud, which the stories implied would prove to be the major source of the wrongdoing. Although the error was noted in a Muskogee paper several days later, the public's perception of the Chickasaw leaders as a gang of swindlers probably was set. Some of the stories identified the law firm of Mansfield, McMurray, and Cornish as the same one "that had recently gained no little notoriety" by collecting a fee of $750,000 for legal services to the Indians. Meanwhile, the stories continued to promise sensational revelations. According to the *Muskogee Times-Democrat*, the graft and corruption had been endemic for years in Indian Territory tribal governments. "If the secret history" was published, "it would be one of the most astounding disclosures of official corruption ever laid before U.S. citizens." The newspaper applauded the action "that seeks to throw open the dark closets of the Chickasaw tribal government and expose the skeletons of alleged official misconduct."[4]

Even though the indictment did not name Governor Johnston, Mosely, and the attorneys, they remained the central focus of press attention. According to the indictment against them prepared by U.S. Attorney William B. Johnson, they were charged with conspiring to defraud the Chickasaw Nation. In particular, Mosely, while governor in 1902, illegally authorized payments of some $28,800 to the law firm. Johnston was said to have authorized $2,500 in illegal payments to the firm in February 1905.[5]

While no transcript of the grand jury proceedings could be found,[6] a summary of the U.S. attorney's case is contained in a document the latter prepared for his boss, the U.S. attorney general. In his lengthy summary, attorney Johnson said that while the school warrants were being investigated, "evidence developed" that incriminated these defendants. Johnson detailed the two Chickasaw legislative acts of 1899 and 1900 approving the contracts with the law firm for legal services and expenses at fixed amounts. Then, he produced records showing that the firm was paid far in excess of the specified amounts. And the records showed that the expenses paid had not been itemized. "Evidence shows that these attorneys, and whoever happened to be governor, had the entire unlimited control of the finances of the Chickasaw Nation from October, 1900, and expended money on any pretext for any purpose they saw fit ... That there has been an extravagant misuse of funds there can hardly be any question."[7]

The defendants all posted bonds before arrest warrants could be issued. Johnston and Mosely posted $2,500 bonds, while McMurray, Mansfield, and Cornish each posted $5,000 bonds. The law firm distributed a statement that the charges were "trumped up" and implied that the Interior Department had instigated them. Several press reports continued to blur the distinctions between the fraud cases and those charged. In one story, the *Times-Democrat* all but said that those indicted were guilty. The newspaper conveyed that evidence "had been gathered carefully by trusted agents of the federal government" and the bulk of the evidence consisted of "original documents." The prosecution would be conducted by Johnson, a "fearless prosecutor, intimately acquainted with affairs in the Chickasaw nation where he has lived for the last fifteen years."[8] In a less judgmental article, *The Daily Ardmoreite* reported that the law firm had been paid $96,000 over the last four years; yet under their contracts, the attorneys had been entitled to collect only $30,800. The story said the balance apparently had been paid in expenses.[9]

As soon as the indictment stories were published, the three law partners not only claimed their innocence but also began contacting influential friends to ask the Justice Department for an investigation of the investigation and the grand jury proceedings. While they said they were anxious to go to trial, behind the scenes they were actually maneuvering to have the indictments quashed. Although the newspapers repeatedly wrote that the news was "shocking," the attorneys certainly were not surprised about their indictments. During the six years that they had represented the Chickasaw and Choctaw tribes, they had been extraordinarily successful, and in the process, they had made powerful enemies.

J. Frank McMurray had used a go-between to contact Cecil A. Lyon of Sherman, Texas, a lumber magnate, member of the Republican National Committee, and friend of President Theodore Roosevelt. McMurray told Lyon that the indictment was a gross injustice and explained why at some length. Could the attorneys substantiate all their claims, Lyon wanted to know. Everything, McMurray answered. After hearing McMurray's version, Lyon agreed to bring the matter to the attention of the U.S. attorney general and the president. Subsequently, Lyon went to Washington and recounted McMurray's version to Assistant Attorney General Charles W. Russell.[10]

On July 31, Russell wrote Attorney General W.H. Moody about a matter that might have prejudiced Secretary Hitchcock against the law firm.[11] Acting for the Chickasaw and Choctaw nations, the law firm had obtained legislation in 1902 establishing a Citizenship Court to review decisions of the judges of Indian Territory that allowed more than three thousand persons to be added to the Chickasaw or Choctaw citizenship rolls, thus making them eligible for land allotments and per capita payments. Since the Citizenship Court ruled against most of these claimants, the savings to the tribes "may have been worth as much as $15,000,000." The firm had contracts with each tribe, specifying that the firm would make 9 percent of the recovered amount, which "would have amounted to considerably over a million dollars."[12]

Hitchcock refused to approve the contract but said he would permit a payment of $250,000. The firm refused that amount and lobbied Congress to permit the Citizenship Court to establish the fee. After Congress enacted that measure, the court allowed the firm $750,000. Mansfield, McMurray, and Cornish accepted that amount and were paid in March 1905. Hitchcock was outraged, charging that the law firm had bought its way through Congress.

Russell also noted that the law firm had made a legion of enemies, the three thousand persons who had been stricken from the tribal rolls as well as numerous attorneys who had represented them— first to gain tribal citizenship and then before the Citizenship Court. He said that he realized that advising the president "to have the indictment dismissed ... may give rise to much criticism" and that he would be "very careful before advising such action."

The letter did not mention that another target of Secretary Hitchcock's animosity was Governor Johnston, who had successfully opposed the secretary's attempt in 1900 to extend his department's control over the Chickasaw schools. Hitchcock previously had decreed that the Atoka Agreement gave the Interior Department authority to supervise Indian schools. Four of the so-called Five Civilized Tribes had relinquished control of their schools.[13] Johnston disagreed with the secretary's interpretation, and when Interior's man showed up to assume control of the tribal schools, Johnston refused to recognize his authority. Hitchcock then withheld the tribe's mineral royalties, the sole source of the tribe's education funding, and a stalemate ensued, which lasted until a compromise was worked out in April 1901.[14] That the Chickasaws maintained control over their school system, however, in exchange for an insignificant concession was interpreted as a Chickasaw victory.

In Washington, Russell talked to both U.S. Attorney

Johnson and McMurray and examined "all the evidence and documents." Johnson must have been vexed by the summons and investigation. Later, he said that of the approximately five thousand indictments that were drawn under his seven-year watch as U.S. attorney, this was the only one to have been investigated.[15] But if he was vexed, he might have been apoplectic when he learned of Russell's September 29 letter to Attorney General Moody: "Sufficient facts were produced to show an apparent case [against the five defendants], but it needed only an explanation and the production of some documentary evidence to make it fall to pieces." As a result of his examination, Russell concluded that the expense money had been used "in good faith for the benefit of the nation," not "embezzled in pursuance of a criminal conspiracy." Russell recommended dismissal of the indictment and said that the defendants were owed an apology for the "grave injustice" done them.[16]

Word of Russell's recommendation leaked to the public in October, and Secretary Hitchcock said he was not satisfied with the investigation conducted by the Justice Department. He secured permission from the President to conduct an investigation of the matter by special agents of the Indian Bureau." [17] In a more colorful account published in *The Daily Ardmoreite*, it was reported that Hitchcock "doesn't disguise the fact that he is after the scalps" of the defendants.[18]

In November 1905, the law firm signed a contract with Cecil Lyon to help them gain the President's approval of the firm's contracts with the Chickasaw and Choctaw nations concerning the proposed sale of their extensive mineral lands. In early December, Cecil Lyon telegraphed President Roosevelt: "In spite [sic] report, Attorney General cases against Johnston, McMurray et al not dismissed. Please so direct."[19]

Attorney General Moody telegraphed W.B. Johnson on December 6 to dismiss the indictment "unless you have, since your return [to Ardmore from Washington], found some reason to the contrary." On December 13, Johnson sent Moody a telegram and letter, providing some new items of interest and his opinion that the defendants were guilty.

While probably all parties would agree that the documentation of the dealings between the Chickasaw Nation and the law firm was far from perfect, Johnson saw this as evidence of embezzlement, while Russell saw only instances of less than desirable bookkeeping but no evidence of fraud. Russell could be dispassionate; Johnson could not.

Why? Because W.B. Johnson had preceded Mansfield, McMurray, and Cornish as the Chickasaw tribal attorney, and it was during his tenure that the three thousand plus fraudulent claimants had been admitted to the Chickasaw and Choctaw tribal rolls. As the tribe's trusted and well-paid ($8,000 annually) legal advisor, Johnson had been unwilling or unable to stem the tide that would have resulted in an immense financial disaster. One possible reason that Johnson had not vigorously resisted the fraudulent claimants was that he was too busy with his other job as U.S. Attorney. When his contract expired, Governor Johnston replaced him with Mansfield, McMurray, and Cornish, who undid the injustice to the tribes that had been perpetrated on W.B. Johnson's watch. Still, Johnson, as U.S. Attorney for the southern district of Indian Territory with authority over both the Chickasaw and Choctaw nations was in a position to render justice or injustice to tribal officials and his successors, Mansfield, McMurray, and Cornish.[20]

On December 18, Johnson received a cable from the attorney general, informing him that the President had removed him from office. Hours later, he received another telegram rescinding his removal. Apparently, President Roosevelt was mistakenly told that Johnson had refused to obey an order to dismiss the indictment. The second telegram was sent when the error was discovered, although no explanation was offered to Johnson. One can only imagine Johnson's reaction to each of the two telegrams. What is known is that he resigned that same day.[21]

Even before Johnson's resignation, there were reports of a "serious rupture" between Hitchcock and Moody, which could force President Roosevelt to request Hitchcock's resignation. A

When Gov. Douglas Johnston, above, insisted on maintaining control of the tribal school system, he made an enemy of Secretary of Interior Ethan Allen Hitchcock. Subsequently, Gov. Johnston was indicted by a federal grand jury in 1905. (Photo courtesy of Chickasaw Library)

newspaper reported that Moody told the President that it was "a case of either Hitchcock or me." [22]

The storm in Washington passed. The case, in effect, was suspended while Johnson's successor, George R. Walker, waited for assistance from William J. Burns of the Secret Service. Secretary Hitchcock announced that in early 1906 Mr. Burns would be responsible for gathering pertinent evidence for U.S. Attorney Walker. Meanwhile, Walker took up the normal heavy workload in his district, including eight court towns. When Burns' help was not forthcoming, Walker himself gathered the evidence and conducted his own investigation. Just before he sent his lengthy report to the attorney general on March 29, 1907, Secretary Hitchcock resigned.[23] In his report, Walker unequivocally recommended the dismissal of the indictment on several grounds.

During the grand jury session, when McMurray was asked to produce the firm's financial records, he said they were at the firm's headquarters in McAlester but could be brought to Ardmore for the next day of court. The jury members agreed to wait but later that day changed their minds. Without examining the books that McMurray claimed would provide grounds for exoneration, the grand jury proceeded to return an indictment. According to U.S. Attorney Johnson, one of the jurors received word that his brother was dying, and "if we had let him go it would have necessitated the reorganization of the grand jury. I told them they could do as they pleased and (then) they asked me to prepare the indictment." [24] Walker wrote that if the jury had seen the financial records of the firm as he had (and they should have) there would have been no indictment.

Moreover, getting a fair trial in Ardmore, Walker wrote, was out of the question. Ardmore was the headquarters of an organization founded to resist paying tribal taxes. The organization sprouted up after Governor Johnston had asked the law firm for assistance, resulting in the attorneys providing both a plan and advancing the expenses to the tribe for collecting livestock taxes, merchandising fees and sales taxes. These taxes had been on the books for years, but the farmers, ranchers and merchants had refused to pay, and the Chickasaws apparently had stopped trying to collect.

In a renewed effort to collect fees and taxes, Indian police working under the direction of the Interior Department shut down any business that refused to pay the taxes, while Chickasaw agents, with Interior's approval, herded up and sold the livestock of non-paying owners. This affected hundreds of people. Lawsuits were filed against the Chickasaws. Nevertheless, the Chickasaws recovered hundreds of thousands of dollars of taxes owed. Amid the bitterness and turmoil, the federal government sought an indictment against the five defendants, Johnston, Mosely, Mansfield, McMurray, and Cornish. Walker learned that some of the grand jury members were Ardmore merchants who belonged to the organization resisting the tribal taxes. McMurray later said he considered the indictment to be a compliment, not a stigma.

Even though Hitchcock had resigned, his successor, James R. Garfield (not to be confused with President James A. Garfield) still wanted the case "vigorously prosecuted" despite Walker's report. In his communiqué, Garfield noted that the Indian Affairs Commissioner Francis Leupp concurred. The new Attorney General Charles J. Bonaparte asked a departmental special assistant W.S. Gregg to go to Ardmore to conduct another investigation. Gregg examined the evidence presented to the grand jury, along with the books and papers of the law firm, and concluded that "the Government could not hope to be successful in prosecuting the case...." He made three key points: the circumstances under which the indictment was obtained were not, to say the least, in keeping with good legal practice; the evidence against the defendants was too scant to justify an indictment much less a conviction; and "not one penny of the money supposed to have been misused reached the pockets of the attorneys." His report reached Bonaparte on May 2, 1907. Six days later, Secretary Garfield wrote that there was no point in continuing to pursue the case.[25]

Inexplicably, President Roosevelt then directed that Charles Nagel of St. Louis be requested to determine if the prosecution of the defendants should move forward. Following yet another complete investigation of the case, Nagel reported on June 24, 1907, that "the indictment can not, in my opinion, be sustained." By September, everyone in the Justice and Interior departments again had agreed that the indictment should be dismissed. There was no action, however, until the day before Oklahoma gained admission to the Union, November 16, 1907. Bonaparte cabled U.S. Attorney Walker to dismiss the indictment. If they had waited another day, the case might have been taken up by a state court.[26]

The matter ended with a whimper, not a bang. After December 1905 when the case went into a long hibernation, there was nothing to report. Probably most people had long since made up their minds about the innocence or guilt of the five defendants. Very few were aware of just how thoroughly the matter had been investigated and how badly the defendants had been mistreated by the justice system, which in this case in 1905 had been temporarily under the control of a few venal and unprincipled men.

On page three of the November 15, 1907 issue of the *Muskogee Times-Democrat*, the newspaper that had so often clouded the distinction between reporting and editorializing on the matter ran a one-sentence story: "U.S. District Attorney George R. Walker was advised by the Department of Justice to drop the case against Mansfield, McMurray and Cornish for conspiracy."[27]

Time of Unrest:
CHICKASAW MASS MEETINGS IN THE 1920S

Outwardly, the mass meeting of hundreds of Chickasaws at Seeley Chapel in November 1922 was reminiscent of the way the tribe conducted business centuries before in its Southeastern domain. Every year, when the first new corn was ripe, tribal members would come together to discuss tribal business and to celebrate the green corn, or busk, festival. The year-old, sacred fire would be extinguished, and a new one was struck to begin four days of national business, purification rituals, feasting, dancing, and stickball playing.

But the busk festival had not been observed for generations, and the only times that the tribe assembled en masse following removal was to collect annuity payments. Still, when Governor Douglas Johnston called for the 1922 mass meeting, it was the first time in many years that such a large gathering of Chickasaws had assembled to discuss their problems and priorities and to feast on *pashofa*, the traditional meal of pork and cracked corn cooked in big pots over firewood.

The governor intended the mass meeting to become an annual event, like the busk festival. While this was a link to the past in a sense, it also reminded many of the Chickasaws of what they had lost or were losing. Aside from the loss of government, relatively few participants at the meeting spoke Chickasaw or knew much about the tribe's customs and traditions, the very aspects of the tribe that had made Chickasaws unique.

Though the governor's idea to hold annual mass meetings might have been in keeping with an ancient tribal tradition, Johnston's main aim was to demonstrate to Congress and the Department of Interior that the tribe was becoming increasingly impatient with the federal government to complete its business. The government was into its second decade of delinquency on its promise to wind up tribal affairs fairly and squarely. This unwillingness to settle their affairs aggravated virtually all Chickasaws, but that was as far as tribal unanimity went.

If, at these meetings and in other ways, the Chickasaws had presented a strong, united front, the unfinished business issues—the negotiations between the government and the tribe—might have proceeded more expeditiously. But throughout the decade of the 1920s, divisiveness within the tribe seemed to grow. Sometimes it involved money, and often the issue tended to pit full bloods against mixed bloods.

Squabbling also characterized Choctaw tribal relations, which further muddied the water because both tribes had an undivided interest in most of their unalloted lands. But intra-tribal dissension was only a contributing factor to the lack of a settlement. More importantly, the fiscally tight-fisted occupants of the White House during the decade (Harding, Coolidge, and Hoover) were philosophically and politically opposed to a settlement with the tribes.

Moreover, the 1920s was a trying period for administering Indian policy. Commissioner of Indian Affairs Charles Burke had the misfortune to be in office while demands for reform increased in frequency and intensity, but no significant changes occurred. "It was a time of unrest and questioning," wrote historian Francis Paul Prucha, "in which

the ground was prepared and the seeds planted in the public mind for the radical change that came in the 1930s."[1]

There was also some public sentiment—whether due to ignorance of the treaties and agreements or not—that the Indians did not deserve special treatment, especially after 1924 when Congress declared all Indians to be American citizens. (Members of the Five Civilized Tribes had been citizens since 1901; by 1924, only about one-third of all Indians were not citizens.) It was said that Indians were no worse off than many other Americans who were competing and pulling themselves up by their bootstraps. Those with this viewpoint were not necessarily racist; they said that any people who had been conditioned to expect "handouts" would behave similarly. In any event, intra-tribal disputes provided the federal government with an excuse for doing nothing.

Worse still, the Oklahoma Legislature in 1919 passed

For the first time in many years, Chickasaws, like this unidentified man, gathered in a mass meeting at Seeley Chapel to discuss tribal problems and priorities and feast on *pashofa*. The meeting was held in this rural setting because it was believed that many full bloods would not come to a town. (Photo courtesy Chickasaw Library) a bill requiring the county courts to develop their own probate rules. This boosted the opportunities of grafters and "professional guardians" who had been feeding off of Indians ever since 1908, when Congress removed minors of the Five Civilized Tribes from federal protection and placed them under Oklahoma's probate courts. In 1924, the Indian Rights Association of Philadelphia published a pamphlet titled "Oklahoma's Poor Rich Indians: An Orgy of Graft and Exploitation of the Five Civilized Tribes—Legalized Robbery." The report did little to stimulate action in Congress or Oklahoma except among the congressional delegation, which condemned the sweeping nature of the charges.[2]

At the 1922 mass meeting, a group of full-blood Indians introduced a resolution calling for the perpetuation of tribal schools by placing all present and future tribal assets into a fund for that purpose. The resolution was defeated, but it was transformed into a petition by the full-blood group and was sent to Washington. The majority group, mainly mixed bloods, passed a resolution opposing a school fund and proposing that all assets be divided among the Chickasaws and Choctaws. The group said that tribal schools were unnecessary and that a school fund could become a slush fund.[3]

The Chickasaws forwarded the resolution to Washington. The mass meeting had been held at Seeley Chapel, a Chickasaw church a few miles north of Tishomingo, probably because many full bloods would not come into towns. According to the minutes, one of the resolutions was seconded by a young man named Jess Humes, who would become one of Governor Johnston's closest advisors and in the years ahead, a leader of various groups and coalitions aiming to restore Indian sovereignty.

Johnston's stand on the school issue was not clear at the Seeley Chapel meeting. Favoring a school fund would have been a reversal for him, but a news article published afterward noted that he was "committed to the plan to preserve the tribal schools."[4] The reporter might have assumed that Johnston favored earmarking tribal funds to education because Johnston did not wish to speak out against the position of Victor Locke, the former Choctaw chief and current superintendent of the Five Civilized Tribes.

Charles Burke, commissioner of Indian Affairs, told Locke, Johnston, and Choctaw Chief William Harrison that the two tribes needed to determine the will of the people regarding the settlement of the tribal estates. Johnston already knew the will of the majority on the school matter, because meetings of opposition had been held throughout the Indian nations.[5]

Nevertheless, Chickasaws held more meetings at which women for the first time were invited to participate.[6] In the late spring of 1923, Johnston announced that even if it were desirable to fund Chickasaw schools in perpetuity, the tribal funds were "at a low ebb," and it was "impossible to sell the remaining common property to good advantage at this time."[7]

Actually, very little remained of the old Chickasaw school system. Of the approximately 2,500 Chickasaw children attending school in the old Chickasaw Nation in 1921, about 2,050 were enrolled in public schools. The balance of students was enrolled in Bloomfield, the one remaining tribal boarding school, or in contract schools. According to a report of the superintendent's office in Muskogee, "tribal boarding schools still have a distinct field of usefulness...to those inantely [sic] timid and reticent Indians who would perhaps not attend public schools where white children are in the majority." Also, the boarding school's curriculum "is adapted to the economic needs of the Indian and affords instruction and training that could not be obtained in the average rural schools. The boarding schools should be continued as long as there are available funds."[8]

If the economic trend continued, that couldn't be much longer. But in 1924 Congress passed a bill permitting the Chickasaws and Choctaws to submit all of their claims against the government to the U.S. Court of Claims. The House bill had been written by Oklahoma Congressman and Chickasaw citizen Charles Carter. Several suits were filed, and by 1929 the total claims exceeded $32 million.

Missing National Papers Create Voids in Tribal History

The original Chickasaw Nation records are housed at the Oklahoma Historical Society in Oklahoma City. From people interested in their family history to Arrell Gibson writing his magnum opus *The Chickasaws*, researchers have used these records to inform themselves and sometimes a much wider audience. Since most Chickasaw history has been written from non-Indian sources, it is essential that whenever tribal documentation is available that it be included in any examination or interpretation of Chickasaw history.

But anyone who has had much experience using the records almost certainly has been disappointed to find unexpected gaps—sometimes huge ones—in the recorded history of the Chickasaws. After examining the records for information on the establishment of the Chickasaw Seal, we found nothing, save a brief provision in the 1855 Constitution stating that there would be a Great Seal. In all likelihood, there was once, or still may be somewhere, written records describing the first seal, as well as addressing the interrogatories who, when, where and how. More recently, we searched in vain for records of action or discussions by the Chickasaw government relative to the sale of the tribal park lands near Sulphur to the federal government in 1902.

There is no doubt that these and a host of other specific documents once were part of the Chickasaw national papers and that what remains today is only a fraction of what did exist around the turn of the twentieth century. Twenty years ago, Bill Welge, who had just been hired as an archivist by the Oklahoma Historical Society (OHS), learned in some detail how the records of the Five Civilized Tribes had come to be housed at the OHS. He was part of the research effort to develop a federal grant proposal to fund the microfilming of those tribal records. "The National Endowment for the Humanities," he said, "had to know how these records came about and so we had to examine our own records to trace the tribal records back to their sources."

In the case of the Chickasaws, the records had been stored in the basement of the Chickasaw Capitol Building in Tishomingo, Welge said. "This would have been after the Curtis Act was passed by Congress in 1898, calling for the abolition of the Chickasaw and Choctaw tribes by 1906. The Dawes Commission, needing the records to document citizenship for the land allotments, requested that the records be transferred to Muskogee and they were, beginning in 1899 when the commission began enrolling Chickasaws."

Welge said he had not seen Dawes Commission records indicating that the federal government made even a rudimentary inventory of the Indian records that they received. "It is likely that the government decided not to use field clerks to do that and go to that expense when the tribes were about to be dissolved."

As the Dawes Commission finished examining the tribal records, they were transferred to the attic of the old federal courthouse in Muskogee. There was nothing to indicate that anyone examined the records or that any security measures were in place until the late 1920s, when they were discovered by famed Muskogee historian, Grant Foreman. The OHS hired Rella Watts Looney as the state's first archivist, and in 1928 she began the immense task of sorting and cataloging the records of the Five Civilized Tribes.

Up until that time, the OHS housed primarily pre-statehood newspapers. To enhance the reputation of the OHS and its collections, Foreman and former Oklahoma governor Robert Lee Williams devised a plan for the development of a great building to house artifacts and historical records. The key to getting the state funding was the acquisition of federal records that were stored in the courthouse attic in Muskogee. Conversely, the Interior Department told state officials that granting custody of the records to the OHS depended upon them being housed in a fireproof building.

The Oklahoma Legislature appropriated the money just in time (on the eve of the Great Depression) and the OHS building, located adjacent to the State Capitol Building, was erected in 1930. In March 1934, Congress passed a bill giving custody of the records to the OHS, and the transfer from Muskogee to Oklahoma City was made later that year. Welge said that the records catalogued by Mrs. Looney matched the inventory of tribal records at the OHS. "The large amount of records that is missing was missing prior to 1928."

Evidence, Welge said, suggested two primary causes. "Many of the records are water stained, and this suggests the possibility that some sort of flood occurred in the basement of the Chickasaw Capitol Building. It is likely then that some of the records were so damaged that they might have been discarded. The other reason that records are missing is that they were withheld by individuals. We know this happened because occasionally someone will donate original tribal papers that had been in his or her family for generations. A Texas man donated a copy of the record book of the Chickasaw Supreme Court from 1837 to 1855. We also know that one person in eastern Oklahoma has the original 1818 Chickasaw Nation census."

Countless other such documents surely have been passed down through generations of families. According to Welge, it was likely that some tribal employees took their records with them. "I've never seen a tribal law requiring departing employees to turn over office or departmental records. Most did so, I suspect, out of tradition. Others may have withheld records from the Dawes Commission purposely—as a gesture of defiance."

Whatever the cause, a large number of records are missing. The most glaring omission, in Welge's opinion, was Panola, one of the four Chickasaw counties. "We

The Chickasaw Nation's tribal records were discovered by Grant Foreman in a federal courthouse in Muskogee in the late 1920s. Federal officials allowed them to be moved to the custody of the Oklahoma Historical Society after its new, fireproof building (above) was constructed adjacent to the state Capitol Building in 1930. (Photo courtesy of Oklahoma Historical Society).

have absolutely nothing from that county and we should have civil and criminal court records, permits issued to non-citizens, wills, tax papers, vital statistics, grazing leases, and so on. I think there is little doubt that some of these records are out there still."

We encourage persons who have custody of these old tribal documents to consider donating them or photocopies to the tribe so that the history of the Chickasaw Nation will expand by that much more. Even one donation could make a significant difference in someone's life.

The Road to Sovereignty:
THE CHICKASAW GRASSROOTS MOVEMENT OF THE 1950s

By 1951, small groups of Chickasaws who were dissatisfied with Governor Floyd Maytubby for one reason or another began meeting to see what could be done to make him more responsive or to get rid of him. Technically, he was in office not to respond to Chickasaw requests for information or help but to close out the affairs of the tribe. Although he was appointed governor by the secretary of the Interior for a two-year term, his reappointments had been so routine that his tenure apparently would be for life, if he so desired. Maytubby was in his thirteenth year as governor.

Probably most Chickasaws in 1951 could not have named their governor or could not have said what he did. But as the decade wore on, more of them became politically active. Even if their activism extended only to signing a petition asking for a tribal election, by the late fifties these letters and petitions were being taken a bit more seriously by some of Oklahoma's congressional delegation and the Bureau of Indian Affairs (BIA).

The leaders of this reformist movement were mainly elders, the group most respected and therefore apt to be taken seriously by Chickasaws. Except for Jess Humes, however, most were politically inexperienced, relatively uneducated and reluctant to make waves. Even Humes, who for years had held elective office in various indigenous Chickasaw organizations, was not a true leader. Though physically imposing at six feet three, Humes was a gentle, soft-spoken man who preferred to make an impression in concise, reasonable, hand-written letters to selected members of Oklahoma's congressional delegation.

Some of the reformers were motivated by a deep distrust over the sale of the Chickasaw-Choctaw coal and asphalt lands. Although in 1949 a majority of the voting members of both tribes had approved selling the tribal coal and asphalt lands to the federal government for $8.5 million, critics of the proposed deal had been around for years, implying or charging a federal conspiracy to defraud the Indians. Since the land had been sold and the per capita payments dispensed, some were willing to be more vocal about Maytubby and his lawyers not acting in the best interest of the tribe.

As a way of heading off any groundswell of support for a tribal gubernatorial election, Governor Maytubby wrote to his friends in the congressional delegation. In a letter to Senator Robert Kerr, Maytubby laid out the objections he would use time and again to holding a tribal election: Chickasaws are scattered all over the country; it would be too expensive; and the Five Tribes Act of April 26, 1906, (continuing tribal governments in weakened forms) made no provision for such an election.[1]

Furthermore, he believed that the tribe would be better off if the leader were selected by a more enlightened, sophisticated authority than by a vote of the people, whose interests, he believed, were often relatively myopic. He also thought he deserved the appointment out of a sense of *noblesse oblige* and because he had done an excellent job, given the narrow limits of his authority.

Ironically, the movement toward tribal democracy was taking root just as Indian policy was in transition from self-determination to termination of the federal trust

status.[2] Assimilation as a federal policy was alive again.
The termination policy had received a big boost when the
Hoover Commission's report on the organization of the
executive branch was completed in 1948. The commission's
task force on Indians stated that assimilation was the only
logical goal. "Traditional tribal organization was smashed
a generation ago," and there was no turning back. While
complete integration was taking place, the commission
wanted the social programs for Indians transferred to the state
governments, thus, in time, putting the BIA out of business.[3]

By 1953, Congress committed to rapid termination of
the tribes by adopting House Concurrent Resolution 108,
written by Representative William Harrison of Wyoming
and Senator Arthur Watkins of Utah. The resolution read,
in part: "It is the policy of Congress, as rapidly as possible,
to make the Indians within the territorial limits of the
United States subject to the same laws and entitled to the
same privileges and responsibilities as are applicable to
other citizens of the United States, and to end their status
as wards and to grant them all the rights and prerogatives
pertaining to American citizenship...."[4] The rush to terminate
tribes began in 1954 with the Menominee tribe termination
bill. Other termination acts were passed during the 1950s,
covering a few relatively small tribes.[5]

Although Reverend Jess Humes was one of a group of Chickasaw elders who favored the restoration of tribal government,
he was not the charismatic leader that the movement needed.
He preferred to make points in short, reasonable, hand-written
letters. (Photo courtesy of Chickasaw Library)

Choctaw Chief Jimmy Belvin was accused by a Muskogee BIA official of "agitating" Chickasaws to write letters to the BIA commissioner asking for the right to elect their own Governor. Chief Belvin was "guilty" as charged. (Photo courtesy of Chickasaw Library)

To promote employment opportunities and to unofficially help facilitate termination, Indian Affairs developed a voluntary relocation program. It was aimed mainly at moving Indians from reservations and rural areas to cities [where presumably jobs awaited them].[6] But the program was not supported by groups such as the National Congress of American Indians and the Association of American Indian Affairs. They pointed out that the bureau had moved untrained Indians to big cities where they formed a pool of cheap, unskilled labor—the type always to be laid off first. Further, they accused the bureau of trying to undermine Indian self-government on the pretext of "freeing the Indian" and "giving him control of his property."[7]

Some three weeks before Governor Maytubby's term was to expire in October 1951, a convention of Chickasaws met at Seeley Chapel and passed a resolution that was telegrammed to President Harry Truman asking that he withhold reappointing Maytubby until an election could be held, an election similar to the one recently conducted by the Choctaws in which Harry J.W. "Jimmy" Belvin was selected chief in a tribal referendum. (The referendum, however, was not binding since the chief was still appointed by the Interior secretary.) The telegram was signed by Jess Humes, chairman, and Eli Goforth, secretary. No response was returned and Maytubby received the reappointment.

Several months later, Myrtle Creason, the long-time activist secretary of the Choctaw-Chickasaw Confederation of Oklahoma County, wrote Senator Kerr asking him to do something quickly about giving the tribes the right to select tribal leaders "without interference or sanction of the Indian Bureau." She noted that the government is "sending billions to foreign nations to help them hold free elections." In conclusion, Creason articulated precisely the sentiments of a growing number of Indians: "It is not our desire to challenge the Government, but we want to be treated like intelligent people, capable of knowing what we want."

A group of Chickasaws meeting at Seeley Chapel in 1954 voted to ask Maytubby to resign immediately. In a letter to Maytubby and the congressional delegation, two of the officers, Jess Humes and Abijah Colbert, cited "negligence of duty" and "failure to protect the rights and interests of the tribe."[8] A Kerr staffer recommended to the senator that he write to Governor Maytubby to see "what the rukus [sic] is about ... These Indians get mad every once in a while."[9]

Apparently, Kerr never got anything more about "the rukus" in writing. What precipitated the Chickasaws' action

Abijah Colbert was another respected elder who was involved in the Chickasaw grassroots movement to restore tribal government. He was a leader of a group which called for the immediate resignation of Chickasaw Governor Floyd Maytubby. (Photo courtesy of Chickasaw Library)

is not known, since the minutes of the meeting (if any were kept) cannot be found. But it is likely that Maytubby simply ignored the Humes' and Colbert letter, especially since the resignation request came in the middle of his term. No other documentation relative to the matter exists in the collections of Oklahoma's congressional delegation. The Seeley Chapel resolution, however, did seem to mark a point of no return for Humes, Colbert and many others.

They stepped up their activity in 1955, delivering petitions with 227 Chickasaw names, asking that a referendum for governor be held that year. In a letter to BIA Commissioner Glen Emmons, Muskogee BIA chief Paul Fickinger said that many of the names appeared to be written in the same handwriting and that the Secretary (of Interior) had the responsibility to appoint the governor, and that it "should not be shrugged off by the subterfuge of a referendum."[10]

Governor Maytubby also wrote to Fickinger, saying that the Choctaws, especially their chief, Jimmy Belvin, had been agitating Chickasaws to write letters to the BIA commissioner, asking for a gubernatorial election. Many of the "agitated" Chickasaws had been candidates for the appointment of governor in 1939 following Governor Douglas Johnston's death. Maytubby wrote that Belvin worked through Humes

in organizing "a small set-up called the Chickasaw Council" and another small group named the Choctaw-Chickasaw Confederation. Maytubby concluded with the total fabrication that no Chickasaw had ever complained to him "on the way I have conducted the affairs of the Chickasaw Nation."[11] In fact, he had received petitions signed by hundreds of Chickasaws asking that he resign immediately.

In 1955, Durant oil man Hollis Hampton announced he wished to be considered for appointment as Chickasaw governor. But the Choctaw-Chickasaw Confederation did not promote a candidate and seemed disorganized. Finally, in October the group wired Commissioner Emmons, asking that a referendum be held to elect the next governor. But four days earlier, the Interior secretary had reappointed Floyd Maytubby for another term.[12]

Tribal elder Jonas Imotichey wrote a short note in 1958 to Representative Carl Albert, Oklahoma's third district congressman, asking that Governor Maytubby be replaced the next year by one Bobby Page Boyd.[13] This may have been the first time that a representative of the out-of-power groups inside the Chickasaw Nation had advanced the name of an individual for governor. Apparently none of the elders wanted the job, so a young man committed to the cause had to be recruited and agreed upon.

Born in Wapanucka, Bobby Boyd grew up in and around Tishomingo and graduated from Murray State College and later Oklahoma City University with a bachelor's degree in dramatics in 1956. Living in an Oklahoma City nursing home in the summer of 1993 following two strokes, Boyd said he went to Hollywood after graduation and made five western movies, always appearing as an Indian who sooner or later took a bullet. Some of his "co-stars" included John Wayne and Will Rogers, Jr., and two of his movies were titled "Scorching Fury" and "Return of the Mayflower." He returned to Oklahoma because he was in love with a Midwest City girl. While he was courting her, he became interested in becoming governor of the Chickasaws because his friends in his hometown told him that Maytubby was doing nothing for the tribe. "I went to see Maytubby at his Oklahoma City office and told him that to his face. We became bitter enemies."[14]

Boyd said that the idea to try for the appointment was his own and that he received little or no help from other Chickasaws. A few letters were written on his behalf, but the evidence supports his claim that he did his own promoting. While he was persistent, he was not persuasive. Whether he had Chief Belvin's support is unknown, but Boyd listed the chief as a reference. Belvin, however, already had a full dance card, as he liked to say. He was a working chief with two major preoccupations in 1958-59. He had worked on and was promoting the Choctaw self-rule bill, and he was lobbying hard for another tribal referendum for chief and, failing that, for another federal appointment as chief. On top of that, Belvin was also an Oklahoma state senator from Durant.

Although Boyd was raised in the heart of the Chickasaw Nation, in Johnston County, he apparently knew little about Chickasaw history or the nation's status at the time. He wrote to Paul Fickinger and Carl Albert, asking for a copy of the Chickasaw Constitution and laws, wanting to know why the tribe could not elect its governor and the date "the current one's term expires."[15] Albert forwarded Boyd's letter to the acting BIA commissioner, who, in a two-page, single-spaced tutorial, pointed out that the Chickasaw Nation had no constitution or laws, that an election would be impractical and "perhaps even impossible," and that Maytubby's term would expire on October 17, 1959.[16] Fickinger also weighed in with a lengthy and officious response, noting that the law did not provide for an election and that the "Principal Chief has no legal responsibility for matters relating to the tribe, but only ministerial duties relating to physical properties which may still remain in tribal ownership."[17]

After Fickinger sent a copy of Boyd's letter to Maytubby, the governor replied with a note that amounted to burial by deprecation. Boyd, he wrote, "had been in Los Angeles posing as a vice-chief of the tribe." Maytubby said he had warned Boyd by letter to stop "this misrepresentation," or he would write to the newspapers and cause him some "adverse publicity." The governor went on to insinuate that Boyd was trying to promote a shady oil deal in Oklahoma and that the Better Business Bureau had assembled "a great deal of information about him on inquiries."[18]

Whether or not Boyd was the con man that Maytubby painted him to be, he did have support of some of the grass-roots' leaders, such as Jonas Imotichey. Boyd wrote Fickinger saying he was looking forward to meeting him in Muskogee to discuss what he said was the city of Tishomingo's offer to give the tribe space in its old capitol building (which had been sold to Johnston County in 1907) for a museum and to name a hospital after the tribe if the tribe would help the city and county acquire a hospital.[19]

Evidently, however, the meeting was never held. And those, like Imotichey, who had supported Boyd for a time, extended only luke-warm support. When Imotichey contacted Carl Albert, instead of playing up Boyd, he wrote: "We have made a number of attempts the last several years to get rid of the present governor." If a groundswell of support had materialized for him, Boyd might have continued campaigning for the job, even after he learned to his chagrin that the governor's salary was only $3,000 per year. But Boyd lost interest sometime in mid-1959 and went into the real estate business. In 1993, he said he probably had no Chickasaw blood anyway. His mother, he said, was a full-blood Choctaw, and his father had only a little Indian blood.[20]

While Boyd's bid for the appointment was fizzling out, coincidentally, another young, college-educated Indian from Wapanucka was beginning to put together a grass-roots movement to unseat Floyd Maytubby. Unlike Bobby Boyd, however, this man was Chickasaw and committed to the cause. His name was Overton James.

1967—Snapshots of Tribal Revitalization

October 21, 1967, dawned cool and clear at Seeley Chapel, a perfect day for the tribe's annual meeting. In many ways, the beautiful autumn day and the air of excitement resembled the annual meeting held there four years earlier when Overton James was inaugurated as governor of the Chickasaw Nation. But while the message to the tribe that day essentially had been, "we have no where to go but up," the 1967 meeting reflected the tribe's increasing viability.

Of the 500 who attended, several had been working to make its revitalization possible: Virgil Harrington, Muskogee Area director of the Bureau of Indian Affairs and his top BIA staffers; Hugo attorney Lon Kile; Chief Jimmy Belvin of the Choctaws and Chief W.E. "Dode" McIntosh of the Creeks; other members of the Inter-Tribal Council of the Five Tribes; and a small contingent from the U.S. Public Health Service (PHS). Some of them gave brief reports (some were not so brief) and while it was obvious that the Chickasaws had come a long way in four years, the tribe's development was still embryonic.

Many of the guests of honor echoed the opinion of Chief McIntosh that "Governor James is a great Indian leader." After greeting the audience, Harvey Homeratha, leader of the Otoe tribe, was returning to his seat when he spontaneously decided to make a presentation. "This blanket I am wearing... A man in my tribe who becomes a worthy tribal leader is entitled to wear such a blanket. Your Governor James, I have seen him at many Indian meetings, and watched him demonstrate his leadership. He is worthy of wearing such a blanket." And he removed the blanket and placed it around the shoulders of the surprised Governor James.[1]

Such ceremony contributed to the unique style and tenor of the meeting. There was periodic singing and traditional dancing.

Yet, at times, the assembly resembled a stockholder's annual meeting, with various reports emphasizing how productive the year had been and how cautiously optimistic these men (the leaders were all men in 1967) were about the future. At other times, the gathering—featuring speeches from "foreign heads of state"— looked like an exercise in diplomacy being held in a small Third World country. And yet, aside from Lynn Gibson, the governor's part-time correspondence secretary, James was the tribe's only employee. (James and Gibson both held full-time jobs with the Indian Education Division of the Oklahoma Department of Education in Oklahoma City.)

The tribe's business in 1967 (and for the next few years) primarily involved complying with federal guidelines and then pressuring the federal officials to allocate and release the money to start needed programs and services. These included among others a health clinic, sanitation project, and a housing program. In the mid-1960s, there were no Indian health-care facilities within the old Chickasaw Nation. When medical services became available for welfare and elderly recipients, Indians were told by the Public Health Service (PHS) to use the public facilities like anyone else who was eligible. This was in response to requests by Governor James and the various county tribal councils to establish field clinics in Tishomingo and Ada.

When Representative Carl Albert (Democrat, Third District) threw his support behind the request, the PHS modified its stand somewhat. Dr. E.S. Rabeau, chief of the PHS Indian Health Division, wrote that a welfare office in Johnston and Coal counties would be used three days a week as a clinic for Indians. Emergency care and prescription drugs also were provided through contracts with area physicians.[2] James told Representative Albert: "This is far from what we felt we need, however, it is a start." James had met with the area Indian health people and his political antennae told him it was time to thank everyone for their assistance. But he wrote to Charles Ward, Albert's assistant, that "if the new program doesn't meet our needs, we will pursue additional services."[3]

Before James could initiate another request, Dr. Rabeau visited Oklahoma in April 1967 and evidently was impressed with the Chickasaw's continuing health-care needs. Later a permanent physician was assigned to the Tishomingo and

In 1967, Carl Albert, Third District Congressman from McAlester, assisted Gov. James in getting expanded health care for tribal members. James believed Rep. Albert in time would help the tribe reacquire its historic Capitol building in Tishomingo from Johnston County (Photo courtesy of Chickasaw Library)

Colgate clinics and within a year a new clinic building in Tishomingo was dedicated by Governor James.[4]

At the same time, what was left of the tribe's cultural heritage—that which had survived the move mainly from Mississippi—had to be shored up. If much more of the traditional culture were lost, the tribe's identity would be gone as well. And if, as some asserted, culture and language are inseparable, the tribe's sad state of cultural affairs could be reflected by the fact that only a few hundred Chickasaws out of more than 6,000 on the tribal rolls could speak their language.[5]

Governor James believed that his mother, Vinnie May Humes, had been right in not teaching him to speak Chickasaw. During the Depression, many Chickasaws felt that being Indian was impediment enough to economic and educational success. Learning Chickasaw as a first language would make it harder to learn English, another obstacle to Indian success in American society. But in 1967, feelings had changed. Overton James knew that within a generation or two only a handful of Chickasaws would know the language, and he wanted it saved from extinction. The only sure way to do that was to produce a Chickasaw dictionary.

Actually, a dictionary had been started in 1929 under the direction of Oklahoma historian Muriel Wright. The Reverend Jess Humes, a fluent Chickasaw speaker and tribal leader, had helped her resurrect the project in 1957, and Governor James brought it to life again in 1965, again under Wright, with $6,000 from the tribal trust fund.[6]

But Humes found he could not work with Wright. Probably they had disagreements over Chickasaw and Choctaw words (the two languages have many similarities).[7] Determined that the project be finished, Governor James asked his mother, another fluent Chickasaw speaker, to help her husband, the Reverend Humes, who spoke both Chickasaw and Choctaw. Vinnie May initially demurred. She didn't know anything about producing a dictionary, and the people would say that the governor was practicing favoritism. "Momma," James said, "you and Jess are the best qualified people. We can't wait any longer."[8]

So by late 1967, they were working most mornings at their kitchen table, using a high school dictionary and a banged-up manual typewriter. Eventually their Chickasaw dictionary was published by the University of Oklahoma Press.

Meanwhile, James and his advisory council took steps to acquire or improve property of historical value in the old Chickasaw Nation. Chickasaw cemeteries Bloomfield, south of Durant, and Ft. Washita, northwest of Durant, were restored and perpetuated with tribal aid. At the latter site, a granite monument was erected and dedicated by James to the memories of several hundred Chickasaws who were buried there in unmarked graves. In 1967, the tribe helped save their 1898 Capitol Building in Tishomingo from a potential Johnston County wrecking ball by working to designate it as a National Historical Site. James believed that eventually the federal government would provide the tribe with the funds to reacquire the building and he periodically reminded Carl Albert and U.S. Senator Fred Harris of the tribe's continued interest.

In one scenario that James mentioned at the tribe's annual meeting in 1967, the old Capitol would be a Chickasaw museum and would comprise a detached part of Platt National Park in Sulphur. Only James envisioned that the park's name would be changed to Chickasaw National Park.[9] The year before, the governor had asked Albert to support the proposed name change with the National Park Service. Albert told his assistant Charlie Ward to get the details from the Park Service, but to have the people of Sulphur to initiate the proposal.[10] In mid-1967, the Chickasaw Advisory Council passed a resolution requesting the name change, and copies were sent to the Oklahoma congressional delegation and appropriate members of the Interior Department and U.S. Park Service.[11] The Inter-Tribal Council of the Five Civilized Tribes passed a similar resolution later that year and distributed copies of it to the same officials.

Everyone seemed to favor the move until Secretary of Interior Stewart Udall killed the momentum. In a letter to Advisory Council member Robert Kingsbery, Udall wrote that while the Council's resolution was "laudable...it would be premature to support or oppose the name change until the views of other interested individuals, organizations and the State of Oklahoma are known...." He noted that Congress in 1906 named the park for the late Senator Orville H. Platt in recognition of his distinguished service to Indians and his country. Platt had been characterized by President Theodore Roosevelt as "the grandest and noblest man" he had ever known.[12]

Subsequently, the proposed name change was incorporated in a Park Service "Master Plan" expanding and consolidating Platt Park and the Arbuckle Recreation Area into the Chickasaw National Recreation Area. Though this had become primarily a Carl Albert-inspired, pork barrel project of epic proportions and complexity, the tribe would be getting its wish when all the dealing was done and the legislation was passed.

That finally occurred, when President Gerald Ford signed the bill into law on March 18, 1976.

One of Governor Overton James's major goals in the middle 1960s was to support and promote the maintenance and even restoration of traditional Chickasaw culture. This painting is called "Memories of Stomp Dancing." (Art by Gary White Deer. Courtesy of Chickasaw Nation)

Chickasaw Headquarters Moves to Ada, 1975-76

After the $150,000 in tribal funds were expended for the purchase and initial renovation of the Chickasaw Motor Inn in 1972, it was clear that no significant outlays from the tribe's remaining $316,000 in trust funds were going to be made.[1] That meant the tribe's future growth was tied almost exclusively to winning federal funds. The means to compete came through a grant to the Five Civilized Tribes Foundation, the non-profit arm of the Inter-Tribal Council.[2] The grant from the Department of Commerce's Office of Native American Programs (ONAP), enabled each tribe to establish a planning department.

The Chickasaws' first planner was Emil Farve, who said that during his first year, (1974-75), the tribe received nearly $2 million in federal grants. "Even though initially we were often competing against cities and counties for funds, we were successful because Indian tribes always met the criteria: educationally, economically, we were the lowest of the low."

Ted Key, who wrote the most grant proposals for the tribe between 1975-79, estimated that 90 percent of his proposals were funded or re-funded. Grants and contracts enabled the tribe to acquire more programs and services, employees to staff them, and even buildings to house them without depleting tribal trust funds.[3] In fact, by late 1976, the trust funds had increased to approximately $450,000 through interest payments and in repayments from the Chickasaw Motor Inn. In fiscal 1976, interest on the trust funds was about twice the amount deducted to cover the tribe's annual budget. The budget, $20,100, included the governor's salary of $5,200, his business expenses and benefits of about $4,200. The balance included expenses not covered by grants, such as tribal meetings.[4]

While revenue exceeded expenses, capital assets through federal grants were growing by leaps and bounds. In 1974-75, funding materialized for three new buildings. A HUD grant provided a new office building and a separate maintenance facility for the Chickasaw Housing Authority in Ada. The move into the new office building in the summer 1975 alleviated the overcrowding that on occasion was manifested with three people sharing a desk. The land on North Country Club Road had been used by government agencies and was deeded to the Chickasaw Housing Authority. The Authority's former building was turned over to the housing authority of the city of Ada.[5]

By 1975, overcrowding was also a fact of life in the Chickasaw Nation's suite of offices in the Motor Inn in Sulphur. In a little more than a year, the number of employees there had nearly tripled to more than fifty. The office that had been reserved for Governor Overton James (who still worked full time in Indian education for the state of Oklahoma) was now being used by others and many of the desks were communal. All available space for offices had been taken, and there was nowhere to go but out. Moreover, Emil Farve, as the governor's assistant in Sulphur, said he was hiring almost anybody who asked for a job. "I wasn't advertising jobs in the newspapers, but when somebody asked, I would hire 'em and then arrange with the agency project officer (overseeing the grant) to revise the budget to create the job."[6]

A new tribal office building was obviously needed. And yet, a grant proposal was not usually submitted unless it had been solicited by a government agency. Although that had not happened yet, the legislative catalyst for the expansion of tribal governments was passed on January 2, 1975. Called the Indian Self-Determination and Education Assistance Act, it was the culmination of President Richard Nixon's belief that tribes should take the responsibility for the programs provided by the federal government. Ultimately, the act was of a more limited nature than the "takeover" bill advocated by Nixon. Because some Indians were fearful that takeovers of programs would lead to termination, the act established a system under which a tribe could contract for parts of educational, health care and other programs. [7]

Because tribal governments were growing in size nationally, it wouldn't be long before RFPs (requests for proposals) for tribal buildings began showing up. Actually, though, the grant that enabled the Chickasaws to get the jump on many other tribes wasn't primarily intended to provide a building but to create employment. The ONAP grant that the Chickasaws applied for and received was intended to combat a high level of unemployment. That is why 75 percent of the $426,000 grant was earmarked for labor. But could the tribe construct a headquarters building with the costs of materials and labor so lopsided? Farve and Governor James decided to worry about that after the tribe had the money. At the groundbreaking ceremony, James turned the first shovelful of dirt, then a large crew of Chickasaws with shovels and pickaxes immediately began digging the foundation. It was expected that the project would provide full-time jobs for approximately thirty-five Chickasaws for a year. [8]

Just where the groundbreaking was to be held was the subject of intense interest among tribal employees and representatives of cities vying to be selected for the Chickasaw Nation's headquarters. Ardmore, the largest city in the eleven-county Chickasaw Nation, was geographically remote from most Chickasaws. [9] Although James considered Ada and Sulpher to be in the running, he privately favored Tishomingo "for historical continuity." To his surprise and chagrin, however, city officials "didn't seem that interested." How would sincere interest be manifested? By donating choice real estate to the Chickasaws. Sulphur was the most centrally located site, plus many tribal employees favored it because they lived in or near the town. [10] In December, Sulphur offered ten acres near the Sulphur Air Park. With an apparent change of heart, Tishomingo offered five acres near the fairgrounds and promised to purchase an adjoining five acres. [11]

While these offers were acceptable, James noted that both tracts were "out in the boonies." He also felt that the offers had come rather grudgingly. Tishomingo wasn't taking the tribe seriously, and Sulphur was taking the tribe for granted. Ada officials, on the other hand, were enthusiastic and positive from the beginning. Immediately recognizing the potential economic benefits of having the Chickasaws headquartered in Ada, Ted Savage and James Thompson took the governor on a tour of the sites owned by the city's industrial trust authority. Savage, director of the chamber of commerce and Thompson, president of the trust authority, did a first-class selling job, according to James. "At first they drove me out around the airport and so on. Then, just in passing, Thompson pointed to some little league baseball fields and said the authority owned that land, too. Said it was 7 or 8 acres. It was in an area of Ada bordering a commercial district and an industrial area. I told 'em, 'You let us have that land, and we'll construct our building there.' They said it wasn't available. I said, 'See what you can do.'" [12]

Savage and Thompson knew that the Chickasaw Nation was already a major employer in the area and that under Overton James the tribe might some day rival Pontotoc County's number one employer, East Central State University. Therefore, the trust authority's priorities needed to be rearranged. First, the authority voted to move the little league

complex near the fairgrounds, and then it deeded the seven and one-half acres, appraised at $100,000, to the Chickasaw Nation for its headquarters building. Meanwhile, James had asked all three cities to submit concrete written proposals by mid-December. In a special meeting in Okmulgee on January 6, the governor's Advisory Council accepted James's recommendation to select Ada. But in a rare occurrence, the council vote wasn't unanimous, and Sulphur ran a close second. [13]

The grant that provided funds for a new tribal head-quarters building in Ada made it almost imperative that the tribe act as its own contractor. With 75 percent of the amount designated for labor, it was necessary to cut expenses to the bone. Because Governor James was still employed by the state education department to run its Indian program, he couldn't oversee the construction on a daily basis. So he gave the job to his top aide, Emil Farve. One-half Chickasaw, three-eighths Choctaw and one-eighth French, Farve was born and raised in the Ardmore area school of hard knocks. But he liked to learn and was bright , found school tedious and couldn't see that it was getting him anywhere. What he wanted most was a good paying job. He had worked selling newspapers and at odd jobs from an early age, but by the time he was 17, Ardmore looked like a dead-end for employment. So he dropped out of high school and prevailed on his parents to let him join the Army.[14]

Five years later he returned to Ardmore with a GED (general equivalency diploma), knowledge of military weapons and no greater prospects for a good job than when he left in 1958. One day just to have something to do, he and his Indian friends decided to have a basketball tournament in a local gym. But they were told the gym was only for students. So, Emil decided they needed their own gym and set about looking for a funding source. In due course, he learned that the Office of Economic Opportunity (OEO), a new federal agency, could provide money for such a project but that the grantees needed a board of directors. He found three of his friends, also day laborers like himself who agreed to be on the board. But before he could find out what the next step was in the process, one of his board members resigned because someone had told him that OEO was a Communist organization. The ensuing confusion among the remaining board members caused the project to unravel. But the episode provided a glimpse of Emil as an incipient grant writer—resourceful, not intimidated, but rough around the edges. He might have gotten his gym built if only he'd known for sure that OEO was not Communist controlled. [15]

A decade later, Farve was in charge of assembling and coordinating a workforce for the construction of the new 8,000-square foot Chickasaw headquarters. Aside from the usual array of skilled workers, Farve hired forty to fifty unskilled Indian laborers from which a cadre of about thirty worked on the building for a year. He did this first because he had a soft spot in his heart for Indians trying to get work. But there was also a practical reason. Because only 25 percent of the grant could go for building materials, Ray James, the architect for the project, suggested to Farve that materials be scrounged wherever and whenever possible. He knew a man, for example, who wanted a barn removed from his property. A farmer whose land abutted the Arbuckle Mountains said the Chickasaws would be doing him a favor to remove large rocks from land he wanted to till. Farve got sixteen surplus 3/4-ton trucks from Ft. Bliss, Texas. Some of the trucks worked and some needed help to work, but they were used by his brigade to transport the disassembled barn and rocks to the building site. [16]

Never having been a contractor before, Farve had logistical problems. At times skilled workers were called in prematurely. And with the almost continuous presence of his group of unskilled laborers, the building site often was crawling with people. Other contractors came by to roll their eyes and make disparaging remarks about "the dumb Indians." Even if some of their criticism was valid, Farve felt their motivation was jealousy. And what he cared most deeply about was that hard-core unemployed Indians were working.[17] Other laborers who were melded into the project came from the tribe's CETA (jobs training) program.[18]

As the building was going up, so was the number of tribal staff members. As a result, even before the building was completed, Ted Key had submitted a $361,000 grant proposal under the Local Public Works Act of 1976 for the expansion of the headquarters building. The expansion would include two new wings totaling 6,000 square feet.[19] The new building was completed on schedule in February 1977. An open house was held on March 26, with an exuberant Governor James saying, "Andrew Jackson did not know what a great favor he did for us by moving the Indian nations from Mississippi to Oklahoma." Some ninety employees in eight departments were now housed in the new building. Fortunately for everyone, word came about this time that Key's proposal had been funded for the building's expansion. Construction was to begin that summer.[20]

It was a bittersweet time for Farve. On one hand, the new building looked great, was badly needed and had provided a year of paychecks for many Chickasaws

The federal money acquired for constructing a tribal headquarters only permitted 25 percent to be spent for building materials. So tribal employee Emil Farve scrounged around for material. A farmer told Farve he would be doing him a favor to remove large rocks from his property. They were transported to the tribe's building site and transformed into a headquarters building. (Photo courtesy of Chickasaw Library.)

and other Indians. On the other hand, Farve knew his men, who had worked so hard and felt pride in what they had accomplished, were very unlikely to find similar employment again. [21] Furthermore, it was widely understood by employees that the cost of the building had exceeded the grant by about $40,000. "Emil did a good job on the building in many ways," said Governor James. "But I told him repeatedly that he had to stay within the budget and he didn't." The only way to pay for the overrun was with trust funds, a move that the fiscally conservative governor found galling and embarrassing. [22]

He called in Farve and told him he was through as his administrative assistant. Aside from the cost overrun, James said, there had been too many complaints from departmental people about his management style. The governor told Farve he could research the tribe's on-going Arkansas riverbed case or head the planning department. Farve thought the riverbed case was all but over and he wasn't a lawyer anyway. Heading the planning department wasn't appealing because he would have had to bump Ted Key, who had been doing an excellent job. Farve didn't believe there had been a cost overrun but couldn't prove it. He also was hurt by his colleagues' allegations. After a few weeks of drifting, Farve resigned and moved on. [23]

Despite this unpleasant ending, during the summer of 1977 few negative thoughts crossed the governor's mind. The bid on the construction of the headquarters' two new wings had been so low that in July the tribe found it could get an additional wing and still be within the grant total from the Economic Development Administration. The three new wings would more than double the size of the existing building. The wings were designed to complement the original tribal office through the use of exposed wooden beams and tilt-up concrete walls inlaid with native stone. [24] The expansion was finished in March 1978. In little more than a year, the Chickasaw government had moved from several small rooms in the motor inn to a beautiful and serviceable 14,000-square-foot headquarters building that was emblematic of the tribe's rapid expansion, credibility, and perhaps even its motto: "the unconquered and unconquerable Chickasaws."

Surveying Chickasaw Sites in Lee County, MS, 1981-83:

THE TUPELO EDUCATION OF A HARVARD MAN

Throughout most of the eighteenth century, the bulk of Chickasaws lived in elongated villages in northeastern Mississippi, in or near modern-day Tupelo, Mississippi. During the century, the villages were not static. As circumstances dictated, some villages expanded, some contracted. Others were abandoned and new ones sprang up in the characteristic pattern of setting on ridge tops overlooking one or more streams.

As a result of this movement over that century, a large number of locations in Lee County, Mississippi contained Chickasaw sites. That is not to say that Chickasaws lived only in modern Lee County, but most lived within its 418 square miles.

But where exactly? The Chickasaws left no enduring signs or monuments, and gradually, natural processes—mainly wind and water—obliterated or covered nearly all the physical remnants of Chickasaw society. Many people, mainly farmers and artifact collectors, knew where some sites were. Often plows and bulldozers accidentally kicked up artifacts and human remains. A handful of archaeologists had excavated a few villages and recorded them on maps kept by the state. But nobody had ever done a county-wide, systematic survey.

Until 1981. That was the year John Stubbs received a bachelor's degree in anthropology from Harvard. He thought he wanted to be an archaeologist, but unlike a lot of others headed into professional careers, he wanted to experience archaeology before committing to graduate school. He was asking about opportunities when his advisor, Dr. Stephen Williams, received a call from Dr. Pat Galloway with the Mississippi Department of Archives and History (Archives and History). Her department was looking for an archaeologist to spend a year in Tupelo doing a surface survey of historic Chickasaw sites. No digging would be permitted.

Galloway didn't just happen to call Harvard. She knew that two Harvard professors Jeffrey Brain and Ian Brown had studied a collection of Chickasaw artifacts on loan to them from the Smithsonian. And she knew that the archaeologists had been contacted by and had met with three of Tupelo's most experienced artifact collectors. These three, Julian Riley, Banks Livingston, and Steve Cook, held perhaps the three largest collections of historic Chickasaw artifacts. They had allowed Brown to photograph their collections. Brown said he and Brain were "flabbergasted" by the extent, diversity and quality of the artifacts that dated from the fifteenth century to the early nineteenth century. Another archaeologist David Dye who also saw the collections, said they were "mind-blowing."

Galloway and others from Archives and History had met with Riley, Cook, and three other collectors in Tupelo to begin a systematic study of those artifacts grouped according to where they had been found. Some 200 sites were to be recorded. In general, the artifacts included trade beads, metal objects, silver, pottery and stone tools. With careful study of their origin, archaeologists would be able to assign date ranges to the sites. While working with the collectors, perhaps Stubbs could persuade them to stop disturbing Chickasaw graves.

On the first day, Galloway's team recorded twenty-five grave lots of artifacts. But before they could reassemble, an article in the next morning's newspaper resulted in the end of the collaboration. The state attorney general ruled that Mississippi's prohibition against disturbing remains in cemeteries extended to Indian graves, even though they were not marked. So collectors could be prosecuted for digging up Indian burial sites. To collectors it seemed that the media that had been presenting them in a positive light as adventurers and educators was now calling them criminals. Furthermore, some sources in the article referred to them as "pot hunters" and "grave robbers."

Although Galloway had asked the attorney general to issue such a ruling, she said that the timing of the announcement was an unfortunate coincidence. Riley and Cook were not named in the article, but they thought they had been set up by Galloway and angrily refused to cooperate with her and Archives and History any further.

A few months later, Galloway on behalf of Archives and History offered the one-year job to John Stubbs, 22. In doing the survey, he was to get help from the collectors and persuade them to stop digging at the sites. Stubbs

John Stubbs, Harvard archaeology graduate student, circa 1982, stands by his transportation in Tupelo, Mississippi. Stubbs was employed by Archives and History to conduct an extensive surface survey of the land formerly occupied by the Chickasaw tribe. Some landowners were cooperative, a few said, "Git!" (Photo courtesy of John Stubbs)

In his archaeological survey, John Stubbs was looking for relatively heavy surface concentrations of pottery sherds, flints and chert, which were associated with Chickasaw occupation like this one in a sketch by Chickasaw artist Joanna Underwood. (Courtesy of Chickasaw Nation)

said it was like "walking into a hornet's nest," but with the confidence bestowed by youth and a Harvard education, he felt up to the task.

Of course, John Stubbs was not an archaeologist in 1981, though the Tupelo newspaper identified him as one. To be recognized by the profession as an archaeologist, a person would have to earn at least a master's degree in archaeology and obtain two years of accredited field work. Stubbs also had no experience with Southeastern Indian artifacts. But Galloway hired him because he would have three experienced and willing tutors at Harvard—Williams, Brown and Brain—who still had the Chickasaw artifacts on loan from the Smithsonian. Stubbs took what amounted to a "crash course in Southeastern Indian archaeology" from December until he reported to Tupelo in June 1981.

The project received state and city of Tupelo support, which was mobilized by some Tupelo citizens. Some of them happily squired this Harvard grad around Tupelo society. Stubbs got a stipend and lived in an apartment in Tupelo. Archives and History provided a vehicle; its logo appeared on both sides. This association served to open some doors and close others. Riley and Cook agreed to help in a limited way by giving him general directions to site locations.

The Chickasaw Nation was not directly involved, but Governor Overton James had been notified by Galloway in 1980 that Chickasaw graves in and around Tupelo were being "desecrated." James wrote a strongly worded letter of protest to government officials, but he could do little more for several reasons. Tribal government was still small and without much income. And laws to protect Indian graves were non-existent or weak and not enforced. Furthermore, officials could do nothing about graves located on private property (where most were). But James realized that surveying Lee County sites and educating landowners could curb the destruction of sites, so he was happy to give the project his blessing. In return, James received from Galloway periodic updates on the project.

Stubbs's formal method of surveying involved dividing the county into eight soil types. Then, he surveyed at random about 10 percent of each of these areas. While such a survey was scientifically sound, he quickly found that he was wasting a lot of time locating the land to be surveyed, getting permission from landowners to survey the land and covering a lot of ground that he could be reasonably sure contained no Chickasaw sites. How could he know? For one thing, sites always seemed to be on ridge tops, so it was a waste of time surveying around stream beds. Furthermore, it soon became apparent that Riley and Cook already knew where a large

number of the Chickasaw sites were, and he could simply ask one of them about the area he proposed to survey.

Stubbs met many times with them, particularly Steve Cook, a civil engineer. Riley, a certified public accountant, was often too busy to attend these sessions. They wanted Stubbs to know that they had only been trying to salvage artifacts that would have been destroyed by bulldozers, road graders and plows. Why, they said, many times they had warned various state officials and archaeologists about the imminent destruction of Chickasaw village sites and had gotten nowhere. No official had ever taken them seriously, they said, adding that they were through butting heads only to be insulted.

While Stubbs believed that they were sincerely interested in protecting the sites and that they had warned state officials in vain, he did not believe that all of their collections had resulted from salvage missions and surface surveys. By their own admission, they were expert with metal detectors, the implement most often used by collectors to find European trade goods. He got the impression that some collectors justified digging sites containing graves by rationalizing that they were saving these artifacts from the destruction associated with eventual development. This attitude was abetted, probably unwittingly, by a well-intentioned civic leader quoted in the paper saying that in the next ten years "all traces" of the Chickasaw past would have been destroyed by farming techniques, natural erosion and community development.

Cook's and Riley's relations with Stubbs were cordial but not trusting. They gave Stubbs a copy of a thirty-page paper they had written in 1980 on the general locations of Chickasaw village sites. In the paper, they supported their speculation with eighteenth century European documents and correspondence but didn't include the crucial corroborating evidence of having found certain artifacts in specific locales. And despite having shown their collections to Brain and Brown, they would not show them to Stubbs or discuss in detail where certain artifacts were found. It wasn't personal. It was more a matter of that being then, this being now.

It was disappointing, however, to not be able to correlate Stubbs's surface finds with European trade goods held by collectors. This was especially frustrating because many trade goods could be dated chronologically, whereas he couldn't detect chronological differences in the Chickasaw pottery. Consequently, Stubbs believed he knew where the Chickasaws had lived, but not when because he could not trace their movements through time.

Nonetheless, Stubbs headed out, sometimes with suggested locations from Cook and Riley, sometimes to do his random sample. In any case, he introduced himself to the landowners, usually farmers. He would tell them he was doing a survey about where the Chickasaw Indians used to live. He had heard that maybe they had some arrowheads or pottery on their land. Would they show him so he could record it for his survey? He told them his work had been publicized in the newspaper, and might show them a copy. His work would be reported on periodically throughout the project. Then, he would tell them that if they would let him look at their artifacts they would be "helping science."

Many of the landowners were agreeable, and took him right to the locations. Then, they wanted to know everything he could tell them about the Indians. Some told him they didn't have time; a few said, "Git!," and produced a shotgun. Wherever he found artifacts, he recorded them and their location in his notebook, took black and white and color transparencies and retrieved a small sample of the artifacts on the surface, usually of the plain pottery pieces favored by eighteenth century Chickasaws.

Areas with relatively heavy concentrations of pottery sherds, flints (for muskets) and chert (a rock used to fashion knives for scraping deer hides) were thought to be associated with village sites. Stubbs tried to estimate village sizes, but this was often not possible because of the poor condition of the land (erosion, overgrown with weeds and cedar).

Survey conditions varied, usually according to the season, from okay to "horrible"—to use Stubbs's word from one report. This meant that some likely sites could not be surveyed if the land was in cultivation or if part of the prairie location favored by the Chickasaws had "returned to nature."

As the first year was proceeding, Stubbs told everybody that a second year would be necessary, not only to cover enough land to make the survey scientifically valid, but also to give him more time to establish a better relationship with the collectors. Support was provided by the city of Tupelo, the Lee County Library and the Mississippi Committee for the Humanities, which funneled its grant money through a group named the Chickasaw Indian Cultural Center Foundation (CICC). With the grant money, the Foundation upgraded Stubbs from archaeologist to "scholar in residence." In addition, Stubbs would be responsible for lining up speakers for six public education programs.

Through the efforts of the CICC, the events were well publicized, but they were not well attended. The box-like Lee County Library was perhaps an unattractive venue, and though most Tupelo residents probably were aware of the former Chickasaw presence, Stubbs got the feeling that most citizens could care less. The city's priorities were Elvis Presley (who was born there) and the Civil War's Battle of Tupelo, in that order.

This was disappointing to Stubbs because one of his main goals was to help develop within the community a mission to protect the remaining Chickasaw sites. He hoped to do this by increasing public awareness and education about the sites generally (for public consumption) and specifically (for landowners). If the leading citizens adopted the idea that it was wrong to plunder Chickasaw grave sites, an official or unofficial mechanism to monitor and protect the sites might emerge from the best of all possible places—within the community.

But it never happened. A reason might have been that the city did not receive information about site locations. Thus, if a developer filled out an application for a permit, there was no one in city hall to warn the developer that there might be Chickasaw burials in certain places on the property.

Stubbs felt the best form of protection probably came through his low-key approach with landowners. But, he walked a fine line in giving out information. He wanted to interest them in his project, not to turn them into collectors.

At the end of the two-year project, Stubbs felt like he had

scrupulously surveyed 200 sites or perhaps 40 to 50 percent of the remaining Chickasaw sites in Lee County. Some he couldn't get to, and some had been destroyed or submerged under roads or housing divisions. Long Town, the village where some of the tribal leaders, the Colberts once had lived, had been obliterated by a subdivision called Lee Acres.

Stubbs moved back to Cambridge and enrolled in the graduate archaeology program at Harvard. He spent part of the first few months completing his report for Archives and History. It filled three, three-ring binders that were a total of about nine inches thick. He took a portion of the artifacts with him but mailed those back to Archives and History after he was through with them. He planned to build on the Chickasaw project after he received his Ph.D. in archaeology from Harvard.

In a 1987 note to Sam McGahey, then chief archaeologist with Mississippi Archives and History, Stubbs wrote that he was about two years from completing his Ph.D. Meanwhile, he wrote that if anyone ever worked seriously with the Chickasaw collection and had questions, "I would be more than happy to help..." And he said that once his professional education was over, he "hoped to get back to the Chickasaw in some fashion." Then, he added, "but who knows exactly what will happen."

Postscript

John Stubbs never did return to the Chickasaw project and is now a college counselor at a private prep school in the Atlanta area. His survey report, photographs and journals are stored at the Mississippi Department of Archives and History in Jackson. The artifacts have been in the custody of Mississippi State University archaeologist Janet Rafferty ever since she re-analyzed them in the early 1990s. Both she and archaeologist David Morgan wrote separate published articles on these artifacts. Stubbs' site designations are included on topographical maps maintained in confidence by Archives and History. Another set is owned by the Chickasaw Nation. Stubbs says his project, which ended twenty years ago, could be part of a promising Ph.D. dissertation.

The Making of the Constitution of 1983, Part I

The 1979 Chickasaw constitution that provided for a democratic government consisting of three branches was approved by the Interior Department and a federal district court and was ratified in 1979 by an overwhelming 92 percent of those Chickasaws who voted.

The constitution provided the means to begin working toward a democratic government. But that government and the process of governing would evolve. Although Governor Overton James continued to dominate tribal government during its first year of the constitution's existence, the Tribal Council had been

fulfilling its minimum requirements by meeting monthly and passing resolutions that approved federal appropriations to the tribe. Council meetings also featured discussions, debate, and dissension, but the members, with the exception of attorney Robert Keel, felt too insecure to test the limits of their constitutional power vis a vis the governor. Consequently, the three judges making up the judiciary had little to do.

Then, on January 27, 1981, the U.S. Court of Appeals in Washington, D.C., lobbed a bombshell into the middle of tribal governments.[1] (It is governments, plural, because the appellate court had combined the Chickasaw and Choctaw cases, both filed originally in 1977, due to the similarity of their circumstances and issues.) The court found that each tribe's constitution, both written in 1867, had not been invalidated by the 1906 Five Tribes Act—as had thought to have been so by the federal government, and Gov. Douglas

In 1981, a federal court held that the Chickasaw Nation's 1867 Constitution had never been invalidated by Congress. This was contrary to the belief of tribal members, 92 percent of whom had ratified a new Constitution in 1979. As a supporter of the new constitution, Gov. Overton James led a faction that opposed the restoration of the 1867 Constitution because it was outdated and impractical.(Photo courtesy Chickasaw Library)

Johnston and his successors. Actually, Chickasaw citizen and plaintiff Charles Tate of Ardmore believed that in 1906 Indian Affairs officials knew that that law did not call for the abolition of tribal governments but "about the time of statehood there was tremendous political force to do away with them" and that Indian Affairs evidently had chosen the politically expedient path.[2]

Although those nineteenth century constitutions were not invalid, the court in 1981 ruled that they were outdated and impractical. Therefore, new constitutions would have to be written and voted upon by the tribal members. To do this, the court of appeals remanded the cases to the lower court with directions to establish a reformation process consistent with that of an earlier and similar case, Harjo vs. Andrus, involving the Creeks. The court said that the new procedures would ensure elections that would accurately reflect the wishes of tribal members. The procedures included input from tribal members on the fundamental differences in the 1867 and 1979 constitutions, adequate voter education regarding the issues and fair balloting and poll watchers. [3]

The court's decision should not have surprised the Chickasaw tribal leadership. They knew that Charles Tate had appealed the district court's decision—approving the 1979 ratification—to the federal appeals court, and they understood that the Harjo case had established a clear judicial precedent. A few years before, the Creeks' 1867 constitution was found to be valid but in need of updating, and the court had ordered that a new constitution be written and ratified by the people.

Unflappable as always, Overton James, and attorney Lon Kile traveled to Washington and told BIA officials that James and the Tribal Council would continue to carry out their duties until and unless they were notified otherwise by the court or the BIA. [4] In April, all parties to the lawsuit agreed to ask the court to allow the tribal government to continue operating fully until a new constitution could be ratified by the people. The court granted the request but stipulated that the sale of any land or property, including the Arkansas riverbed jointly owned by the Cherokees, Choctaws and Chickasaws, could not be negotiated during the interim. [5] In a press release, Governor James called this "a major victory for Tribal officers elected under the 1979 Constitution." He also reported that a letter outlining the fundamental differences between the 1867 and 1979 constitutions would be submitted to Washington by April 17, "so we hope we can get back to 'business as usual' in the near future." [6]

In his letter to the BIA, Governor James noted eleven fundamental differences. The 1867 document established a bicameral legislature and governor with no blood quantum requirements serving two-year terms and limited to four years in any six years. The 1979 version prescribed a nine-member Tribal Council and a governor who had to be at least one-fourth degree Chickasaw blood and could serve an unlimited number of four-year terms. In 1867. voters had to be male, at least 19 years of age, and residents of the nation for six months preceding the election. Elections were held by voice vote. The modern version included females, lowered the voting age to 18, had no residence requirements and assigned voting procedures to the Tribal Council. Other differences included four voter districts (1867) versus seven voter districts (1979) and the provision in 1979 for a lieutenant governor.[7]

The plaintiffs were represented by Ellen Leitzer, a New Mexico-based attorney, while the defendants were represented by Lon Kile and his partner Bob Rabon. Both sides said they were hoping to have a new constitution in place by the end of the year. In June, both sides signed a court-approved consent decree specifying certain steps in the reformation process and providing that it would be run by an Election Commission (consisting of three members from each side). Also, three elections would be held: one to decide the fundamental differences, a second to ratify the amalgamated constitution and a third to elect tribal officers. For the defendants, Governor James appointed Ted Key, director of

the Chickasaw Housing Authority; Pat Woods, of James's staff; and Chickasaw citizen Jack Hensley. The plaintiffs were represented by Tate and Chickasaw citizens Sally Bell and Clarence Lee Cravatt.[8]

They met for the first time in the Carter County Courthouse in Ardmore on June 26, 1981, and it was almost immediately obvious that quick agreements were not in the cards. The two sides could not agree on the wording of a court-ordered news release that was to appear in the *Chickasaw Times,* or on a time to hold their meetings. Both sides advanced what they called "compromises," but nobody budged. Although exchanges of letters occurred periodically, they didn't meet again until February 16, 1983.

The Chickasaw Nation's new form of government, provided for in the 1979 constitution, operated without interference from the federal government through 1982. But in 1983, that could change if the Election Commission did not get down to business. (Originally the case was designated *Cravatt v. Andrus.* But since 1981 when James Watt had been named secretary of the interior, it had become *Cravatt v. Watt.*) Governor James led the group advocating the 1979 constitution, while Charles Tate's group wanted the tribe governed by the 1867 Chickasaw constitution. There was so much animosity between members of the two sides that they could not even agree on meeting times.

Each side had a prepared list of fundamental differences when the impasse occurred in June 1981. In November, the attorney for the Tate side (plaintiffs), Ellen Leitzer, suggested that a "mediator/arbitrator and/or administrator" might be involved to handle disputes. She said employees of the Federal Mediation Board had been used effectively in the 1975 Pine Ridge (Sioux) elections and the Hopi and Navajo land dispute.[9] The two sides liked the idea but their responses were guarded. Leitzer then suggested the person's specific powers and duties, ending with the understanding that the ultimate decision of the mediator/arbitrator/administrator on a specific issue would be final and binding.[10]

Chickasaw citizen Charles Tate, an Ardmore attorney, was the leader of the Chickasaw plaintiffs who favored a 1983 Constitution that included some of the elements from the 1867 Constitution. To decide how much of an amalgam the new constitution would be, tribal elections were held. Probably Tate's biggest victory was the provision that legislators, not the governor, should set employee salary ranges. (All photos courtesy of Chickasaw Library.)

Governor James and tribal attorney Bob Rabon recommended that each side select three names to advance for the arbitrator position. Final details were worked out as 1982 was running out. Simultaneously but coincidentally, President Ronald Reagan signed Public Law 97-385, permitting the Cherokees, Choctaws and Chickasaws to sue the government for the value of property taken without compensation. The property affected by this law was the Arkansas riverbed land and lands used many years before for the construction of railroad station houses. The sooner the constitutional reformation was over, James said, the sooner negotiations could begin on those two issues. [11]

On January 6, 1983, the District of Columbia District Court named Fred L. Ragsdale, Jr. as arbitrator/administrator. All parties had agreed on Ragsdale, who only recently had been named professor of law at the University of New Mexico. Ragsdale had extensive experience in teaching Indian law, acting as counsel to a number of tribes and working on Indian-related affairs in the Carter administration. The first meeting with Ragsdale as chairman of the Election Commission was set for February 16 in Ardmore and he would earn his pay. The old animosities were in place and everyone seemed to understand that the problems and differences would not just go away. At the meetings, there was more a sense of urgency than of anxiety. Most often, Ragsdale was like a good baseball umpire; when he was doing his job right, he would scarcely be noticed. He allowed a good deal of discussion and arguing, sometimes heated arguing. But pejoratives (dictator! liar!) and inflammatory language were out although Ragsdale occasionally had to pound his gavel and try to yell over the combatants. The defendants sometimes disagreed with his pronouncements, but they considered Ragsdale to be fair.

Pat Woods did not like attending the meetings with their unpleasant overtones, and she said the mischievous Ted Key often would try to increase her discomfort by maneuvering to place her next to Tate, whom she was sure hated her. She disliked Tate's rude behavior, but she was impressed by Sally Bell. "Sally was partially influenced by Tate but she also had a love of Chickasaw history and told of an ancestor's role in the framing of the earlier (1867) constitution," Woods said. "I didn't agree with her being for the older document, but I could appreciate where she was coming from. I think Tate had told her that Governor James was a dictator, and she initially believed him. But at the meetings, observing Tate and being around the governor, she could start drawing her own conclusions." The result, Woods said, was that Sally Bell became more conciliatory.[12]

The Making of the 1983 Constitution, Part II

The defendants, led by Governor James, were basically defending the status quo, since the government was being run according to the provisions of the 1979 document. In a way, that gave the plaintiffs, led by Charles Tate, an advantage because their proposals seemed relatively fresh and innovative. For example, they were proposing a bicameral legislature, but not a body with the 32 members of 1867.

Rather, they advanced a plan for a house with one representative per 1,500 population (initially eight or nine members) and a senate composed of one senator from each of the nation's historic four districts. Furthermore, while the plaintiffs conceded that moving the seat of government from Ada back to Tishomingo probably would be prohibitively expensive, they did propose that the Legislature should hold its monthly meetings in Tishomingo. They argued for this concession because Tishomingo had been established as the legislative seat by the 1867 document and because the people had not been consulted prior to the seat being moved to Ada.[1]

The Election Commission meetings were open to the public, but the Commission could go in to executive session. The audience could not make comments or ask questions. How the commission did depended mainly on what side the observer was on, but Tate seemed to do most of the talking for the plaintiffs and clearly was their leader. For the defendants, Kenneth Meeler, a retired schoolteacher, had replaced Jack Hensley, but Meeler seldom contributed. Pat Woods and Ted Key—both with experience defending policy decisions—stated the defendant's case that was developed by James and attorney Bob Rabon. [2]

In March, both sides finally agreed to seven fundamental differences that would be submitted to a vote of the people.

The differences involved the length of the governor's term, whether to have term limits and whether to have a lieutenant governor. In addition, voters would decide whether to have blood quantum requirements for executive branch candidates, whether employee salaries should be set by the governor or the legislature, whether tribal judges should be elected or appointed, whether vacancies in elective offices should be filled by special elections or by the governor with legislative approval. Finally, voters would decide the location of the seat of government. In the May issue of the *Times*, each side defended its position on each issue and announced to readers that the federal district court had added three more fundamental differences.[3]

Judge Richey added the differences in late March at the behest of Robert Keel and two other Chickasaws who had petitioned the court for intervention in *Cravatt v. Watt*. The additional fundamental differences included residency requirements for legislative and gubernatorial candidates and the boundaries for legislative districts.[4] Keel raised these issues because the proposed constitution would not have permitted anyone not residing within the Chickasaw Nation for at least one year to run for the Legislature or governor. Keel lived in the Oklahoma City area.[5]

The first of three elections was held on June 18, 1983,

with 65 percent of those registered voting. Governor James got most of what he wanted. Tribal government would remain in Ada, the lieutenant governor would be retained and the governor would not have a term limit, although this last issue was decided by just 120 votes out of 2,396. On the other hand, voters decided to elect judges rather than having them appointed by the governor, and in James' biggest setback and Tate's greatest victory, the voters decided that legislators, not the governor, should set employee salary ranges. The vote on this employee salary issue was very close, 1,218 to 1,162, but the results diminished the governor's power and became a focal point for future power struggles between the executive and Legislature.[6]

The people also voted to retain the 1979 requirements that candidates for governor be at least one-fourth Chickasaw (neither side took a position on this issue) and that vacancies in elected offices should be filled by special elections rather than by gubernatorial appointment with legislative approval. The voters approved the recommendations of Tate and the plaintiffs on three issues and rejected them on three others. Each side could claim victory and the governor did. But Tate was more circumspect. He had wanted to get rid of Governor James and Lt. Gov. Bill Anoatubby, and he had failed. The voters would have a more direct opportunity to vote them

out of office in October, if they first ratified the proposed constitution drafted by the Election Committee.

That election was scheduled for August 27. Meanwhile, the Commission met on July 26 and adopted an apportionment plan for the initial legislative election. The four districts would elect thirteen members. Voters living outside the Chickasaw Nation were asked to affiliate with one of the four districts: Tishomingo, Panola, Pickens and Pontotoc. Once those numbers were in, the representation was based on population. Pontotoc would have six representatives, Pickens and Tishomingo received three each and Panola was allocated one representative. Chickasaws had to affiliate with a district to vote in the legislative races. [7]

The big loser in the first election was Robert Keel. One of the fundamental differences he succeeded in getting on the ballot backfired. Since the people, by large majorities, had voted to require candidates for the Legislature and governor to reside within the Chickasaw Nation for at least a year before being eligible for office, Keel could not run for either the legislature or governor. [8]

When the voters ratified the Chickasaw Election Commission's 1983 constitution by a vote of 1,595 to 232, [9] the election of tribal officers was set for October 8. If Tate had had any desire to run for governor in 1983, as some had suspected, the results of the prior reformation elections probably convinced him that he would lose. He supported Bob Imotichey, who was vice chairman of the Tribal Council. Tate paid for ads favoring Imotichey and two legislative candidates from the Pickens district: T.S. Colbert and Kirk Perry, the former deputy director of the Chickasaw Housing Authority.[10]

James' opponents had received a boost in late August when the state's largest newspaper, *The Daily Oklahoman,* ran a story about the governor having sent a letter to dozens of suppliers, implying that they might lose the tribe's business if he were to lose the election. The story also reported that James urged contributions as "an investment in the future." James denied that the letter was a veiled threat or a vehicle for extorting money from the vendors. He said most business with the tribe was done by bids. Council member Gene Williams said he was upset because such a letter made the tribe look bad in the community. Council member Keel demanded an apology from James. U.S. Attorney William R. Price said there was "obviously a threat" used in the letter, but he would not say publicly if a crime had been committed. At the time, James said he expected to have at least one opponent and would need to raise $15,000 to $20,000 for his campaign. He said that his letter was no different from other politicians' attempts to raise money and that strangers do not contribute money to campaigns.[11]

Bob Imotichey had virtually no campaign experience but even if he had been a veteran campaigner, he would have been hard pressed to win. Probably the only chance he had to win was to attack the honesty and integrity of Governor James, but he did not run an aggressively negative campaign.

Ultimately, three other teams opposed the James-Anoatubby ticket, and they suffered a resounding defeat: Overton James-Bill Anoatubby, 1,502 votes; Bob Imotichey-Bill Wade, 639; Cy Harris-J.D. Leslie, 243; and Douglas Hatton-Duane McClure, 116. Still, James, taking nothing for granted, campaigned like he was in the race of his life. [12] Anoatubby campaigned more effectively than he had in 1979, but he was still learning. Gov. James was a master of

~~~~~~

After the Constitution of 1983 was ratified, Gov. James and Lt. Gov. Anoatubby were re-elected in October. Although the outcome was never in doubt, James campaigned like he was in the race of his life. The governor was confident in his ability, but on election eve he had prepared three different statements: one for victory, one preparing for a run-off, and one that was a concession speech. (Photo courtesy of the Chickasaw Library)

the art of campaigning; he enjoyed it almost as much as his first campaigns. If anything he thought he was even better at it in 1983. He had great confidence in his ability and always thought he would win. But on election night as the ballots were being counted, he had with him copies of three different speeches.

One was the victory speech that he needed to remind him to mention certain people or future goals. Another was a short speech if a run-off were necessary. The third speech contained four paragraphs that said, in part, "I regret that Bill [Anoatubby] and I will no longer be able to serve the Chickasaw people, but it is not a regret filled with selfishness. It is rather a regret that we will not be able to complete all our goals....The voters have made their choices, and we must all continue on the path which leads the Chickasaw Nation to many successes. Bill and I both wish success to the victors, and offer our willing assistance whenever it is needed."[13]

The other races included several old names, some of who won and some whose time had passed. Collectively, these tribal members who made up the most democratic Chickasaw government of the twentieth century would begin a struggle to govern almost immediately. Over the next decade, it would seldom be easy, often would be contentious, and the harmony that was a universally espoused goal was always ephemeral because nothing was static. New issues and persons would materialize steadily, presenting a stream of challenges and problems, and often the tribe would lack both resources and expertise to deal with them adequately. Things would change constantly, and those in power would usually resist the change. For those in tribal government, the next decade would be a roiling mixture of fun, excitement, aggravation, volatility, pain and depression. Many involved would experience both the highest and lowest moments of their lives, their greatest achievements and their most glaring failures.

February 2005 *Times*

Indiana Professor "Excavates" Lost Chickasaw Words

John Dyson does not speak fluent Chickasaw, but this Indianian considers himself an archaeologist of the language. Actually, he spent his academic career teaching Spanish and Portuguese at Indiana University. But his analogy is apt; for the last decade, he has been poring over eighteenth and nineteenth century documents, maps, books, and picking the brains of Chickasaw and Choctaw speakers in an effort to discover and restore Chickasaw words and their meanings that have not survived the last two to three centuries. "These words and phrases are my artifacts," says Dyson.

His is a daunting task, given the multitude of thorny obstacles. For example, the same word from some eighteenth century source may have numerous different spellings since Chickasaw was not a written language before the tribe's removal to Indian Territory. So, a word that was recorded in a trader's journal or a village name that was on a surveyor's map was subject to many factors, including the pronunciation by the informant, the hearing and spelling by the recorder and, in many cases, whether the informant was Chickasaw or not.

To achieve any success, Dyson has to be creative, resourceful, tenacious, patient, and to have good sources of information. He evidently possesses them all to some degree, given his track record so far. He wrote an article in which he claims to have restored the original Chickasaw names back to all of their respective pre-removal villages. He also discusses the presumed or known meanings of the names. And to strengthen the archaeologist analogy further, Dyson's article appeared in the Winter 2003 issue of *Mississippi Archaeology*.

Publishing in a Mississippi periodical was like a homecoming event for Dyson in a sense. Born in Batesville, Mississippi, he remembers childhood visits to his uncle's farm near New Albany (northwest of Tupelo). "The land went directly from Chickasaw ownership to my family's ancestors," he says. "I used to walk right behind my uncle when he was plowing because occasionally he'd plow up arrowheads and other artifacts."

"I don't know whether geography is destiny," he says, explaining that when the family moved, it was to Paducah, Kentucky, located close to the Chickasaws' historical northern border. Furthermore, the Dysons' new home was in a city named after Chickasaw chief Paducah. Or so everybody thought.

Years later in the early 1990s while teaching at Indiana University, Dyson decided to research the chief's life and the city's name. While reference searches were not helpful, he eventually and coincidentally found the real explanation in a letter from William Clark [of Lewis & Clark] to his son. Dyson says, "Clark, who had been named superintendent of Indian Affairs at St. Louis, said he wanted to name the land that became the city of Paducah after the Paducah Indians (also called the Plains Apaches)." He published his research in a small journal, and when some of the local citizenry heard about the article and Dyson's claim that their city's namesake was bogus, Dyson says he became "persona non grata" for a spell.

The professor's research ignited in him a "fascination to know how the Chickasaws had been so influential in the southeast and beyond—way out of proportion to their [low population] numbers." Dyson was disappointed initially to discover how little had been written about the tribe in colonial documents. But he came to understand the reasons. "For one thing, the Chickasaws were relatively remote physically from the Europeans and Americans in the eighteenth century," he says. "Also, because the Chickasaws were so warlike, the white colonists' interest in the tribe was not cultural, but political. To the whites, the Chickasaw were either your ally or your enemy."

As he read the eighteenth and early nineteenth century primary source material on the tribe, the language professor especially noticed the Chickasaw words, or words purported or assumed to be Chickasaw. Early in his research, Dyson could sometimes tell or sense that some word was not Chickasaw. But intuition was not good enough. If he really wanted to

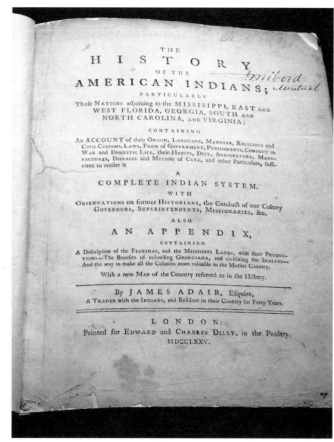

In his work of discovering and restoring eighteenth century Chickasaw words and their meanings, Professor Dyson said that the book, *History of American Indians*, containing numerous Indian words spelled phonetically, was invaluable to his effort. But the text often added to the mysteries Dyson was trying to unravel. The book pictured here is an original edition owned by the Chickasaw Nation. (Photo courtesy of Chickasaw Nation)

carve out a research niche in studying these words and their meanings, he would need to get more serious. He did.

Dyson has found words that have no meaning to today's speakers or have a different meaning than the original. For example, eighteenth century English trader James Adair wrote in his book, *History of the American Indians,* that Chickasaws spoke of *ishtahollo'* as priests or sacred beings. But the consensus of the tribe's Chickasaw Language Committee holds that the word means witch.

How could today's meaning be almost exactly the opposite? Dyson says the difference probably is associated with the tribe's conversion to Christianity. "To eighteenth century Chickasaws, *ishtahollo'* did sacred and supernatural things. Missionaries called these beliefs superstition, and after removal when more and more Chickasaws became Christian, the word stayed the same but the context changed."

Dyson also looks for words that once existed but apparently have vanished. He knows, for instance, that Chickasaws used to make their dugout canoes from cypress and tulip poplar trees, but when he consulted the Chickasaw dictionaries, no words for either tree were included. "There are no swamps [where the trees grow] in Ada that I know of, so you can see how these words might have been lost simply from disuse over the last 170 years."

Dyson did find the words elsewhere. He says *sipsi'* (tulip poplar) appears in Adair's book. *Sh a kolo'* appears for a cypress swamp on Bernard Romans' 1772 map of northern Mississippi.

The divide between the Chickasaw spoken in the eighteenth century and that spoken today is particularly wide because of the profound disruption to the Chickasaws' continuity caused by their forced removal to Indian Territory in the late 1830s and '40s. Furthermore, no Chickasaw dictionary existed until the 1960s when one was produced by Chickasaw speakers Vinnie May and Jess Humes. (A second dictionary was produced by Pamela Munro and Chickasaw speaker Catherine Willmond in 1994.)

However, Cyrus Byington compiled a Choctaw dictionary which was published by the U.S. Bureau of Ethnology in 1909, and another Choctaw dictionary was compiled and published by Ben Watkins in 1892. And because Choctaw and Chickasaw are similar languages, Dyson has found the books to be essential to bridging the two-century Chickasaw language gap. Both Byington, a missionary, and Watkins spent years with the Choctaws, learning from people "whose ways of living and thinking and looking at the world are long past," writes Dyson.

The books contain a treasure trove of synonyms, which strongly suggests "a former period of bountiful Chickasaw synonyms," Dyson writes. "The words that evidently existed have been lost to history and to the elders. In the two Chickasaw dictionaries, I am lucky to find one synonym for a word."

Since he started his research, Dyson has consulted a number of Chickasaw and Choctaw speakers. In 2004, he attended a meeting of the Chickasaw Language Committee and asked for the members' comments and help. He also speaks periodically with Oklahoma Choctaws and Mississippi Choctaws and not surprisingly finds differences in their vocabularies and word usages. Members of both groups were helpful as he plowed through the nineteenth century Choctaw dictionaries while researching his article on Chickasaw village names.

One of his major findings was that some of the Chickasaw village names in the literature were actually Choctaw. Because the Choctaw and French were allies before 1763, French documents reflect Choctaw information about the Chickasaws. For example, in March 1736, French and Indian forces attacked the Chickasaw village of Chokkilissa. But in his article, Dyson writes that *Okla Chitoka* is how the Choctaws referred to the attacked village. *Okla* is town; *chito* is large; and *ka* emphasizes the importance of the town. Being French and using French spelling, the recorder wrote it as *Ogoula Tchetoka*.

Thus, the account of the great Chickasaw victory has appeared in history articles and books as the "Battle of Ogoula Tchetoka." From a Chickasaw perspective, it should be the "Battle of Chokkilissa'."

In this article, Dyson proceeds chronologically through the major sources of information, narratives (such as Adair's book), and maps, all of which provide Chickasaw village names. Naturally, he says, this entails repetition, especially since the names of some of the villages did not change or change much. But, the "greater and more varied the number of spellings, the better the clues we have as to what was actually being said."

A good example of the same village name spelled numerous ways is Foli' Cha'a', which in Chickasaw literally means "chopped off switches," according to Dyson. Tying the diverse spellings together, he says, gave him fits. "I spent probably weeks cross-checking in the Chickasaw and Choctaw dictionaries and other sources, verifying alternate spellings in numerous languages, and pestering native speakers and language colleagues to death." The village's first mention, Dyson writes, appeared on a sketch drawn in about 1684 for the French crown by an Italian mapmaker named Coronelli. He spelled it Fabatchaoux. It was later written as Falatchao and Falatche in French, Hollachatroe in English by Nairne, and Phalacheho in English by Adair in his 1775 book.

Dyson believes "chopped off switches" refers to the cut saplings known as wattle that were used to construct Chickasaw buildings. *Foli'* is obsolete in Chickasaw, but *fuli* means switch in modern-day Choctaw and is the old Choctaw word for wattle. In the article's introduction, Dyson notes that the village names are almost unfailingly practical or pragmatic; their meanings describe some aspect of the village or its natural setting. By extension, Dyson believes that the early-day Chickasaws were as pragmatic as the names of their villages.

Four of the villages listed by Coronelli appear with divergent spellings on virtually all of the major documents and maps throughout the eighteenth century, Dyson says. While historical and archaeological evidence clearly shows that the village locations changed (usually for self-defense against the French and their Indian allies), the village names did not. Dyson writes that Chickasaw identity and continuity were explicit in the persistence of seven village names throughout the eighteenth century. He identifies them as Chokkilssa', Chokka' Falaa', Aamalaata', Chisha' Talla'a, Tokaabilowa', Foli'Ch a 'a', and Aahikki'ya'.

Though Dyson's article is thirty-eight pages long (including the bibliography and notes), he says he hopes it is a good beginning. "I do not pretend to have gotten every name correct," he says, inviting comments and alternative interpretations from Chickasaw speakers and scholars.

Another project that he is researching for publication is an examination of all the old-fashioned or obsolete Chickasaw words in James Adair's 500-page book. He says the words and phrases include clothing, food, musical instruments and even cursing the enemy. But what Dyson is perhaps most excited about are the words associated with traditional Chickasaw spirituality. He says, "Adair is quite detailed about their different religious ceremonies; who performed them; and why, when and under what circumstances."

Although Dyson identifies Adair's book as "definitely the one to consult for eighteenth-century Chickasaw words, the trader had a maddening habit of inserting Indian words in the text often without identifying tribal origin." Since Adair spent most of his time with the Chickasaw Indians and admired them most, scholars assume that the majority of the Indian words in his book are Chickasaw. But, Dyson will spend considerable time teasing out words that are Catawba, Cherokee, Choctaw, and Creek.

The professor reports that he is burrowing ahead, but wisely refrains from predicting when his paper will see print. When this work is available, it will be reviewed in the *Times*.

In October 2006, John Dyson received the first Heritage Preservation Award from the Chickasaw Nation for his article on Chickasaw village names from 1540 to 1835. He received the award from Governor Bill Anoatubby, center, and Lieutenant Governor Jefferson Keel. Dyson, an emeritus professor of languages at Indiana University, said he wished he had "a second lifetime to devote to the Chickasaw language and culture…" (Photo courtesy of Chickasaw Nation)

Archaeology Controversy with Tribe Swirls in Tennessee

Early in August, when land was being graded for constructing a new library building and parking lot in Brentwood, Tennessee, some skeletal remains, possibly prehistoric, were uncovered. In accordance with state law, construction was stopped, and the state archeologist's office was contacted to conduct a survey. Also, in compliance with state law, the city obtained a court order from a local judge to "terminate the cemetery," meaning that any remains could be disinterred and placed in the custody of the state archeology office.

After a preliminary survey, state archeologist Nick Fielder stated that the site contained a village and cemetery and that the remains were characteristic of Mississippian Indians who lived roughly between 1300 and 1350 A.D. Although Fielder estimated that the property might contain from two hundred to three hundred human remains, city officials believed that only two to four would have to be disinterred. But during the next two weeks, many more human remains were found and, by order of the city, were disinterred by a private archeological firm hired by the city for that purpose. (The state archeology office takes charge only when the remains are contained on state land.)

By August 28, eighteen skeletal remains had been removed from the site, and the city manager told the Brentwood mayor and city council that as many as forty might have to be removed.

Representatives of state Indian groups protested the city's decision to remove more remains not located directly under the proposed library building. On September 22, the city council voted to move fifty-eight of seventy-eight graves identified on the construction site. Protesting the action was Mike Sims, identified by the Nashville Banner as a resident of Gainesboro, Tennessee, and a "Cherokee Indian on hand as an observer for the American Indian Movement." "They're destroying more history here than they could ever contain in their library," Sims said.

Conceding the sincerity of the Indian protestors, Mayor Ann Dunn stated that the city (a suburb of Nashville) was in a position where "we have to try to satisfy the needs of our community and the Native Americans. It's a no-win situation. We don't know what else to do. We're not enjoying this." The next day Sims contacted Jerry Bray, the Chickasaw Nation's historic preservation officer, and informed him "of a mass excavation involving a prehistoric village site in Brentwood." Bray telephoned Tennessee officials, including archeologist Nick Fielder, and learned from him that the matter was being handled by Tennessee public officials in conformity with state law. Fielder said federal law did not apply because the library project did not involve federal land or federal funding. Bray informed Fielder that the Chickasaw Nation had a "substantial historical interest in Tennessee" and recommended that he consult the tribe, which, Bray noted, was federally recognized.

On September 25, Chickasaw Lieutenant Governor David Brown wrote Fielder, noting the possibility that some of the remains could be ancestral Chickasaw and requesting Fielder's office to contact Jefferson Keel, Governor Anoatubby's special assistant for cultural resources so that

Media by Joshua Hinson, titled Hika! (Stop!). (Courtesy of the artist)

"immediate consultation arrangements can be made."

Fielder arranged a September 30 meeting in Brentwood that was attended by himself, Keel, Brown, and Brentwood City Manager Mike Walker. Brown stated that tribal policy held that Chickasaw remains and artifacts should be reburied as closely as possible to the original site. Could any of the remains be ancestral Chickasaw? he asked. Fielder said it was possible, apparently not making clear at that point his later contention that no evidence existed of a connection between the fourteenth century Indians and any historic tribe.

When Brown and Keel summarized the meeting for Governor Anoatubby, they reported that Fielder said the remains and artifacts could be ancestral Chickasaw. Fielder also said that possibly 150 to 200 of the approximately 1,000 remains stored in the archeology division might be Chickasaw. Although Fielder said that most were "culturally unidentifiable" like the remains from the Brentwood site, he apparently did not stress that he was talking in theoretical terms. He must have realized his mistake when he received a copy of a letter from Governor Anoatubby to the Brentwood city manager in which the governor said that Fielder agreed that the remains "may indeed be those of ancient Chickasaw people."

Fielder wrote Anoatubby that the governor's impression of Fielder's belief "is not correct" and that "[t]here is no archaeological or historical evidence of the Chickasaw ever have [sic] lived in this area although they apparently did hunt here in the early 1700s." Perhaps to clarify his remarks, Fielder said he told Brown and Keel that he considers the "Chickasaw tribal government to be a potential claimant" under federal provisions for "culturally unaffiliated, unassociated prehistoric artifacts from Middle Tennessee."

Anoatubby believes that any time human remains "could be those of our forefathers, we have an obligation to do something." While the governor recognized that other tribes may have an interest, he thought the Chickasaw Nation should have a say in the reinterment, if not on behalf of the Chickasaw people, then on behalf of all Indian people.

Fielder told Anoatubby that he would notify the tribe of "any future prehistoric Native American cemetery relocation prior to its removal." But he also said that he could not unilaterally rebury the artifacts with the remains, as per the governor's request, "without consultation with the Department of Interior and other potential claimant tribes."

While Tennessee state law required that disinterred remains be reburied within a year, the law "is silent" on burial artifacts, according to Fielder. He said artifacts were usually held by his division for repatriation under federal law (Native American Graves Protection and Repatriation Act [NAGPRA]) governing culturally unaffiliated, unassociated objects. That meant the artifacts were held for a specified time during which tribes could make a repatriation claim with the federal government.

However, Fielder said that there had been instances where he had recommended to the court that artifacts be reburied with the remains and that the court had so ordered. In his affidavit filed in the Brentwood case, he stated that the artifacts would be held by the archeology division and eventually would be made available to claimants under NAGPRA provisions. "Our distinction is, if we find the artifacts on public property, then we feel we have an obligation to share and interpret our findings with the public," Fielder said. Fielder's affidavit notwithstanding, the court order only provided for the disposition of the remains, not the artifacts.

No party to this matter has been satisfied with the course of events. Ultimately, some seventy-eight skeletal remains were removed from the site. Removal took about three months and cost Brentwood more than $100,000 and some negative publicity. The locally based Alliance for Native American Indian Rights protested every step of the way with face-to-face meetings with Brentwood city officials and by sending faxes with messages seeking to update and influence all levels of public officials, media outlets and tribes, including the Chickasaw Nation. Alliance members accused the city of Brentwood of having acted in bad faith. They charged that while city officials talked about minimizing the removal of burials, their main goal was always to finish the library on time.

As its main goal for the future, the 150-member Alliance appealed to the Tennessee Legislature when it convened in January 1998 to change the applicable state law to recognize that Native American graves needed special protection. According to Alliance President Toye Heape, it was both "reasonable and realistic" to amend the law to prohibit the termination of burial grounds that have been recorded by the state archeology division. "That would not protect every prehistoric site, but would apply to approximately one hundred sites in the Nashville area, and literally thousands of prehistoric Native American recorded sites in Tennessee."

Of the tribes the Alliance contacted, only the Chickasaw Nation responded. But Heape noted that Chickasaw interest, credibility and prestige could be pivotal in bringing about a change in the state law. Governor Anoatubby felt that the tribe's stated interest in playing an active role in the disposition of the Brentwood remains and artifacts and sites similar to it had not been taken seriously by state officials.

Fielder acknowledged that unfortunate misunderstandings had occurred, but said the basic problem had been that Tennessee law simply provided no legal role for the Chickasaw Nation or any other tribe. He said that would remain the case until and unless the state law was changed. He said "it would make things easier on my office if the law were to be clarified, as to the disposition of artifacts. I am not philosophically or professionally opposed to reburying culturally unaffiliated prehistoric artifacts with the remains, but there are many archeologists in this state, including some on my own staff, who are adamantly opposed to such action."

In the Brentwood case, Fielder mentioned a possible solution that might satisfy tribal needs. "If the city of Brentwood would agree to recommend changing the wording of the court order to include reburying the artifacts with the remains on the Brentwood site, the court might go along." But Fielder said he would not change the wording in his affidavit to the court. Jefferson Keel intended to explore the option with Brentwood officials and planned another trip to Nashville, probably with David Brown and an archeologist of the tribe's choosing, to examine the Brentwood remains and artifacts. Among them were three "museum quality pieces,"

according to Fielder. One was an effigy bottle, and two others were pieces of pottery shaped in human forms.

Meanwhile, Fielder asked for a membership to the Chickasaw Historical Society so that he could receive future issues of The Journal. "It is obvious that our contact with the Chickasaw Nation will be ongoing," he said.

Acknowledgements

This anthology would not have been possible without the encouragement and support of Governor Bill Anoatubby. From the beginning of our relationship, he demonstrated his commitment to discovering, presenting and preserving the tribe's history and culture. This is all the more remarkable for a Chickasaw who didn't grow up in a traditional tribal way, had an accounting degree, and knew very little about Chickasaw history prior to 1975 when he first went to work for the tribe.

But if not for a Chickasaw attorney named Jim Jennings, I would never have come to the governor's attention. As a member of the tribe's cultural committee, Jennings shared the governor's vision of developing a permanent tribal division devoted to the promotion of history, language and culture.

As the chief legal counsel of one of Oklahoma City's largest banks, Jim was meticulous and scrupulous about details, rules and regulations. But he also had an intuitive streak. He sized up people and played hunches. After we had met a couple of times, he decided on some basis known only to him that I might make a good historian, and he recommended me to Governor Anoatubby. Jim already had terminal cancer when we first met and was often very much "under the weather" when we got together in the late summer of 1992. He was going downhill fast that fall but summoned the reserves to avoid a posthumous induction into the Chickasaw Hall of Fame. He died a short time after his induction.

I only knew him a few months, but I still think of Jim sometimes, particularly when I'm having a hard time writing an article. I remember showing him some of my first writing and holding my breath: I didn't want to disappoint him or betray his trust. Those memories play a role in motivating me still.

Over the years, I've been aided and schooled by dozens of other Chickasaws. Those who have made the biggest impression on me are Jeannie Barbour, LaDonna Brown, Senator Helen Cole, Glenda Galvan, Governor Overton James, Lieutenant Governor Jefferson Keel, Kelley Lunsford, Kirk Perry, Carlin Thompson, and one Choctaw, Gary White Deer.

Thanks to Chickasaw artist Joshua Hinson for his cover concept and illustration and Skip McKinstry for the book's layout and design.

For help, support and friendship, I also want to thank Bill Welge and his staff at the Oklahoma Historical Society, John Lovett of the University of Oklahoma Western History Collection, and the staff of the Manuscript Division of the Library of Congress.

I can't fail to mention the contribution of my wife, Gail Fites, who has reviewed and improved every article.

Finally, I thank Paul Lambert and Bob Blackburn for their novel idea of developing the Chickasaw Press. It is an honor to have this book published in the Press's initial year of operation.

Bibliography

Origin: The Chickasaw Migration Stories
1994 *Journal*

Adair, James. *The History of the American Indians*. New York: Johnson Reprint Corp., 1968. First published in 1775.

Cushman, H.B. *History of the Choctaw, Chickasaw and Natchez Indians*. Greenville, TX: Headlight Printing House, 1899.

Gibson, Arrell M. *The Chickasaws*. Norman, OK: University of Oklahoma Press, 1971.

Humes, Jess J. and Kingsbery, Robert. "The Big White Dog and the Sacred Pole, " *Frontier Magazine* (February-March, 1965).

Lincecum, Gideon. *Autobiography of Gideon Lincecum*," Volume 8, Oxford, MS: Publications of Mississippi Historical Society, 1904.

Malone, James. *The Chickasaw Nation*. Louisville, KY.: John Morton and Co., 1922.

Swanton, John R. "Indian Tribes of the Lower Mississippi Valley," Bureau of American Ethnology, (Washington, D.C.: GPO, 1911).

Warren, Harry. "Chickasaw Traditions and Customs, etc., " Volume 8, (Oxford, MS: Publications of the Mississippi Historical Society, 1904).

Editors of Time-Life Books. *Tribes of the Southern Woodlands*. Alexandria, VA: Time-Life, Inc., 1994.

Moundville Linked to Chickasaw Past
December 2000 *Times*

Peebles, Christopher S. "The Rise and Fall of the Mississippian in Western Alabama: The Moundville and Summerville Phases, A.D. 1000 to 1600." *Mississippi Archaeology,* 22, 1, (1987).

All of the following selections are contained in Knight, Jr., Vernon J. and Steponaitis, Vincas P., eds., *Archaeology of the Moundville Chiefdom*. Washington, D.C.: Smithsonian Institution Press, 1998.

Knight, Jr., Vernon J. and Steponaitis, Vincas P. "A New History of Moundville."

Knight. "Moundville as a Diagrammatic Ceremonial Center."

Powell, Mary Lucas. "Of Time and the River: Perspectives on Health During the Moundville Chiefdom."

Welch, Paul D. "Outlying Sites within the Moundville Chiefdom."

Schoeninger, Margaret J., Lisa Sattenspiel, and Mark Schurr. "Transitions at Moundville: A Question of Collapse."

The English Come to Call
May 2001 *Times*

Crane, Verner. *The Southern Frontier*. Durham: Duke University Press, 1928.

Axtell, James. *The Indians' New South*. Baton Rouge: Louisiana State University Press, 1997.

Corkran, David. *The Carolina Indian Frontier*. Columbia: University of South Carolina Press, 1970.

Salley, Alexander *Narratives of Early Carolina, 1650-1708*. New York: Charles Scribner's Sons, 1911.

Moore, Alexander Moore, ed. *Nairne's Muskhogean Journals*. Jackson: University Press of Mississippi, 1988.

Galloway, Patricia. *Choctaw Genesis, 1500-1700*. Lincoln: Univ. of Nebraska Press, 1995.

The French-Chickasaw War of 1736, Parts 1 and 2
July 2003 *Times*

Rowland, Dunbar and Sanders, A.G. eds. *Mississippi Provincial Archives, French Dominion, Volume I,* Jackson: Press of the Mississippi Department of Archives and History, 1927.

Gayarre, Charles. *History of Louisiana*, Volume I. New York: W.J. Widdleton, 1866.

Reynolds, Alfred W., *The Alabama-Tombigbee Basin in International Relations, 1701-1763*, doctoral dissertation, 1928.

Ethridge, Robbie. *The French Connection: The Ethnohistorical Evidence for Interactions between the Chickasaw and French,* paper presented in Macon, Ga., Nov. 10, 2000.

B.F. Riley, *Makers and Romance of Alabama History*, n.p.(1915?) Western History Collection, University of Oklahoma Libraries, Norman, OK.

Galloway, Patricia, ed. *Mississippi Provincial Archives, French Dominion, Volume 4.* Baton Rouge, LA: Louisiana State University Press, 1984.

Foret, Michael J. "War or Peace? Louisiana, the Choctaws, and the Chickasaws, 1733-35." *Louisiana History* 31, 3, 1990.

White, Richard. *The Roots of Dependency*. Lincoln: University of Nebraska Press, 1988.

Gibson, Arrell. *The Chickasaws*, Norman: University of Oklahoma Press,1971.

Foret, Michael J. *On the Marchlands of Empire: Trade, Diplomacy, and War on the Southeastern Frontier, 1733-1763.* Ph.D. dissertation, College of William and Mary, 1990.

U.S. Congress, House. "To Provide for the Commemoration of the Two Hundredth Anniversary of the Battle of Ackia." Report to U.S. House of Representatives, 1934.

Cabaniss, Allen "Ackia: Battle in the Wilderness, 1736,"*History Today.* December 1975.

King, Grace. *A History of Louisiana.* New Orleans: L. Graham, 1893.

Atkinson, James, *Splendid Land, Splendid People*. Tuscaloosa: University of Alabama Press, 2004.

1750s: A Decade of Crisis at Chokkilissa
March 2004 *Times*

Foret, Michael. "On the Marchlands of Empire: Trade, Diplomacy and War on the Southeastern Frontier, 1733-63," Ph.D. diss. College of William and Mary, 1990.

St. Jean, Wendy. Personal communication with author, based on her doctoral dissertation, March 3, 2003.

Atkinson, James. *Splendid Land, Splendid People,* Tuscaloosa: University of Alabama Press, 2004.

Wells, Mary Ann. *Native Land* Jackson: University Press of Mississippi, 1994.

Gibson, Arrell. *The Chickasaws* Norman: University of Oklahoma Press, 1971.

McDowell, Jr., William L. *Documents relating to Indian Affairs, 1750-54; 1754-65.* Columbia: South Carolina Department of Archives and History, 1992.

Rowland, Dunbar, A.G. Sanders, and Patricia Galloway, editors, *Mississippi Provincial Archives, French Dominion, Volume V, 1749-63.* Baton Rouge: Louisiana State University Press, 1984.

Martini, Don. "Chickasaw, A History, 1540-1856" (unpublished manuscript) Chickasaw Nation Library, Ada, OK; *Who Was Who Among the Southern Indians, A Geneological Notebook, 1698-1907.* Ripley, MS, 1998.

Craig, Robert E. "The Colberts in Chickasaw History, 1783-1818." Ph.D. diss. University of New Mexico, 1998.

Cook, Steve. Personal communication with author. February 13, 2004.

Hearts and Minds of the Chickasaws in the 1780s
June 2003 *Times*

Cotterill, R.S. *The Southern Indians,* Norman: University of Oklahoma Press, 1954, 56-114.

Gibson, Arrell *The Chickasaws* Norman: University of Oklahoma Press, 1971.

Berry, Jane M. "The Indian Policy of Spain in the Southwest 1783-1795," *Mississippi Valley Historical Review*, 3 (1916-17): 462-77.

McGee, Malcolm interviewed by Lyman Draper. 1841. Draper Manuscripts, Vol. 10, State Historical Society of Wisconsin, Madison.

Crabb, A.L. ed. "Notes and Documents: George Washington and the Chickasaw Nation, 1795l." *Mississippi Valley Historical Review* (December 1932): 404-407.

Endnotes

Winter of Discontent
1997 *Journal*

1. *Narratives of the career of Hernando De Soto in the Conquest of Florida, as told by a Knight of Elvas and in a relation by Luys Hernandez de Biedma, factor of the Expedition*, ed. Edward G. Bourne, New York: Allerton Book Co., 1922, 133. This book is based on the diary of Rodrigo Ranjel, De Soto's private secretary. Hereafter *Narratives*.
2. David Duncan, *Hernando De Soto, A Savage Quest in the Americas* (New York: Crown Publishers, 1995), 398.
3. Mary Ann Wells, *Native Land* (Jackson: University Press of Mississippi, 1994), 12-14.
4. Ibid., 13.
5. Patricia Galloway, "The Emergence of Historic Indian Tribes in the Southeast," ed. Barbara Carpenter, *Ethnic Heritage in Mississippi*, (Jackson: University Press of MS., 1992), 6.
6. Patricia Galloway, *Choctaw Genesis 1500-1700* (Lincoln: University of Nebraska Press, 1995), 108.
7. Wells, 17-18.
8. *Narratives,* 92.
9. Duncan, 395.
10. Wells, 18.
11. Duncan, 396.
12. Galloway, 118.
13. Ibid., 119.
14. *Narratives*, 93.
15. Galloway, 119.
16. Wells, 21; Duncan, 396.
17. Duncan, 397.
18. *Narratives*, 133.
19. Ibid.

20. Ibid.
21. Ibid., 96.
22. Arrell Gibson, *The Chickasaws* (Norman: The University of Oklahoma Press, 1971): 32.
23. Duncan, 399.
24. Wells, 23.
25. Ranjel, 135.
26. Wells, 23; Duncan, 400.
27. Wells, 27.

Eighteenth Century Deerskin Maps Chickasaw Diplomacy October 2003 *Times*

Note: Gregory Waselkov's article appears in *Powhatan's Mantle: Indians in the Colonial Southeast*. Permission to use the 1723 map was granted by the University of Nebraska Press, the publisher of *Powhatan's Mantle*.

Forced Removal of the Chickasaw, 1837: An Epic Tragedy 1998 *Journal*

1. Stephen Ambrose, *Undaunted Courage* (New York: Touchstone, 1996), 346.
2. Ibid., 348.
3 Arrell Gibson, *The Chickasaws*, (Norman: University of Oklahoma Press, 1971), 105.
4. Leroy Stewart, "A History of the Chickasaws" (Master's Thesis, University of Oklahoma, 1938),14.
5. Ibid., 22.
6. Thomas McKenney, *Memoirs, Official and Personal*, (New York: Paine and Burgess, 1846), 160.
7. Gibson, 168-69.
8. Blue Clark, "Chickasaw Colonization in Oklahoma," *The Chronicles of Oklahoma*, 54 (Spring, 1976): 49.
9. Stewart, 45.

10. Guy B. Braden, "The Shadow of Andrew Jackson," *Tennessee Historical Quarterly* (1958): 326.
11. Gibson,177.
12. R.M. Johnson, *Oklahoma History, South of the Canadian* (Chicago: S.J. Clarke Co., 1925): 129.
13. Braden, 327.
14. John Millard's Journal of a Party of Emigrating Chickasaw Indians, 1837. Letters received, Office of Indian Affairs, (1824-81), Chickasaw Agency, National Archives, Washington, D.C., Microscopy 234, Roll 143.
15. Grant Foreman, *Indian Removal* (Norman: University of Oklahoma Press, 1989), 206.
16. See note 14. Millard's Journal may be found not only at the National Archives, but also at the Oklahoma Historical Society and in the Tribal Library in Ada.
17. Ibid.
18. Stewart, 55-56.
19. Gibson, 185.
20. Ibid., 186-87.
21. Foreman, 214.
22. John Parsons, ed. "Letters on the Chickasaw Removal of 1837," *New York Historical Society Quarterly* XXXVII (1953): 273-83.
23. Committee on Public Expenditures, H.R. 454, 27th Cong., 2nd Sess.
24. Foreman, 214.
25. Ethan A. Hitchcock, *A Traveller in Indian Territory: The Journal of Ethan Allen Hitchcock,* (Norman: University of Oklahoma, 1996), 12.
26. Committee on Indian Affairs, H.R. 271, 27th Cong., 3rd Sess., 1.
27. Ethan A. Hitchcock, Fifty Years in Camp and Field, A Diary of Major Ethan Allen Hitchcock, ed. W.A. Crofutt, (New York: G.P. Putnam, 1909), 156-57.
28. 27th Cong., 3 sess., House Report 27, 1.
29. Gibson, *The Chickasaws*, 214.
30. Foreman, 218-219.

31. Gibson, The Chickasaws, 213-32
32. Same as 26, 117-122.
33 House Executive Doc. 42., 50th Cong. 1st Sess.
34. Ibid., 189.
35. Foreman, 217.
36. Clark, 56-57.
37. Foreman, 225.
38. Ibid.

The History of the Chickasaws' Great Seal
1996 *Journal*

1. The 1840s were of interest because the Chickasaws were moving toward separation from the Choctaws by enacting laws to that effect and by writing and ratifying a constitution in 1848. Arrell Gibson, *The Chickasaws* (Norman: University of Oklahoma Press, 1971), 248-49.
2. Muriel Wright, "The Great Seal of the Chickasaw Nation," *The Chronicles of Oklahoma* (hereafter *Chronicles)*, 40, no. 3, (1962): 388.
3. Muriel Wright, "Official Seals of the Five Civilized Tribes," *Chronicles*, 18, no. 4, 357.
4. Ibid., 361-62. Chickasaw Speaker Pauline Brown says *Ishpani* is a Choctaw, not a Chickasaw, word.
5. Ibid., 362.
6. W. David Baird, *The Chickasaw People*, (Phoenix: Indian Tribal Series, 1974).
7. No laws or other data are provided in her article, and no references or citations to the article or the 1940 Alabama flag ceremony are included in the Muriel Wright collection of papers at the Oklahoma Historical Society.
8. Chickasaw Nation Code, Appendix 1, Great Seal of the Chickasaw Nation, Chickasaw Legislature, David Stout Building, Ada, OK
9. In one of her articles on Chickasaw history, Wright cited John R. Swanton, the Smithsonian Institution ethnologist, who wrote "Social and Religious Beliefs and Usages of the Chickasaw Indians," 44th Annual Report, Bureau of America Ethnology, (Washington, D.C.: 1928): n.p.
10. Gary Childers, Ted Key and Overton James, telephone interviews by author in March 1996.
11. Wilson Seawright, telephone interview by author on May 15, 1996.
12. Gibson, *The Chickasaws*, 271.
13. Gary Childers, telephone interview with author in March 1996.
14. It was donated by Charles Tate, who said he believes it once belonged to the Love family.
15. Kelley Lunsford, personal communication with author, April 1996.
16. Zane Browning, interview with author, March 1996.

The Paradox of Sulphur Springs
1996 *Journal*

1. Opal Hartsell Brown, *Murray County, Oklahoma* (Wichita Falls, TX: Nortex Press, 1977), 104.
2. Frank C. Churchill and Joseph A. Taff, Report on Sulphur Springs Reservation to Secretary of Interior, October 10, 1902, Archives of Chickasaw National Recreation Area, Sulphur, OK (hereafter CNRA Archive).
3. Palmer Boeger, *Oklahoma Oasis* (Muskogee: Western Heritage Books, 1987), 33.
4. Ibid., 38.
5. Ibid, 42.
6. "Perry E. Brown, "A History of Platt National Park," 12, CNRA Archive; Opal Brown, *Murray County*, 105-106.
7. Opal Brown, *Murray County,* 108-109.
8. Boeger, *Oklahoma Oasis*, 47.
9. Ibid., 48-49.
10. P.E. Brown, "A History of Platt National Park," 18.
11. Boeger, *Oklahoma Oasis,* 50-51.

12. Thomas Ryan to J.G. Wright, September 21, 1901, CNRA Archive.
13. Eugene White to J.G. Wright, October 31, 1901, CNRA Archive.
14. White to Wright, November 29, 1901, CNRA Archive.
15. Ibid.
16. White to Wright, December 17, 1901, CNRA Archive.
17. Wright to Secretary of Interior, March 3, 1902, Dawes
    Commission, microfilm #29, Oklahoma Historical Society (OHS),
    Oklahoma City. I tried in vain to find documentation regarding
    why the name Chickasaw Springs was not recommended by
    Inspector Wright.
18. Boeger, *Oklahoma Oasis*, 51.
19. Ibid.; Annual Reports of the Department of Interior, 1903, Indian
    Affairs, Part 11, 226. OHS Archives.
20. Frank C. Churchill to Secretary of Interior, March 11, 1903,
    Arbuckle Historical Museum, Davis, OK, Sulphur folder.
21. Boeger, *Oklahoma Oasis*, 55.
22. P. Brown, "A History of Platt National Park," 2.
23. Ibid., 24.

Trails To Atoka
1997 *Journal*
1. Letter of Indian Delegation to the Five Tribes, February 18, 1893,
   Phillips Collection, misc. 5CT, Western History Collections
   (WHC), University of Oklahoma Library, Norman, OK.
2. In an oblique way, the case the delegates were referring to
   was probably *United States v. Kagama*, May 10, 1886. While it
   addressed another matter, upholding the right of Congress to assert
   jurisdiction over internal crimes of Indians against Indians, the
   decision denigrated the integrity of Indian tribes and cleared the
   way for the government to interfere in the affairs of Indians.
3. Report of Commission to the Five Civilized Tribes, November 20,
   1894, Congressional Serial Set (CSS) 3281, 3-4.
4. John Bartlett Meserve, "Gov. Jonas Wolf and Gov. Palmer Simeon
   Mosely," *The Chronicles of Oklahoma* 18, no. 3, (September 1940)
   246, 249.
5. "Editorial on P.S. Mosely," *The Caddo Banner*, Caddo, I.T. August
   24, 1894. Actually, Wolf resigned before the end of his term, which
   was served out by Acting Governor Tecumseh A. McClure, who
   had been president of the Senate.
6. "Message of P.S. Mosely," *The Alliance Courier* (Ardmore, I.T.)
   September 4, 1895. Mosely Collection, M-44, WHC.
7. Report of the Commission to the Five Civilized Tribes, 1895, CSS
   3381, XCIII-XCV.
8. F.P. Prucha, *The Great Father* (Lincoln: The University of Nebraska
   Press, 1986), 258-59.
9. Ibid., 259.
10. Angie Debo, *The Rise and Fall of the Choctaw Republic* (Norman,
    University of Oklahoma Press, 1934), 255.
11. "New Item of P.S. Mosely," *The David Progress* (David, I.T.), July 30,
    1897.
12. L.A. Benton, "The Situation," *Atoka Indian Citizen*, July 30, 1896, 1.
13. Debo, *Rise and Fall*, 255.
14. D.M. Wisdom, Indian Agent, Union Agency, Annual Report,
    Report of the Secretary of the Interior, Vol. 2 (1896), 154.
15. "Editorial on Message of R.M. Harris," *The Purcell Register*,
    September 24, 1896.
16. E.N. Wright, Communication," *The Indian Citizen*, August 27, 1896,
    1.
17. Loren N. Brown, *The Work of the Dawes Commission Among
    the Choctaw and Chickasaw Indians* (Ph.D. diss., University of
    Oklahoma, 1937), 97-98.
18. Act of Chickasaw Legislature, Chickasaw Manuscripts, No. 7075,
    Archives, Oklahoma Historical Society (OHS), Oklahoma City,
    OK.
19. Act of Chickasaw Legislature, Jan. 15, 1897, Chickasaw Tribal
    Records, Microfilm CKN 5, OHS; "An Act Signed by R.M. Harris,"

The Daily Capital (South McAlester, I.T.), January 23, 1897.

20. Ibid.
21. Brown, *Work of the Dawes Commission*, 107.
22. "Chickasaws Protest," *The Daily Ardmoreite*, February 2, 1897, 1.
23. Report, Chickasaw Commission, February 12, 1897, Atoka Agreement folder, Chickasaw vertical file, OHS Indian Archives, Oklahoma City, OK.
24. "Chickasaw Commission," *Daily Ardmoreite*, February 17, 1897,
25. "The Message, *Daily Ardmoreite*, February 28, 1897, 1.
26. Brown, *Work of the Dawes Commission*, 110.
27. Arrell Gibson, *The Chickasaws* (Norman: University of Oklahoma Press, 1971), 303.
28. "An Act Creating a Commission to Negotiate with the Dawes Commission," *Constitution and Laws of the Chickasaw Nation*, (Parsons, KS: Foley Railroad Printing Co., 1899), 381.
29. Brown, *Work of the Dawes Commission*, 113.
30. "Important Announcement," *The Indian Citizen*, March 29, 1897.
31. "Dawes Commission," *The Indian Citizen*, April 8, 1897, 1.
32. No headline, *The Indian Citizen*, April 15, 1897, 1.
33. Joseph Ralls, Jr., Indian-Pioneer Collection (IPC), Vol. 41, 128-29, OHS Indian Archives, Oklahoma City, OK.
34. D.A. Homer, IPC, Vol. 5, 156, OHS Indian Archives, Oklahoma City, OK.
35. "Agreement," Report of the Commissioner of Indian Affairs, 1897, 409-415.
36. Daniel F. Littlefield, Jr., *The Chickasaw Freedmen*, (Westport, CT: Greenwood Press, 1980), 173.
37. Brown, *Work of the Dawes Commission*, 115.
38. "An Agreement Reached," *The Indian Chieftain* (Vinita, I.T.), April 29, 1897, 2.
39. Report of Commissioner of Indian Affairs, 1897, 39-40.
40. Brown, *Work of the Dawes Commission*, 119.
41. Letter from Choctaw-Chickasaw Union Party, December 17, 1897, U.S. Congressional Serial Set 3563, 1-2.
42. "Message of R.M. Harris," *The Indian Citizen*, September 16, 1897.
43. Brown, *Work of the Dawes Commission*, 122.
44. "Message of R.M. Harris," *The South McAlester Capitol*, February 17, 1898.
45. Brown, *Work of the Dawes Commission*, 116.

Alfalfa Bill's Work for the Tribe
February 2003 *Times*

1. Keith L. Bryant Jr., *Alfalfa Bill Murray* (Norman: University of Oklahoma Press, 1968), 22.
2. Ibid, 27.
3. Although Johnston's house, called Breezy Meadows, was larger than most houses in the area, it was far from a mansion. According to the Oklahoma Historical Society, which maintained the home for years, Johnston's home was 1,854 square feet. Perhaps Bradley's choice of words was a sign of the house's prestige and elegance rather than its size.
4. William H. Murray, "Address at Gov. Johnston's Funeral, June 29, 1939," Carl Albert Center, Murray Collection, Box 5, Folder 1, University of Oklahoma, Norman, OK.
5. Gordon Hines, *Alfalfa Bill* (Norman: University of Oklahoma Press 1932), 124.
6. Bryant, *Alfalfa Bill Murray*, 27.
7. Hines, 134-35.
8. William H. Murray, *Memoirs of Governor Murray and the True History of Oklahoma*, vol. 1 (Boston: Meador Publishing Co., 1945), 237.
9. Bryant, 31.

The Symbol on the Hill:
A History of the Chickasaw Capitol Building of 1898
1998 Journal

1. James J. Flink, "Automobiles," in *The Reader's Companion to American History*, eds. Eric Foner and J.A. Garraty (Boston: Houghton Mifflin Co., 1991), 65.
2. "Chickasaw Capitol" *The Daily Ardmoreite*, November 20, 1898, 1. In checking the area's newspapers that existed in 1898 at the newspaper division of the Oklahoma Historical Society, I found only two accounts of the dedication of the Capitol Building on November 17, 1898. Aside from the *Daily Ardmoreite*, there was a shorter account in Atoka's *Indian Citizen Press*, December 1, 1898.
3. The Chickasaws and Choctaws were linked together through the ownership of common lands.
4. The existing tribal records on microfilm in several locations and in the Davis Homer 1899 publication *Constitution and Laws of the Chickasaw Nation* almost always reflect only decisions not debate.
5. "Program for Ball and Banquet Dedicating The New Chickasaw Capitol, November 17, 1898," *Press of Tishomingo Herald*, Chickasaw Capitol folder, Chickasaw Library, Ada, OK.
6. Dawson Phelps, "The Chickasaw Council House," *Journal of Mississippi History*, July, 1952, 171.
7. Ibid., 171-72.
8. The late Beverly Wyatt, former long-time museum curator, conducted research on the Chickasaw capitol buildings in 1992. None of her findings and information on the log building were documented.
9. Overton James, "Dedication of the Chickasaw Council House, July 4, 1965," Overton James's papers, Ada, OK.
10. Research by an ad hoc committee of the Chickasaw Historical Society, Buck Cheadle, chair.
11. Arrell Gibson, *The Chickasaws* (Norman: University of Oklahoma Press, 1971), 280.
12. Jonas Wolf, Annual Message, *The Indian Champion*, Atoka, November 8, 1884.
13. No headline, *Muskogee Phoenix*, March 9, 1893, 4.
14. *Muskogee Phoenix*, October 13, 1892, 1; March 9, 1893, 4.
15. Gibson, *The Chickasaws*, 300-301.
16. *The Daily Ardmoreite*, November 2, 1896.
17. Davis A. Homer, *Constitution and Laws of the Chickasaw Nation* (Parsons, KS: Foley Railway Printing Co., 1899), 401-02.
18. Articles of Agreement and Contract, April 7, 1898, Capitol Building file, Chickasaw Council House Museum, Tishomingo, OK.
19. "Will it Succeed?," *The Daily Ardmoreite*, January 26, 1898, 1.
20. No headline, *Purcell Register*, February 10, 1898.
21. No headline, *The Daily Ardmoreite*, March 27, 1898, Council House Museum, Tishomingo, OK.
22. "Articles of Agreement and Contract," April 7, 1898, Capitol Bldg. file, Chickasaw Council House Museum.
23. Sandy Busby, "Century Old Secret Found in Johnston County Courthouse," *The Daily Ardmoreite*, May 18, 1992, 1.
24. *The Daily Ardmoreite*, April 28, 1898, 1.
25. Ibid., May 4, 2.
26. Gibson, *The Chickasaws*, 304.
27. *"Election of Douglas Johnston" Marietta* Monitor, Aug. 19, 1898.
28. "Big Day at Tishomingo," *The Daily Ardmoreite*, June 17, 1898, 3.
29. No headline, *Purcell Register*, August 29, 1898, 2.
30. "An Act Appropriating The Sum of Fifteen Hundred Dollars for the Further Improvement of the Building and Grounds of the National Capitol of the Chickasaw Nation," n.d.,Capitol Building file, Council House Museum.
31. Mrs. John Lokey, "72 [sic] Years of History Here," *The Daily Ardmoreite*, February 17, 1975. Since so many of the tribal records are missing today, it is tantalizing and frustrating to read about Mrs. Lokey's 1975 discovery.
32. For one: Busby, "Century Old Secret Found in Johnston Co.

Courthouse." See Note 23.

33. Chickasaw Nation Records, Microfilm CKN 21-3, "Buildings 4597-4627," Chickasaw Library, Ada. One warrant for $7,500 was issued on June 10, 1898, and three warrants for $2,500 each were issued on the same date, August 31, 1898. Perhaps Harris was paid from three separate accounts in August.

34. "Memories of the Son of C.P. [sic] Shaeffer," n.d., 4, Capitol Building file, Chickasaw Council House Museum.

35. See Note 31.

36. William H. Murray, *Memoirs of Governor Murray and True History of Oklahoma* vol. 1 (Boston: Meador Publishing Co., 1945), 236-37.

37. "Chickasaw Capitol," *The Daily Ardmoreite*, November 20, 1898, 1.

38. Oscar White interview by Beverly Wyatt, June 21, 1972, audio tape, Chickasaw Library, Ada, OK.

39. Ibid.

40. William H. Murray, "The Constitution," *The Daily Ardmoreite*, November 21, 1898, 1.

Thousands of Fraudulent Citizenship Claimants Foiled
January 2002 *Times*

1. Editorial on Message of D.H. Johnston," *South McAlester Capital*, September 18.

2. W. David Baird, *The Chickasaw People* (Phoenix: Indian Tribal Series, 1974), 74.

3. "General Review of McMurray Contracts," "Investigation of Indian Contracts," Burke Commission, 61st Cong., 2nd Sess., Report 2273, ix-x.

4. "Election News Item," *South McAlester Capital*, August 21, 1902, Johnston Collection, Box 1, Folder 54, Western History Collections, University of Oklahoma, Norman, OK.

5. Gordon Hines, *Alfalfa Bill* (Norman: University of Oklahoma Press, 1932), 149-54.

6. Ibid.

7. John Bartlett Meserve, "Gov. William Leander Byrd," *The Chronicles of Oklahoma*, Vol. XII, 441; "Editorial on P.S. Mosely," *Wapanucka Press*, September 4, 1902.

8. Loren N. Brown, "The Choctaw-Chickasaw Court Citizens," *The Chronicles of Oklahoma*, XVI, 439.

9. Two good sources give two different numbers. McMurray says 3,850 (McMurray testimony, Indian Contracts investigation, 651), while historian Loren Brown citing the Dawes Commission Report of 1904 says the number was 3,520. (Brown, "Choctaw-Chickasaw Court Citizens," 442-443.

10. Brown, "Choctaw-Chickasaw Court Citizens," 442-43.

Pursuing Justice: The Prosecution and Persecution of Five Chickasaw Nation Leaders in 1905
1996 *Journal*

1. "The Alleged Frauds," *The Daily Admoreite*, June 22, 1905, 1. The Phoenix story ran in the *Ardmoreite*.

2. "Different Phase of Chickasaw Muddle," *Muskogee Times-Democrat*, June 28, 1905.

3. Among those indicted in the school warrant case was U.S. Marshal Ben H. Colbert, a former Rough Rider and personal friend of President Theodore Roosevelt. He was also a director of the recently failed Chickasaw National Bank of Tishomingo. Others included former Chickasaw treasurer W. T. Ward; two Chickasaw school officials S.M. White and E.B. Hinshaw; and the former cashier of the Chickasaw National Bank Kirby Purdom, who was identified as a "fugitive from justice." The school warrant case will not be dealt with here.

4. "Grafters of Various Kinds and Degrees," *Muskogee Times-Democrat*, July 6, 1905.

5. "Text of indictment prepared and signed by W.B. Johnson," 60th Cong., 1st Sess., 1907-08, S. Doc., Vol. 35, Doc. 398, Washington, GPO, 1908, 33-34. Hereafter, S. Doc. 398.

6. I contacted several archival repositories of government records, and the records of this case held in the U.S. Court for the southern district of Indian Territory in May and June 1905 could not be found. It is alleged that many of the federal court records that were stored in the Carter County courthouse in Ardmore have been stolen over the years. However, I did find many pertinent records in S. Doc. 398, a report prepared by the U.S. attorney general for the U.S. Senate pursuant to a Senate Resolution of March 3, 1908. The report appears in S. Doc., Vol. 35 and is part of Doc. 398. (see note 4).

7. W. B. Johnson to U.S. Attorney General, October 20, 1905, Exhibit L of S. Doc. 398, 38-43.

8. "Grafters of Various Kinds and Degrees, " *Muskogee Times-Democrat*, July 6, 1905, 2.

9. "Origin of the Frauds," *The Daily Ardmoreite*, June 29, 1905, 1.

10. "Statement of Cecil A. Lyon," "Investigation of Indian Contracts," Report No. 2273, 61st Cong., 2d Sess., HR, Vol. 1 (Washington, D.C.: GPO, 1911), 404. It is also quite likely that on this occasion McMurray discussed a possible business arrangement to work together to sell the vast coal and asphalt holdings of the Chickasaw and Choctaw nations. Collaborating with a friend of Teddy Roosevelt could be a decisive asset to the attorneys, who needed Roosevelt's approval of the attorneys' contracts with the two Indian nations before any of the mineral land could be sold.

11. Charles W. Russell to U.S. Attorney General, July 31, 1905, Exhibit J of S. Doc. 398, 35-36.

12. An average value was assigned to each allotment, and that was multiplied by the number of fraudulent claimants.

13. "Governor Johnston," *The Atoka Indian Citizen*, undated , 1900.

14. No headline, *Holdenville Times*, April 18, 1901, Douglas Johnston Collection, Box l, folder 32, University of Oklahoma Western History Collections.

15. "Testimony of W.B. Johnson, Esq.," "Investigation of Indian Contracts," 61st Cong., H.R. 2273, 643. Hereafter "Indian Contracts."

16. Russell to Moody, Sept. 29, 1905, Exhibit K of S. Doc. 398, 36-37.

17. no title, *The Mounds Monitor* (Mounds, I.T.), October. 9, 1905.

18. "Chickasaw Warrants," *The Daily Ardmoreite*, October. 11, 1905, 1. The article is another example of the improper mixing together of different indictments and those indicted.

19. Indian Contracts, xii.

20. George R. Walker to Attorney General, March 29, 1907, Exhibit C, Document 398,14-15. You cannot blame the Chickasaws for employing the attorney who was in a position to prosecute them. But how could the Justice Department have allowed its chief prosecutor for the southern district of Indian Territory to be on the Chickasaw payroll?

21. Ibid.

22. "Rumors at Washington," *The Daily Ardmoreite*, December 17, 1905, 1.

23. Walker to U.S. Attorney General, March 29, 1907, Exhibit C, S. Doc. 398, 11-18. It is not known if the impending release of Walker's report was a factor in Hitchcock's resignation. But it is known that Hitchcock had invested a lot of his own prestige in the matter and resigning before the report was made public could save more embarrassing questions.

24. W.B. Johnson testimony, "Indian Contracts," 464.

25. Attorney General Bonaparte to President of U.S. Senate, March 17, 1908, 2-5.

26. Ibid., 4-5.

27. "Case Dismissed," *Muskogee Times-Democrat*, November 15, 1907, 3.

The Road to Sovereignty:
The Chickasaw Grassroots Movement of the 1950s
1995 *Journal*

1. Floyd Maytubby to C.A. Cravatt, October 4, 1951. National Archives, Southwestern Branch, Ft. Worth, TX. E-327, Chickasaw tribal folders, 1947-65 (hereafter NA SW Branch)
2. Donald F. Fixico, *Termination and Relocation, Federal Indian Policy, 1945-1960* (Albuquerque, N.M.: University of New Mexico Press, 1986), ix.
3. Francis Paul Prucha, *The Great Father*, abridged ed., (Lincoln: University of Nebraska Press, 1984), 341-42.
4. "Federal Indian Policies ... from the Colonial Period through the 1970's," Bureau of Indian Affairs, No date, Chickasaw Library, Ada, OK
5. Prucha, *The Great Father*, 349-50.
6. Fixico, *Termination and Relocation*, 135.
7. Joy Miller, "What's the Deal on Indians?" *The Daily Oklahoman*, March 11, 1956.
8. Jess Humes and Abijah Colbert to Floyd Maytubby, January 2, 1954. Robert Kerr Collection, Carl Albert Center, University of Oklahoma, Norman, OK.
9. "V" to Sen. Kerr, Jan. 6, 1954. Kerr Collection. I believe V is Sen. Kerr's secretary.
10. Paul Fickinger to Commissioner, Indian Affairs, January 20, 1955. NA SW Branch.
11. Floyd Maytubby to Paul Fickinger, January 21, 1955, NA SW Branch.
12. Jack Davidson to Glenn Emmons, telegram, September 17, 1955, NA SW Branch.
13. Jonas Imotichey to Carl Albert, October 14, 1958, Carl Albert Collection, Box 30, Folder 67, Carl Albert Center, University of Oklahoma, Norman.
14. Bobby Boyd, interview by author, September 16, 1993.
15. Bobby Boyd to Carl Albert, n.d., probably July 1958. NA SW Branch.
16. Acting BIA Commissioner to Carl Albert, August 15, 1958. Carl Albert Collection, Box 30, Folder 67, Carl Albert Center, University of Oklahoma, Norman, OK.
17. Fickinger to Boyd, September 11, 1958. NA SW Branch.
18. Maytubby to Fickinger, September 11, 1958. NA SW Branch.
19. Boyd to Fickinger, September 11, 1958. NA SW Branch.
20. Boyd interview.

1967—Snapshots of Tribal Revitalization
August 2001 *Times*

1. "Report of the Eighth Annual Meeting of the Chickasaw Indians," Seeley Chapel, October 21, 1967, Chickasaw tribal papers, Ada, OK.
2. Charles Ward to Overton James, September 23, 1966, author's papers.
3. Overton James to Charles Ward, October 24, 1966, author's papers.
4. "Dedication Ceremony of Indian Health Clinic at Tishomingo, OK," July 13, 1968, caption on photo, Overton James' papers, Ada, OK.
5. Overton James, interview, October 1992, author's papers.
6. Minutes, Special Meeting of the Chickasaw Advisory Council, Oklahoma City, OK, March 18, 1967, Chickasaw tribal papers, Ada, OK.
7. Overton James, interview by author, January 18, 1993.
8. Vinnie May Humes interview by author, September 23, 1992.
9. Report, Annual Meeting of the Chickasaw, Seeley Chapel, October 21, 1967, Chickasaw tribal papers, Ada, OK.
10. Notes between Charlie Ward and Carl Albert, April 25, 1966, Carl Albert Collection, Box 58, Folder 14, OU, Norman, OK.
11. Resolution, Chickasaw Advisory Council meeting at Tishomingo,

June 30, 1967, Chickasaw tribal papers, Ada, OK.

12. Letter, Stewart Udall to Robert Kingsbery, August 2, 1967, Chickasaw tribal papers, Ada, OK.

The Making of the Constitution of 1983, Part I
November, 2003 *Times*

1. *Morris v. Andrus* and *Cravatt v. Andrus*, U.S. Court of Appeals, D.C. Circuit, January 27, 1981.
2. Joyce Peterson, "Indian Tribe Lawsuit Ruling Leaves Interpretations Open," *The Daily Oklahoman* April 27, 1981.
3. Ruling, Court of Appeals, January 17, 1981.
4. Minutes, Tribal Council, February 20, 1981. David Stout Building, Chickasaw Nation Headquarters, Ada, OK.
5. Court Order, Motion for Provisional Relief, *Cravatt v. Watt* (Watt had replaced Andrus as secretary of Interior), U.S. District Court, April 3, 1981.
6. J.Y. Tomlinson, Jr., Press Release, Chickasaw Nation, April 6, 1981.
7. Overton James to Anne Crichton, solicitor, BIA, April 8, 1981. folder—1983 Constitution Chickasaw Library, Ada, OK.
8. Minutes, Tribal Council meeting, June 19, 1981.
9. Ellen Leitzer to Bob Rabon et. al. letter, Nov. 3, 1981. Folder—1983 Constituion, Chickasaw Library, Ada, OK.
10. Leitzer to James Brookshire, Department of Justice, February 16, 1982. Folder—1983 Constitution,Chickasaw Library, Ada, OK.
11. Gary Childers, "Bill Passed that Allows Tribes to File Suit," *Chickasaw Times*, XII, no. 1.
12. Pat Woods, interview by author, December 16, 1993.

The Making of the Constitution of 1983, Part 2
December 2003 *Times*

1. Tribal Plaintiffs to Defendants, memo on fundamental differences between the two constitutions, undated, Chickasaw Library, Ada.
2. Ted Key, Pat Woods, Overton James, Wilson Seawright, and Zane Browning, interviews by author, cited in endnotes of Part I.
3. "Constitutional Issues Aired," *Chickasaw Times*, XII, no. 4. (1983), p. 1.
4. "Additional Differences Presented," *Chickasaw Times*, XII, no. 5, (1983), p. 1.
5. Robert Keel, interview by author, June 3, 1993.
6. "Chickasaw Constitutional Reformation Election Held," *Chickasaw Times*, XII, no. 6. (1983),p. 1.
7. "Apportion Plans Announced," *Chickasaw Times*, XII, no. 8, (1983), p. 1.
8. "Chickasaw Constitutional Reformation Election Held," *Chickasaw Times*, XII, No. 6, (1983),1.
9. "Chickasaws OK Changes," "Ada Evening News," August 29, 1983.
10. Campaign ad for Imotichey, Chickasaw Library, 1983 election.
11. Mike Hammer, "Chickasaw Council Fighting Leader's Campaign Tactics," "*The Daily Oklahoman*," August 26, 1983.
12. Lynn Gibson, interview by author, February, 23, 1993.
13. Overton James' personal records, Ada, OK.

Index

S

Sacred Pole (*fa-bus-sah*), 3-7
Sacchuma, 20
St. Jean, Wendy, 45
Savannah, 43
Sealey, Samuel, Chickasaw chief, 81
Seawright, Wilson, Chickasaw judge, 91
Seeley Chapel, 148, 150-151, 162, 164-166
self-determination, 158, 174
Seminoles, 84
Shawnees, 66
slave raids, 25-26, 49
Smith, Marvin, 10
sovereignty, 157,
Squirrel King, Chickasaw chief, 44, 66
starvation, 85
Stubbs, Jr., John, 32-34, 180-186
Sulphur, Oklahoma, 174-175
Sulphur Springs description, 93-94, 96, 100
Supplementary Agreement (of 1902) to Atoka Agreement, 97-98, 135, 137-139
Swanton, John R., 4, 6

T

Tallaposies (Upper Creeks), 27, 40
Tascalusa, 18
Tate, Charles, 189-194, 197
termination, 158-159

Tishomingo, Chickasaw capitol, 103, 115-116, 119-120, 122-123, 125-128, 130-131, 138, 151, 154, 165, 175, 194
Tishomingo, Chickasaw warrior, 87-88
Tombigbee River, 18, 39, 45, 59-60
trade goods, 28-29
Treaty of Doaksville, 1837, 79
Treaty of Hopewell, 1786, 70, 78
Treaty of Mobile, 1784, 70
Treaty of Paris, 1763, 68
Treaty of Pontotoc, 1832, 78
Treaty of San Lorenzo, 1795, 74
Tupelo, Mississippi, 18, 30-33, 64, 179, 185, 200
Tuskahoma Party, Choctaw, 105, 114

U

Ubabeneli (Great Spirit), 4
Ugulaycabe, Chickasaw chief, 69-70, 73
Upshaw, A.M.M, 79, 85

V

Virginia Colony, 25

W

Waselkov, Gregory, 43-45
Washington, George, 70-71, 73
Welch, Thomas, 27, 37
Welge, Bill, 154-155

Wells, Mary Ann, 23
Westoes, 25-26, 28
White, Eugene, 97-98
White Deer, Gary, viii
white dog, 6
Williams, Stephen, 180, 182,
Willmond, Catherine, 202
Wolf, Jonas, Chickasaw governor, 103, 105-106, 122
Woods, Pat, 190, 192, 194
Woodward, Henry, 25-27
Wright, Allen, Choctaw chief, 89
Wright, Muriel, Choctaw historian, 87-92, 169